Beyond the border post, I can see a watchtower. It is on the other side of a bare stretch of land, and because my passport is safely checked, and I am obviously an Allied Traveller, I start walking across the invisible Iron Curtain.

"You can't walk in there!" call out the guards.

To Bill and his widespread
and loving family in the USA

COUNTRIES ALONG THE IRON CURTAIN, MARKED WITH CROSSES, THROUGH WHICH BRIDGET TRAVELLED.

BRIDGET ASHTON

Cold War, Warm Hearts

a memoir

The Book Guild Ltd

First published in Great Britain in 2023 by
The Book Guild Ltd
Unit E2 Airfield Business Park,
Harrison Road, Market Harborough,
Leicestershire. LE16 7UL
Tel: 0116 2792299
www.bookguild.co.uk
Email: info@bookguild.co.uk
Twitter: @bookguild

All photos by the author, except for three from the 1960s
for which the photographers are unknown

The events in this book all took place over half a century ago. They all
really happened, but some perhaps slightly differently owing to the tricks of memory.
In only one case has a name has been changed to protect an identity

Typeset in 11pt Minion Pro

Printed and bound in the UK by TJ Books LTD, Padstow, Cornwall

ISBN 978 1915603 326

British Library Cataloguing in Publication Data.
A catalogue record for this book is available from the British Library.

Endorsements

"Bridget Ashton has written a vivid memoir of her time crossing the Iron Curtain in the 1960s. Based on her diaries and letters, and enlivened by her fresh, contemporary photographs, it shows how this fundamental barrier was never completely closed. The people Ashton encounters in the East freely show her their humanity, even as they are sometimes forced to contend with inhuman regimes. A life-affirming book."

Timothy Phillips, author of *The Curtain and the Wall*, 2022

"Bridget Ashton's travel writing is utterly authentic and restlessly curious. She is an intrepid, 'unquiet' woman adventurer, exploring in the grand tradition of Celia Fiennes and Freya Stark. Her memoir of life in post-war Soviet Europe is a vivid reminder of how much Europe has changed; and how much it has not."

Max Adams, author of *The King in the North*, *Unquiet Women*, *In the Land of Giants* and *The Wisdom of Trees*

"*Cold War Warm Hearts* transports us back half a century, to an era when a trilingual peasant woman wondered whether England also had a moon, and a young man could recall his childhood friend being carried away on a Nazi cattle truck. Through innocent student eyes, Bridget Ashton evokes the world she discovered as she hitch-hiked across the Iron Curtain, determinedly criss-crossing Eastern Europe and the Balkans on an extraordinary journey that uncovers boundless hospitality but also tensions that are no less relevant today."

Fiona Hall, author and Member of the European Parliament 2004–2014

By the Same Author

Hay Before the Bookshops or The Beeman's Family, 2022

Bridget Gubbins' Morpeth Local History series
De Merlay Dynasty, 2018
The Conquest of Morpeth, 2017
Juliana and Ranulph of Morpeth Castle, 2016
Newminster: Monks, Shepherds and Charters, 2014
The Mysteries of Morpeth's Workhouse, 2013
The Drovers are Coming to Morpeth Town, 2012
The Curious Yards and Alleyways of Morpeth, 2011

Power at Bay, 1997
Generating Pressure, 1991

Contents

Introduction

In 2022, when I finished writing this book, Eastern European countries were in a state of uncertainty. Russia had absorbed Crimea and was actively fighting in Ukraine. Another version of the Cold War seemed possible. Many older people who remembered life under Communism, closely shadowed by the Soviet Union, were trembling.

In 1966 and 1967, I travelled among people who were trapped behind the Iron Curtain. I was alone, young and inexperienced, throwing myself on the hospitality of strangers.

Stalin had died in 1953. Khrushchev's 'Thaw' had softened some aspects of Communism, but this had led to the Hungarian uprising which was ruthlessly quelled in 1956. All of this happened before I went there. But the gloomy atmosphere which I sensed in Czechoslovakia erupted in the 'Prague Spring' in 1968, shortly after I left.

People's lives in the former Soviet bloc have certainly changed. Since the Berlin Wall came down in 1989, capitalism has taken over. Many of those countries now belong to the European Union.

Yugoslavia no longer exists, and the nations into which it broke have suffered dreadful wars. Russia remains strong and brittle to the East, sensitive to the influence of the West, and is a constant shadow hovering over the countries it once dominated.

My stories tell of the people I met in Eastern Europe during the Cold War of the mid-twentieth century. They were trapped and had to make the best of things. Oddly, at the end, I too found myself escaping from a different kind of entrapment. Times have changed, but their stories may perhaps warn us of how history repeats itself.

1

Across the Iron Curtain?

Sometimes a girl may have a simple encounter which changes her life. This way or that way? One way or another? Thus it was with me.

"Bridget, why don't you just drop everything and come travelling with me?" this good-looking young man says. We are chatting in a café in town. He is a Polish American called Steve. I've never met such a person before.

It is early summer, 1966, in the town of Hereford, near the border of Wales, where I have been studying to be a teacher for nearly three years. My natural course through life is to become a teacher and find a man who wants to marry me.

"It is quite impossible," I tell him. "I've almost finished my course. And anyway, I don't even know you."

I am unwilling to drop into the expected route of work and marriage. I have a vague idea that I might hitchhike to Israel to work on a kibbutz. But Steve has started off some different thoughts in my mind. Poland?

I have hitchhiked with my student friends through many countries in Europe. We have learned how to find our way easily enough through France and Spain, Germany and Switzerland, with barely more than a few coins in our pockets. Meeting Steve is making me think about another reality, in the East. What do I know about the lands behind the Iron Curtain, beyond that boundary which divides Europe into two parts?

I have been living in the safe world of post-war Britain with its National Health Service, student grants and free education. To me, Communism is an unknown system of gloom, of prisons and fear, shortages and queues, despondent people, hammer and sickle emblems, red stars, Russian tanks. Is it really like that? Are young people over there in the 1960s anxious, fearful, unhappy and longing to escape? While we laugh and dance to The Beatles, are they confined and miserable? Should I be afraid to enter their world?

My friends and I live in the relative backwater town of Hereford, in our women-only teacher training college. We are not particularly part of the drugs and music scene of the 1960s world. Yet between our studies, whenever we can get away, ours is a world of hitchhiking, the open road and travel wherever the spirit leads us. We love the landscapes and the rural lifestyles we learn about in different countries. We carry the music of The Beatles and The Rolling Stones in our heads, and we enjoy jazz and folk music, Bob Dylan and Joan Baez. We head off for France or Spain, or further afield to Italy and northern Africa. At weekends, we may hitchhike to London with no more than a pound or two in our pockets, working the underground trains without paying the fare. We go to Glasgow, to South Wales or take a boat to Ireland. A long weekend in Paris too – it is perfectly possible if all goes smoothly. Several of us, me included, are geography students, and we justify our travels by believing we will be better teachers.

On the long summer days, road junctions in the UK and across Europe are frequented by youthful hitchhikers like us. With our thumbs up, we smile charmingly at the approaching drivers. Who would object to giving young girls like us a lift?

We stay overnight in youth hostels where we pay the minimal fee for a bunk bed in a dormitory. Sometimes we are so short of money that we must choose between food or the hostel overnight fee, and then we might ask a farmer if we can stay in the barn. We put our blankets down in the hay, sleeping amid the rustlings of rodents and the biting of insects.

But Poland? Behind the Iron Curtain? What about young people there? Are they able to travel around as we do? How do they feel about living in their locked-up lands? Perhaps they like their countries, and we have been given the wrong idea. Perhaps it is fine living under Communism, or socialism, however it is defined. After all, the principles of equality are appealing. Sharing wealth, everyone being equal, what is wrong with that? How would I know what young Polish people think unless I go there?

"I have an interview for a teaching job in Birmingham," my friend Mary tells me one day, soon after my encounter with Steve. Birmingham is where the jobs are. Three of my friends go there for interviews: Mary, Jenny, a dreamy languid philosopher, and Tonie, who is in love with her Welsh lorry-driver boyfriend. Others of my fellow students have serious boyfriends, and one is already married. A job for a few years and a loving relationship leading to marriage and a home. This is the expectation, the normal route for young women like us in the 1960s.

But not for me, not yet.

"Bridget, what will you do if you meet someone and fall in love?" my friends warn me. "You might get trapped. Who will know where you are if you end up in gaol? You don't know anyone. You don't speak Polish."

I ignore their warnings.

I look at my atlas. To get to Poland, I must pass through West Germany and then cross the Iron Curtain into East Germany, a fearsome land with the notorious Berlin Wall within it. President Kennedy had said *Ich bin ein Berliner* when he looked over it. The frontier of Poland, my destination, lies beyond East Germany.

I find a map showing the line of the Iron Curtain, which I can see zigzagging through Europe from north to south, from the Baltic to the Mediterranean and the Black Sea. I know the line is guarded with watchtowers to keep us out and the people over there in.

"I'll go to Poland if they'll let me in," I say to myself. I manage to get a skimpy, tightly printed book called *Teach Yourself Polish* at Hereford public library and struggle with a language full of *sz, cz,* other strange sounds and completely unknown verb systems.

Compared to slipping away to France or Ireland or the Netherlands, going to Poland is a different matter. I am not even sure if it is possible. Poland is behind the Iron Curtain, and I have never met anyone who tried to get there.

I learn that the application must be done through Orbis, the Polish state's travel agency, and their London office posts me a typed information sheet. It is not impossible to go there, but there are rules and conditions. There are two sides of detailed rules and regulations, including these stern words:

Information concerning individual arrivals to Poland of the members of the International Youth Hostel Federation:
The tourist desiring to reserve places in the youth hostels applies to the: Polskie Towarzystwo Schronisk Młodzieżowych Warszawa, Al. I Armii Wojska Polskiego 25, telegraphic abbreviation TESEM, telephone 28-04- 61, int. 228.

My International Youth Hostel Federation handbook shows the detailed network of youth hostels in Poland. I have no particular route in mind, and despite the grim language and heavy black typing, I decide that I will chance finding accommodation when I get there.

I pay £30 to Orbis for the obligatory vouchers to be exchanged for money once in Poland. You can't get Polish money in England to take along with you. The official exchange rate is sixty zlotys to one pound sterling. This I would later learn is much less than the unofficial illegal rate of two hundred zlotys to the pound. I would live on £1 per day in zlotys.

With my vouchers secured, on Saturday the 11th of June, I send off my passport and application for a thirty-day visa to the Polish embassy in London. Entry and exit points must be specified. Any stay longer than thirty days would mean registering with the police at every place where I would be staying, which I certainly don't plan to do.

By the end of June, my passport with the stamped-in visa has been returned. Soon after that, my three years of college come to an end, and I face the reality of my choice, all triggered by that chance meeting with Steve. How shall I get to Poland? Flying is not even a consideration for someone on my budget. Travelling means physically progressing over land and sea, crossing border controls between different countries as I go along.

DEUTSCHE DEMOKRATISCHE REPUBLIK

It is the 1st of August 1966, and I am heading for Berlin, isolated amid the lands of East Germany, the *Deutsche Demokratische Republik*, the DDR. The name rings with gloom. I've hitchhiked from Hanover along the Autobahn through West Germany. The closer I come to East Germany, the less the traffic. I have several short lifts, the cars dropping me off in inconvenient places as they divert onto the side roads, leaving me walking illegally along the Autobahn. I try to look inconspicuous as squads of helmeted mounted police on motorbikes pass me by. They don't stop. A young woman on foot, like me, isn't much of a threat here in the

West. A car stops and the driver takes me to the border post leaving the West, where he drops me off.

"You must do the rest by yourself," he says, unwilling to risk trouble with the East German border guards just ahead.

I take a photograph of a notice in English:

ALLIED CHECKPOINT
HELMSTEDT
ALL ALLIED TRAVELLERS
REPORT HERE

The English-speaking border guards check my passport and return it. They are smiling and friendly. Cars and travellers are mingling around.

Beyond the border post, I can see a watchtower. It is on the other side of a bare stretch of land, and because my passport is safely checked, and I am obviously an Allied Traveller, I start walking.

"You can't walk in there!" call out the guards.

I'm surprised but not willing to defy armed soldiers. I turn back and look out for an opportunity to cross over the no man's land, the invisible Iron Curtain.

A Volkswagen car with a B for Berlin on its number plate pulls up, and the driver moves towards the passport control. He can see my rucksack and my Union Jack flag. I look at him enquiringly.

"*Ja, Berlin. Sie können mitkommen,*" he says, or something like that which I understand. Yes, you can come with me to Berlin. When his passport is checked, I climb into the Volkswagen, and we drive slowly across the few metres of no man's land between the Allied border guards and the next barrier. The watchtower is on our right, high up on criss-cross legs, where armed soldiers must be on lookout. They would have seen me walking towards them. Who are they watching out for? People trying to get in, or people trying to get out?

At the grey concrete control post, the East German border guard approaches.

"*Reisepass bitte.*" Passport please. I don't like handing it over. We are directed towards a small building where we must fill in forms. Where are you staying? In my case, a youth hostel in West Berlin. I must pay a visa fee because I wish to enter the Soviet Zone of East Germany. This costs fifteen Deutschmarks, about £4 at this time.

Simple, you would think. Just pay, sign on the dotted line, get your visa stamped into your passport and away you go. My diary tells more:

> *It's not so easy. It means queuing for hours in tiny passport rooms filled with sweaty, frustrated people, pushing in towards the bars, tempers flying, everyone hot and annoyed, many forms to be filled in and queues to be queued in again. The whole process took two hours.*

Here I see my first 'Communist' soldiers in grey uniforms. I don't know if they are soldiers from the army or border guards. And there are some Soviet soldiers around too. I catch myself staring at them as if they have come from outer space. Russians! Soldiers from the Red Army! And I am looking at them, standing near them. Little me, from England, looking at the representatives of the Cold War, our enemies.

The customs officers closely examine the contents of my driver's car, but other than a quick look at my rucksack, they leave me alone. Thus, I retain my copy of Boris Pasternak's *Doctor Zhivago*, which I suspect may be forbidden literature.

The border crossing makes it clear that East Germany, the *Deutsche Demokratische Republik*, doesn't welcome visitors like me. We are tolerated, but it is difficult and unpleasant to enter, and hard Western currency is extracted from us for the privilege. I am in, but I am a representative of an enemy system.

When we are finally through the checkpoint, we travel through East Germany. My driver speaks only a little English, and I am left to my thoughts. His car registration bears B for Berlin, like nearly all the vehicles in both directions. I hope to arrive in Berlin before dark, into the city with its notorious Wall.

I am brooding. On the western side of Europe, which I have left behind, we are free to say what we like and go where we will, even though we are influenced by advertising and the media. I have learned that people on the eastern side are subjected to political propaganda and a socialist system under heavy surveillance from Moscow. They can't say what they like, and they are brainwashed and unfree. It is only four years since the stand-off between Kennedy and Khrushchev when the Soviets were delivering nuclear missiles to Cuba. When I am eighteen, I have absorbed some of this. I am curious, and I am a little fearful.

I can see on my map that there are only four road crossings along the full length of the 1400-kilometre boundary between the East and West of Germany. From Sweden, the ferry across the Baltic arrives at Sassnitz on the island of Rügen. From Denmark, the ferry arrives at the small port of Warnemünde near Rostock. In the very south of the country, travellers from Munich cross near the little town of Juchhöh. We have crossed in the main route from the West European countries to Berlin, the *Grenzübergang Helmstedt-Marienborn*.

We follow the Autobahn, passing between great empty open fields, and sometimes I can see compact villages. They fill me with curiosity. Who lives there, and what do they think about? The countryside looks bare, cold and unloved.

My driver approaches West Berlin, a little island of capitalism isolated in the midst of this desolate landscape. I have another boundary to cross. West Berlin's Wall goes all around its outer rural areas, and the driver drops me off just inside the boundary at a Y junction in the Autobahn. "*Danke sehr,*" I say. Thank you very much. There is a sign:

YOU ARE NOW ENTERING THE
U.S. SECTOR OF BERLIN

I must take the branch into the British zone of Berlin to look for my youth hostel, and I am a little scared. It is getting dark, and I imagine that there are soldiers creeping around in the undergrowth on the sides of the road. I cross over the road, get a lift and soon find my way to the youth hostel.

I'm in my own sphere again where, as a westerner with a blue British passport, I can feel at ease. Even though the Soviet army surrounds the city, an ever-present reminder of the dominance of Moscow, I am in a safe zone. This is the island of West Berlin, where the Americans, British and French are in charge.

BERLIN

"We'll go into the city today to look at the Wall, right?" says Rob to me the next day. He is my new friend, a Londoner who has found his way to the youth hostel.

I find the city beautiful and luxurious. Wide streets with gorgeous shops, plenty of coloured advertising and neon signs, yellow buses and smartly dressed people. We walk along the Kurfürstendamm and see the bombed Kaiser Wilhelm Memorial Church.

Rob and I don't spend much money in the enticing cafés. Youth hostel meals and self-cooking are more to our budget. And there is no point in buying souvenir items to add weights to our rucksacks. My diary on Sunday the 7th of August 1966:

We walked a lot today, right into Berlin. We went to the Wall which divides the city, saw the barbed wire and the Communist guards. The Wall itself is not as high or ferocious-looking as I'd imagined, but the patrolling guards – always looking towards the west – with their guns ready to shoot any erring person, seemed dreadful. We saw the large areas of parkland and wasteland – no man's land – not worth being built on. There were also bomb sites not worth repairing on both sides.

When we arrive at the Wall, we clamber up the steps to the lookout point where important visitors like President Kennedy were always pictured and where, in 1963, he'd said: "*Ich bin ein Berliner!*"

"This isn't like I imagined it," I say to Rob. We gaze over barbed wire to those strange, criss-crossed tank traps which we learn are nicknamed Czech hedgehogs. Behind them is a large bare concrete area with guard posts at the sides. Beyond that we can see plain four- and five-storey buildings. There is not a vehicle in the great square of Potsdamer Platz, which had been one of the busiest places in pre-war Berlin. Guards are patrolling with their guns at the ready, always looking in our direction. Perhaps they feel foolish.

If so, they have good reason. A big notice, written in German, is facing us:

WER
DIE STAATSGRENZE
MIT GEWALT
EINRENNEN WILL /
WER AN DER MAUER
PROVOZIERT /
MACHT ALLES
NUR SCHLIMMER!

This is what it means:

ANYONE
WANTING TO BREAK DOWN
THE STATE FRONTIER
BY FORCE /
ANYONE BEING PROVOCATIVE
AT THE WALL /
ONLY MAKES
EVERYTHING WORSE!

How annoying for them that westerners might want to break down their lovely frontier, and what is more provoking to their dignity than being laughed at?

THE UNDERGROUND INTO EAST BERLIN

Next morning, as Rob and I are getting ready to leave for our day trip into East Berlin, we are chatting with two Australian boys. One makes humorous comments about the red straight-up-and-down dress I am wearing. An enthusiast for Communism, perhaps?

"Come on, I'm not having any bearded Aussies walking around with us!" Rob says, and we go off by ourselves.

We have purchased tickets in the Anhalter Bahnhof station, and the underground train creaks slowly forward towards East Berlin. It moves through dark tunnels and then into a sombre station where the border guards stare at us through the windows of their posts. Our eyes meet for the briefest of moments, the tiniest of split seconds. This is a look which I shall not forget. I get a shivery feeling. Rob tells me that the guards are always paired with someone they don't know to reduce the chance of them making plans together to escape.

This is a *Geisterbahnhof*, a ghost station. It is underneath the Potsdamer Platz which we'd seen the day before. Our train moves slowly between the platforms, allowing the border guards to look carefully for spies or escapees.

We move on until we reach another station, and similarly creep through without stopping, this time beneath Unter den Linden.

We pull in at Friedrichstrasse station where we know we must get off for East Berlin. We are funnelled down a barely lit corridor along with the other passengers where we divide into various specialised lines heading to kiosks behind glass barriers. People from East Berlin and the DDR each have short lines, and West Germans a third. However, we foreigners must take the longest, slowest line. A uniformed officer demands our passports. He checks every page and looks at our photographs. He isn't in a hurry. Finally, we get our visa stamped into our passports and are required to hand over five Deutschmarks, hard West German currency. In exchange, we are given five flimsy, lightweight Reichsmark coins which we know are worthless outside the DDR.

We escape from the station with a sense of relief and go out into the sunshine of East Berlin. Walking south down Friedrichstrasse, we head for the landmark of *Brandenburger Tor*. The city feels soundless with hardly any cars even though this is a main thoroughfare, and there are very few people. There are no obvious shops or kiosks in which to spend our Reichsmark.

It has taken us all morning to get from the youth hostel in West Berlin to this point. We are ambling rather tiredly along, looking at nothing much, chatting about this and that. Rob likes to tell me about his adventures in Africa.

We arrive at Unter den Linden, 'Under the Lime Trees', the great east-west route through the city. Here, the newly planted lime trees are struggling into life, the old ones having been razed in Berlin in May 1945.

Ahead of us, as we turn to the west, is the great *Brandenburger Tor*, the Brandenburg Gate, surmounted by the four-horse chariot looking our way. Flying above the chariot is the DDR's black, red and yellow flag with its hammer and compass emblem.

We approach a flimsy single-bar crossing post, a hundred metres before the Brandenburg Gate, beyond which we can see the Berlin Wall. Some soldiers wearing Soviet army uniforms are laughing and leaning against the barrier. The thought comes to my mind that the Soviet Union is still significant twenty years after the end of the Second World War here in East Germany. For how many more years must this go on? The soldiers appear casual and relaxed, with perhaps a sense of superiority in this dreary city. I daringly take a photograph, but as it is mid-afternoon, the sun is in my face, and they are silhouetted. Still, we can see their smart military peaked caps and neat jodhpurs tucked into long, shiny, black boots. A few tourists like us are looking westwards over the barrier.

After that we wander back through open streets with bombed sites and buildings. The area is still devoid of traffic, and there are hardly any passers-by. Clearly not many people live in this part of the city. We pass through the Gendarmenmarkt, another great square, and here, always frugal with my film, I take a photo of an enormous building. I don't know what it is at the time. There are no signs explaining anything. It is big, black and derelict, just left standing presumably because there are no funds, and no interest, in doing anything about it. Later I learn that it was a prestigious and historic theatre called the *Schauspielhaus*. The SS destroyed it at the end of the war, but its four-metre-thick walls survived, and it is there for us to stare at in 1966. That is what we are, visitors, blankly looking up at the building in this dreary city.

We've had enough for one day. It is time for us to return to our Western retreat.

On the underground on the way back, looking again at the border guards glaring through their windows, Rob says: "Bet they wish they could be getting out in this train with us."

"How do we know?" I reply. "Perhaps they like their country."

THE WALL OF PEACE

In the youth hostel, a little booklet is circulating called *The Wall of Peace*. This explains to westerners why the East German government and people are protecting themselves from us, by building a strong wall around themselves.

It says things which turn our heads inside out, text like this:

> 'On 13 August 1961 peace-loving Berliners won a battle
> for peace. The battle groups of Berlin's working class, along
> with comrades in the National People's Army and comrades
> of the German police of the capital of the GDR [it uses the
> English form, the German Democratic Republic] put an end

to subversive activity against the GDR by spies, slave traders, and revanchist organisations based in West Berlin.

'The Socialist Unity Party of Germany thanks all the comrades in the battle groups, the Society for Sport and Technology, and the German Red Cross for the readiness, the determination, the courage and discipline, with which these comrades and friends protected peace. We thank comrades of the National People's Army and the German police who, by their determination, demonstrated that our young workers' and farmers' state is willing and able to guarantee peace in Germany and that it has the necessary means to do so.

'As the morning dawned, the border was sealed. As Sunday came, the Government's measures were completed. The morning newspapers reported: "The governments of the Warsaw Pact states call upon the Volkskammer and the Government of the GDR, and all workers of the German Democratic Republic, to establish order along the border with West Berlin, in order to prevent subversive activity against the nations of the Socialist bloc, and to establish effective control of the entire border with West Berlin, including its border with democratic Berlin'.

So from that point of view, visitors like Rob and me are included among the 'spies and slave traders'.

Does anyone believe words like this? Is it even possible to imagine that they might?

THE SIGNIFICANT POST – BERLIN

When I arrive at the youth hostel in Berlin, some post is waiting for me. In 1966, letters are important. This is how I maintain links with home. Phone contact is unrealistic because public phones are few and far between and often don't work. Anyway, not many people that I know at home have access to a phone, and calls are reserved for important, urgent messages.

Hence the postal services are of principal importance. People write letters, on real paper, with pens, put the pages in envelopes which they lick and stick down. Then they must buy the relevant postage stamp for the country concerned and go out to put the letters in a postbox.

In this way, we work out where we all are and tell each other what we are doing, although the information is generally out of date by the time we receive it. I had planned ahead and asked my friends and family to post letters to me at Berlin youth hostel.

I have one from my father mentioning a job he was applying for in Aberystwyth as a Bee Advisor, similar to his job in Northumberland. My brother signed his off affectionately after telling me he hasn't enough time to go to Italy or Spain but had £20 and would probably go to Brittany, Paris and Benelux. With frugal management, £20 could cover two weeks' food, travel and accommodation after paying £4 return on the ferry. Mary, my college friend, with whom I'd had so many exciting travels and who would soon be teaching in Birmingham, informs me that her father is instructing her reading, which she finds very annoying. Sergi, a friend from Spain, and Ans, a friend from Holland, also write with their news.

All these letters, which are my link to the world I have left behind, have safely arrived at the youth hostel. While I am there, I have another letter from my mother with news about the travels of my sister Rosie and my brother Richard:

We've had cards from Rosie in Cologne, and I believe she is on her way to Norway or Sweden. Richard is going to France soon. What a family! Be sure to let us have addresses. Where will you be on your birthday?

To reply I'd have to think ahead. I am heading for Poland and have only a tentative route in my mind. It is fairly likely though that

I'll go to Kraków, the historic city in the south. I spend a whole morning at the hostel replying to my letters and asking people to reply to me at the Kraków youth hostel. My birthday is due on the 17th of August, a week or so from the date I plan to enter Poland. Thus, I have a focus and should be in Kraków somewhere around that time. If I get lost, or end up in a Communist prison, and no one hears from me after that time, they will be right to start worrying.

Despite Rob being my new and supportive friend, and despite the love and assurance I receive from my letters, I am not always my cheerful and confident self. I stay for three days in the Berlin hostel, giving myself a little breathing space and helping with cleaning to pay for my keep. And I find myself struck with self-doubt. What am I doing, wandering alone in these strange lands? My younger sister is married and living in her new house; my friends are starting their professional teaching lives; and I am floating around, unsure of myself. But then, after sleeping it off, I wake up, full of fun and bounce. The pull of the unknown, the idea of walking along foreign roads all by myself: these are magnetic ideas. I'm off to Poland, land of good lookers like Steve.

So I go happily down to the Zoologischer Garten station with Rob and buy my ticket for the next day. Always needing to save every pfennig, my ticket would take me through the part of the DDR where it is forbidden to hitchhike and as far as the first village across the border. On the other side of the river Oder, it would take me to Kunowice.

The large, pink cardboard ticket costs me eight Deutschmarks. It is written in German and also Russian, the language of our Cold War enemy. It is valid for two calendar months, from the 8th of August to the 7th of October:

Die Buchfahrkarte ist gültig vom
08 08 1966 bis 07 10 1966

18

THE GRINDINGLY SLOW TRAIN JOURNEY

At the gate controlling entrance to the platform, the German woman inspector smiles as she checks my pink cardboard ticket.

"Fahren Sie nach Moskau?" Are you going to Moscow? She hasn't noticed that my journey is a very short one.

"No, I am going to Kunowice," I explain. She looks surprised, but it is nice to be sent off by a friendly face. A few moments later, the huge black engine comes steaming into the station. It rushes past us so quickly before it pulls its big strength to a halt that I jump up with fright. It is the Moscow Express, train number 02038. As the train begins to move, Rob runs along behind the barrier waving goodbye.

Once again, the journey involves me crossing from the island of capitalist West Berlin into the surrounding eastern Soviet Zone. I can do it, but without a friendly passage. There will be more visa and passport inspections.

The train halts after the short journey to Friedrichstrasse station in East Berlin. The grey-uniformed border guards come on. Everyone has to show their passports and their visas. There is a tense atmosphere in my compartment, people avoiding each other's eyes. *What are these guards thinking about as they do this?* I wonder. There is no point in trying to charm them with friendly smiles. Their steely indifference is so unlike our train guards at home. Eventually, the train leaves for the next station in East Berlin, the Ostbahnhof, where there are more delays.

It takes one and a quarter hours from the time we left Zoologischer Garten in West Berlin station, through Friedrichstrasse, until we pass out of the Ostbahnhof. In doing so, we've crossed the city and passed through the railway equivalent of the Berlin Wall.

We lumber on through the suburbs of East Berlin. *This is where the people live*, I think. The backs of the apartment blocks could have been in the outskirts of London: junk in the yards, washing hanging out, children's bicycles left outside.

I start chatting with two Australian girls, Therese and Margaret. Their tickets are for Poznań, the first major city in Poland, but I will get off before them, immediately over the border. We explore the train as it makes its way through the bleak DDR countryside, and we make the acquaintance of a single girl traveller from Sunderland, in the north of England. I am not the only western young person crossing into Poland, rare though we are.

More border paranoia is waiting for us. The East Germans have let us through, but the Polish state has yet to let us in.

The part of Poland which we'd soon be entering had been part of Germany before the war. The train timetable in Berlin showed Kunowice as Kunersdorf, its original German name. I'd be walking into fields which would still have been in Germany if it had not been for the Second World War and decisions made between the Soviet Union, the USA and the UK after the war.

On this day, in 1966, the river Oder is the border. Our train reaches the no man's land of the flooded river bed, with the chimneys of Frankfurt an der Oder on the skyline. The floods extend right into the edge of Poland. Now we must call the river by its Polish name of *Odra*. Once across the bridge, the screeching and clanging train pulls up into the border station of Kunowice. Trembling a little, I pick up my rucksack and prepare to get off. I struggle to open the door of my carriage. Big metal steps swing into position, and I clamber down into an unknown land.

2

Travelling without a Man

POLAND, AUGUST 1966

GET BACK ON THE TRAIN!

A few uniformed soldiers approach quickly. Are they looking for enemies? Am I officially acceptable in this land of Poland?

"*Dzien dobry*," they say. "*Dzien dobry*," I reply. Good day – among the few words of Polish I've learned.

I surely can't look much of a threat to the great socialist world I am entering in August 1966. But they are unsure. Speaking to me in Polish, they indicate to me that I must get back on the train, gesticulating towards the carriage door. People like me don't get off here. But I know I am in the right place. I'd looked out of the window as we crossed the Oder river, and Kunowice was the first stop over the border. I show them my pink cardboard ticket, partly in Russian, partly in German, with the word Kunowice stamped on as the destination. The train waits while they discuss my ticket and look at the visa in my passport. I am holding up the Moscow express.

Eventually, they decide everything was probably in order and hand me back my ticket and passport.

I turn round to look at Therese and Margaret. We wave to each other as the engine slowly pulls away, leaving me behind. The passengers are heading for the cities of Poland, first Poznań, then Warsaw, after that across the eastern boundary into the Soviet Union, through Brest, Minsk, Smolensk and finally to Moscow, to cities and lands which to me are shadowy and unknown, a constant presence and threat.

The soldiers go back to their hut. I've made a small diversion in their day. They leave me to myself with £30 worth of vouchers and a rucksack on my back. The river Oder and the Communist-ruled *Deutsche Demokratische Republik* are behind me, separating me from the familiar Western world. I am all alone in Poland.

I turn to look eastwards, my eyes following the great lumbering train from which I've just climbed. It steams on towards Warsaw and, ultimately, Moscow. I am going in that direction too but more slowly, and on foot.

I walk into the land which has borne invading armies marching east, and retreating in devastation in their turn, where refugees in their thousands have trudged, in carts, on foot or in whatever vehicle they could find. This is a land where unloved rulers oppressed the population, putting dissenters into prison, or worse. These are vague, unclearly formulated ideas in my mind. My ignorance of the land into which I am walking is profound.

Should I be afraid? I am not sure, but I am optimistic. I check the direction of the sun. I know if I keep it on my right, I'll be heading towards the first main city of Poznań, in the direction of Warsaw. There is only one road and no evidence of road signs.

A road mender sees me with my Union Jack flag. "Why are you travelling without a man?" he says in English. Where did he learn English? Perhaps he'd lived in Canada or the USA before coming back to Poland.

I laugh and reply jokingly and go on my way. But that is a significant question. What on earth am I doing, entering a closed land, with no Polish money, £30 worth of vouchers in my pocket and a visa for a month? No one knows where I am, or where I'd be found if I should be trapped in a Communist gaol. I haven't got round to informing the British consulate in West Germany about my travels. I have no contacts in Poland, no one to meet me or look after me and very little of the language.

The fields smell of hay, and the countryside is quiet. I walk past unfenced open fields, separated by ditches with purple flowers. Horses are grazing in a field next to a farmhouse. A woman wearing a headscarf is in the farmyard where hens peck and a dog is tied by a rope to its kennel. It is delightfully warm.

Not a car is going either way along this quiet road. A few kilometres later, I reach a small raggedy town called Rzepin where people stare at me politely. The houses and main street look unkempt and poor. I pass by a Soviet army tank and war memorial and gaze at the indecipherable Russian writing. This marks the route of the Red Army as it passed on its way to Berlin through a defeated Germany.

With my shoulder-length fair hair, I know I can be mistaken for a German girl which, in these years, in this place, is not helpful. Thus, I make sure my Union Jack flag is conspicuous as I need to focus on getting a lift. Sooner or later, a vehicle will come. This, I remind myself, is the main route between Berlin and Warsaw, two of Europe's capital cities.

Eventually, a car with a French registration comes along. That's hopeful.

"*Bonjour. Vous allez où?*" I ask. Where are you going? I haven't yet needed to try my Polish.

The French couple take me to Poznań, the first major city and my destination for the day. "*Au revoir. Bon courage!*" they say, as I leave them. Goodbye. Good luck.

In Poznań

"*Proszę Pani.*" Please, madam. I approach a woman, happy to try my little bit of Polish, pronouncing 'please' like 'proshang'. "*Gdzie Orbis?*". Where is the Orbis tourist information office? I needed to change my vouchers into zlotys, the local currency.

"*Skąd Pani jest?*" she asks. Where are you from? Aha. I know how to say 'Anglia' in response, which elicits a stream of Polish because she thinks I understand.

At the Orbis office, I change my £30 worth of vouchers for 2100 zlotys. I pick up a brochure in English.

Then I ask: "*Gdzie youth hostel?*" Where is the youth hostel? I know the Polish language has no words for 'a' or 'the'. The Polish words for youth hostel, *schronisko młodzieżowe*, are beyond my ability to pronounce. She seems to understand and points irritably. *Why bother me when you can't speak Polish?* her look seems to say. I wander off in the general direction.

I am still carrying my Union Jack flag on its stick when I arrive at the youth hostel.

"Hello. Where are you from?" says one of two dark-haired Bulgarian young men in English. They are sitting outside the door. We chat and I look at them, I hope not too rudely. I've never seen Bulgars before. I am not sure why, but I'd imagined Bulgar men riding horses, tearing over the mountains with cloaks flying, attacking peaceful villagers. These two good-looking boys are friendly but hardly wild horsemen. This is the first time I've thought about young people having the freedom to travel on their side of the Iron Curtain, Bulgaria being at the extreme south of the line of Eastern European socialist countries. What is difficult for us is perhaps easy for them.

It isn't exactly equal, though, because here I am behind the Iron Curtain, in their area, whereas it would be very difficult for them to come to mine.

In the hostel, I meet Therese and Margaret again, who stayed on the train as far as Poznań. A Polish girl is there with her East German boyfriend. She learns that we plan to hitchhike to Warsaw.

"You must get your Autostop cards," she explains. "All young people have them. You hold them up, and the driver sees you and stops. Then you give the driver some stamps for the distance he has taken you, and later he can exchange the stamps for money."

As I'd passed through on my way to the youth hostel, Poznań had seemed settled and normal. I don't know it then but guess that it had been largely destroyed and much rebuilt at the end of the Second World War, like the much smaller Rzepin that I'd seen earlier that day.

In the Orbis office, I'd picked up a detailed coloured brochure in English. Later, I cut out pictures and text from the brochure and stuck it all in my diary. The state-approved wording assures the readers that this had been a Polish city since the Middle Ages and until the present century, despite being taken over by Prussian rule, and hence being German-speaking, in the nineteenth century. The brochure:

The years 1918 and 1919 brought independence for the city...

After a short time of independence, the Great War II broke out and the barbarian Nazi occupation followed. The Nazi actualised the biological destruction of the Polish nation at any cost. Mass executions, arrests, deportations to the labour and extermination camps became a daily routine. Plundering of Polish property, destroying of Polish culture and Germanisation increased day after day.

During the siege in 1945 the city suffered severe damages but on 23 February 1945 the Soviet army, with the aid of inhabitants of Poznań, liberated the city. After the Great War II Poznań belonged to the most destroyed cities in Poland. The town was gutted in 55%: the Old City and mostly the centre. Industrial plants, communication, railway station, bridges and communal buildings vanished.

Every word in those paragraphs has been written with care, to ensure that the Soviet occupiers would approve, to applaud the Polish citizens and to emphasise the wickedness of the Nazis. But when I think about it, it is not really different from the way that we would write about a city in the West suffering war damage from our enemies.

Although it looks peaceful, Poznań had been the focus of a rebellion only a decade ago, in October 1956. Workers rioted to protest against shortages of food, bad housing and decline in real income. Quickly quelled, this rebellion was part of a movement against the Soviet influence in Poland, preceding the Hungarian uprising later the same year. I don't know this at the time. It all looks sunny, calm and pleasant to me.

The single photo I take in Poznań that afternoon is of the town hall, the *ratusz*, in the market square, showing rows of four-storey arcaded market houses. There are five parked cars, no more, one possible minibus, and not one item of traffic moving along the road.

Deszcz pada – it is raining

Our bags are heavy, and the rain is falling. We buy our Autostop cards, Therese, Margaret, Theo – a Dutch boy – and me.

I've never thought about buying a Communist cup of coffee before. However, we head towards a *bar mleczny*, a milk bar. We enter a great tiled space in a modern building. There is a long queue up to a cubbyhole, and a menu in Polish written up on the wall. You choose from the menu and tell the attendant what you want when you reach the cubbyhole. She gives you a ticket, and then you go to the far end of another line. You move slowly along and, at last, hand your ticket over.

Jajecznica for me. Scrambled eggs and a big, thick mug of coffee. *Jajko* means eggs. The cook cracks an egg in front of me onto a hot pan and roughly stirs it with a fork. She throws it onto a plate, half cooked, and hands it over indifferently. What does she care if it doesn't look appetising?

We pick up some sliced rye bread and our coffee and join the workers in their hearty breakfast. It costs merely pennies. A Polish boy who helped us decipher the menu was eating a dish of cream, cheese and sugar. Cheap, filling food for the workers, we learn at the *bar mleczny*, will fill us up in many a town.

We walk to the outskirts of Poznań in the pouring rain, carrying our heavy bags. *Deszcz pada* – rain is falling – will come in handy today.

Soon we learn how young Polish people travel around. A big lorry stops, which is going all the way to Warsaw. We clamber into the back, all four of us. My diary:

> *It was a kind of wagon train lorry, with a wooden frame covered in canvas. There were lots of leaks and draughts and drips, but it was better than nothing. Soon the driver picked up two Polish boys, so we had fun trying to speak to them in Polish and English. The journey was long. More and more young people, all boys, were picked up. It was dark in the back, the open end of the lorry sending in splashing, driving rain. It was cold and jolting, and all the boys sat there quiet and patient, waiting for the lorry to get to Warsaw. I thought of how many times such a thing must have happened in the war and how many of them would never have arrived at their destination. The journey took five hours.*

In a land with little traffic, the Autostop system seems eminently sensible.

We find accommodation at the International Student Hostel in Warsaw's Akademicka Street. The socialist state is providing young people with decent, inexpensive summer accommodation. And there is a *bar mleczny* nearby. Although the hostel staff need to see my passport, no one expresses surprise that I haven't reserved a bed. I don't get any idea here, nor had I in Poznań, that the Communist state wants to keep an eye on me.

Next day, Theo and I are gazing over the huge wedding cake tower of Stalin's gift to the Polish people.

"I think it is a beautiful palace, but it is too propagandist. Of course, all buildings are propagandist, even the old ones. But they were built to the glory of God. That one is built to the glory of the God of Communism, so I don't like it." That was Theo's opinion of the Palace of Culture and Science in Warsaw.

It was originally called Joseph Stalin's Palace of Culture and Science, but by our time the Stalin name had been removed. Completed as recently as 1955, it is still sparkling new as we look at it. It is in huge contrast to the rebuilt old town which is where we are heading.

It is hard to understand that the perfect brick buildings and cobbled streets have been reconstructed, brick by brick, tile by tile, block by block, in the twenty years since the war. Theo and I had been born around the time the war ended. Our parents would have understood. They'd lived through wartime. We watched a film in the tourist office, which I record in my diary as 'horrifying because even though we both knew what had happened, really to see it did not make us feel any more easy'.

The city's tourist brochure in English tells us more:

As recently as twenty years ago, Warsaw was a wasteland of ruin and rubble. Some 700,000 people were killed in battle or by genocidal Nazi activities, while 85 per cent of the buildings were destroyed – such was the tragic outcome of the war years 1939–1945.

The old town market square has normal everyday traffic flowing past its rebuilt seventeenth- and eighteenth-century houses as we roam around. Blue and white buses, and occasional cars, pass by, causing little disturbance to the pedestrians. Visitors are few and far between, even at the brick barbican gatehouse with its pointed towers and restored sixteenth-century walls.

Theo and I make our way towards the Vistula river. On the other side of the bridge is the suburb of Praga. This is where the Soviet troops had been camped, unmoving, in summer 1944. They were watching while the Nazis destroyed the final stages of the desperate Warsaw uprising, and then blasted the city to smithereens in their ultimate act of revenge.

All this is hard to visualise on this sunny August day in 1966. It is, however, a reminder that the Soviet army puts the interest of its own nation before that of the people of Poland.

OFF TO THE POLISH LAKE DISTRICT

I want to leave the hot, stifling city atmosphere and, based on conversations with the multilingual young people at the student hostel, decide to head for Masuria, the Land of a Thousand Lakes, in the north-east of Poland. This I know from my geography studies is a region where the great Scandinavian glaciers had deposited their loads of soil and gravel, blocking the streams and forming lakes.

If I want to get to know Polish young people, I need to stop talking English. The others feel the same way, and Theo, Therese, Margaret and I agree to separate and exchange addresses. My next address is Kraków youth hostel. In this way we can keep in touch, and our paths might cross again. Theo, like me, but in his own time, is heading north to Masuria, and the Australian girls will later go by train to Prague.

I locate the main road I want to take north from Warsaw and jump on the first bus that comes along. When it goes no further, I start walking.

Ambling along with the sun behind me, between the roadside trees, and with the silence of very little traffic, I soon encounter Marian, a young Polish boy about my own age. After *dzien dobry*, a few smiles, the name of Masuria and indications in the general direction, we begin to walk together. We both have our Autostop cards. My diary:

> *Almost everything that went by stopped, but the only trouble was we walked for ages before anything went by, and the distances were short. The roads grew more and more deserted as we went north. In the end, we found a barn where we camped for the night.*

Next morning, at about 7am, the horse in the stable below our hayloft is being taken out to work. We need to move along because we hadn't asked the farmer for permission to sleep in his barn. I don't have any particular aim, but Marian clearly does. He is heading for Wilkasy where he will meet his friends. I am happy enough to go along with this. My diary:

> *We went out onto the deserted road again. The early morning sun glinted through the trees and onto the soft mossy grass, and as we walked along, carts and peasants were making their way towards the market in the opposite direction.*

Now I am feeling closer to the life of the countryside, which is what I've been longing for. Marian and I communicate with signs and our own languages. He knows the words 'good' and 'bad'. I already know *dobry* for good, but he laughs at my difficulty in pronouncing *zły* for bad. My diary:

> *Eventually we came to the lake country, little lakes in fields or surrounded by pine forests. It was really hot and we had*

to walk miles, so we were really exhausted by the time we reached his destination in a tiny forest glade where his friends had a large tent. We swam and washed in the lake. The boys cooked supper and we sat chatting over the pine fire. I am thinking, what more can anyone want from life than pleasant company, the sweet scents and sounds of an outdoor life and good food and drink inside you?

THE SAUCY RASCALS IN WILKASY

These four boys are the focus of my life for the next few days. They tease me and call themselves *zbereżniki*, a word I learn to banter back at them, which means something like 'saucy rascals'. They've all hitchhiked here from the southern city of Wrocław and are out for their summer college holidays. At Wilkasy, on this campsite beside the lake, their days are their own to do as they like. Taking me, the foreigner, on board seems the obvious thing to do.

Tomasz is the only one of the group who has a few words of English. Short and cheerful, cleanly dressed, he is a philology student at the University of Wrocław. Dionysus is younger than the others, tall, lanky and shy. While Dionysus has the name of a Greek god, Julo, with his blond curls and tight physique, looks exactly like one.

We have had the usual communication sessions.

"*Ti govorish' po Russki?*" they asked, thinking this very funny. Do you speak Russian? They all had to learn Russian at school, but they much prefer to try some English.

"What you do?" asks Dionysus as I rest by the lake, busy drawing a map of the lake district.

"Dionysus, say 'What are you doing?'" I reply. I show them a few English phrases, and in return they help me pronounce phrases like *lubię Polskę*, I like Poland, or *dziękuję bardzo*, thank you very much, putting the slight nasal sound on the ę.

The boys enjoy challenging me with the famous Polish tongue twister, *chrząszcz brzmi w trzcinie*. It means something like 'the beetle is buzzing in the bullrushes'. It is hard enough for a Polish person, never mind an English speaker, and we giggle together at my efforts.

They improve my pronunciation of *Mówię trochę po Polsku*. I can speak a little Polish. I make it sound like *Moviang trochang po Polsku*. I am improving. I can use numbers and buy food in the shops, say what I like and don't like and ask for directions.

Except for voracious *komary*, the hungry mosquitoes who feast on us every night, this lakeside camp is perfect. For a couple of days we swim, lie around enjoying the sun, wander among the woods and go into the village of *Giżycko* to buy food.

During conversation, they get across to me that they are socialists. They accept the values of equality of all the people, the virtues of education for everyone to a high level, full employment, working for the general good and free healthcare. They have plenty to criticise about their country, but so did I and my student friends at home. None of them, though, are members of the Communist Party.

Tom sees me reading my copy of *Doctor Zhivago*, provocative illegal literature which I'd managed to bring right through the DDR into Poland.

"You shall have it when I've finished with it," I tell him.

I have a tin whistle in my rucksack and am keen to collect simple folk songs for my future teaching career.

"We'll show you how to dance the *trojak*," says Tom on one of our fireside evenings.

"*Zasiali górale żyto…*" The Gorals sowed the rye… They roar with laughter as they sing. They demonstrate how it is danced by three people, arms around shoulders, first kicking to the left, then to the right. Then one partner jigs around on the spot, while the middle partner goes down on one knee and gives his finger to the third partner who skips quickly round him, before they change roles. The song starts slowly and then doubles in speed. This is a dance of the Gorals, the mountain people. I am really happy. This is what I had wanted, to learn something about Polish life and become friendly with young Polish people.

Despite that, after three nights and two days, I begin to think I should move on.

"You must leave tomorrow. No cars on the road today," says Tom, early on Sunday. I've been sorting out my rucksack in preparation for leaving for my next destination, the Baltic coastal cities of Gdańsk and Gdynia.

On Monday, Marian and I leave together. We then discover that all the other young people from across Poland who are roaming around the lake district have the same idea. There are so many prospective hitchhikers on the road, and so few vehicles, that there is no hope of a lift. We will wait until Tuesday.

I spend the rest of the day wandering and then writing about the land around us. My diary:

All the little hills created by the glaciers had blocked the tiny streams and caused a thousand lakes and many more little pools. And now the Polish peasant farmers had built up a patchwork of scenery with their cultivated strips, their cottages in the clearings. Many an acre of ancient pine forest had survived the farmers' attacks, and they made the picture even more enchanting, especially when they surrounded the lakes.

The cottages themselves were built with red bricks and red tiles. They had overgrown gardens with sunflowers and potatoes beside every gateway, maybe an old woman bending low in the garden. Pigs, chickens, calves and cows seemed to belong to every house, ducks and geese too. Every farmer seemed to own some horses, and long, wooden carts rattled along the roadside far more frequently than cars. Usually, a whole family would be in the cart, the brown-faced man at the reins, scarved wife beside him in gaily coloured cotton clothes, children and animals behind. The horses were working in the fields too, a chestnut and white straining at the hay wain or a bay pulling the rake. All the horses were beautifully cared for and more sleekly built than English workhorses.

I don't understand that the rural life which I am observing has not always been like this. I know little or nothing about the history of this area, that it had once been part of Prussia. When we walk to the little town of Giżycko, the crow-stepped roofs of the older brick buildings and the church look Baltic, but the boys do not explain anything to me.

On Tuesday morning, the five of us set out together, and this is the strangest experience of

my hitchhiking life. They plan that we'll get lifts together, five people with our rucksacks and baggage. I'd assumed that we'd be splitting up into smaller groups. Nevertheless, this is what we will do. We establish ourselves at the roadside, and we wait. Taking turns, one person watches out for vehicles, holding my British flag in readiness, and the Autostop card. The rest of us sit around occupying ourselves reading the newspaper, in my case writing my diary, playing hopscotch, learning English or Polish, or just doing plain nothing. Time passes. Then, deciding it is lunchtime, we get out everything to make sandwiches: bread, tomatoes, onions, margarine, knives, packets and tins. The bread is being sliced when, at that exact moment, along comes a large pick-up truck.

"*Szybko, szybko,*" the driver calls. Get in quickly. My diary:

Everything was bundled up somehow and we all clambered into the back. Five minutes later, we were deposited again, still hanging on to all the bits and pieces and having lost many slices of tomato in the process.

We wander along, sometimes resting, getting lifts from one village to another, from Mrągowo to Olsztyn, from Morąg to Pasłęk. Passing by a wooden cottage, an old woman dressed in black calls us over.

"What are you doing? Where are you going?" The boys respond politely. She tells us to wait a moment and then hands us some home-grown cucumbers. It is like being in a fairy tale, an old woman in her flowery cottage garden, offering us her gift.

In one village, the boys get chatting in a suggestive manner to two local girls. This I find disquieting as I know that they had no intentions of anything serious, and soon we leave the girls behind.

It becomes clear that we cannot make Gdańsk that day. By 8.30pm, I am getting tired and bad-tempered because I don't know how much longer they plan to keep going on and can't understand their explanations in Polish. In the end, they find a barn where we pull out our sleeping bags and settle for the night.

Next morning, the 17th of August, my birthday, they rouse me at 5am, and on we go along the country road. My diary:

Then, all of a sudden, beside a little shop, the four boys presented themselves to me with pink smiles on their faces.

They said the equivalent of Happy Birthday in Polish and produced a bunch of flowers for my present, pink and red snapdragons and blue daisies. Julo had stolen them from some cottage garden. The flowers sparkled with morning dew, and they smelled good. I was tickled pink with the thought. One of my nicest presents ever.

GDYNIA

I will soon learn about Polish hospitality. Dionysus has an aunt in Gdynia, the port town adjoining Gdańsk. Her family will accommodate all five of us. As it is no use suggesting anything else, I go along with the plan, and we are welcomed into their flat. Our group of five is added to the two adults and four little girls already staying there.

Near their house is a beach of golden sands, and I look over the Baltic Sea, which is as blue as the Mediterranean. Brown and healthy-looking sunbathers are enjoying the glorious sunshine. This is not my image of the gloom of Communism.

I obtain an Orbis tourist brochure about the three cities of Gdańsk, Sopot and Gdynia. It is in the same mode as those I've had in Warsaw and Poznań, with its own view of history. Gdańsk had always been a Polish town, and there was no mention of the German name of Danzig. The brochure:

'In remote times, Gdańsk was a Slav fishing settlement which in the early Middle Ages became a citadel and a port. It reached its peak period between 1450 and 1650.

'After the First World War Gdańsk became, under the Treaty of Versailles, a free city where Polish installations included a Post Office and railways.

'The postal workers and the Polish military detachment, some 200-strong, wrote their names in history by their

heroic fight with the Nazi invaders in 1939. The shells fired on Westerplatte from the German man-of-war Schleswig-Holstein heralded the outbreak of the Second World War.

'The city became prosperous again after the liberation in 1945. The harbour was rebuilt and the old districts carefully renovated. Old Gdańsk used to be surrounded by systems of walls, bastions and gates. Those which remain now date from the turn of the 15th century.

'Sopot was the bathing resort of the inhabitants of Gdańsk. The 19th century gave it the names of "Northern Riviera" and "Pearl of the Baltic".

'Gdynia, barely forty years old. In 1923, the first ship docked in the port then being built on the site of a small fishing village; a few years later, Gdynia outdistanced Gdańsk as regards tonnage handled. In 1933, it was already the largest and most modern Polish port on the Baltic Sea.'

I cut out pictures from the coloured brochure and stick them alongside black-and-white postcards into my diary. I am readying myself to leave on my own, with the plan that I'd join the *zbereźniki* in Wrocław later.

On the morning of the 19th, I pack my bag in preparation for leaving, heading for the mountains in the south. In Poland, all roads lead in and out of Warsaw, so that is my first destination.

The father of the family gives me two ten zloty coins – collector pieces, he explains – as a present. Pleased at last to be going off on my own, I join the youthful hitchhikers who are thronging the roads in the direction of Warsaw. It doesn't work well. Often the drivers take us along routes which we hadn't expected, and we must retrace our steps. I am tired and hungry most of the day. However, we pass through the little town of Pasłęk, which has an attractive medieval brick gatehouse, and I see some of the great formerly Prussian farms of this area with their half-timbered, pillared farmhouses.

At last I find a farm, knock on the door to ask if I can sleep in the barn, but then I am invited into the house by the man and woman and given a bed. It is astonishing to receive such easy hospitality. What on earth could this farming couple make of an English girl travelling, knocking on their door wanting to sleep in the barn. Next morning, I am plied with fresh eggs, tomatoes, coffee and bread and honey for breakfast.

Then my Autostop card and Union Jack are brought out once again. Amazingly, a lorry soon stops, and I am jolted around in the back for four or five hours with all the other hitchhikers the driver has picked up. He takes us all the way to Warsaw.

I am becoming familiar with the Polish method of hitchhiking by this time, this my thirteenth day in Poland. Next day, my first lift is with a family from the north of the country who feed me with a delicious picnic breakfast in a wood, followed by one with a man whose attitude is not welcome and from whom I quickly departed. As I come further south, I find myself on rolling plains of a soft, chalky limestone. Here, for the first time, I see stone-built cottages. The car which picks me up on the last stage to Kraków had also stopped for a boy whom I'd met along the way earlier. I am becoming one of the crowd! Once in Kraków, I have reached the south of the country, two and a half days' travel from Gdańsk and not a penny paid other than the cost of the bus to the outskirts of Warsaw. And all this thanks to the government-approved Autostop scheme.

THE SIGNIFICANT POST – KRAKÓW

Letters are wating for me in Kraków youth hostel, so I am still linked to my network. My sister Rosie in Germany tells me that instead of continuing with German she is learning American slang from Werner, her new American boyfriend. Therese and Margaret, the Australian girls, are off to Czechoslovakia and send me a forwarding address at an Australian bank in London. Theo wishes me luck. My college friend Jenny tells me stories about our Irish friends. Rob sends a letter telling me the two days he spent in Berlin with me are the best of his trip. My mother tells me that my father has appeared on the local TV programme talking about foot and mouth disease.

In the hostel is a Scottish girl called Isobel with her Polish boyfriend. We have acquaintances in Edinburgh who know each other, and we agree to keep in touch. It feels like a small world. The following day I go around historic Kraków, but I am not in the mood for walking around alone among the tourists. I return to the hostel, which is in a quiet convent. While drinking Russian tea, I write my return letters with a Poste Restante address in Wrocław for replies. Wandering beside the Vistula river, I am feeling homesick.

There is an old woman in the hostel who talks to herself a lot. I begin to wonder if I'll end up like that when I become old, talking to myself because I have no one to talk to. Isobel, the Scottish girl, had said: "I really envy you, having the chance to travel for a year, and I do think you're brave." I don't feel at all brave at that moment. I decide to leave the city at once and move on into the mountains.

THE CARPATHIAN FOOTHILLS

The landscape is of rolling green hills with small farms dotted everywhere and villages with rows of little houses, many made of wood, each in their own plot. I wander along from Myślenice towards Wiśniowa, and the next day from there to Rabka. My diary:

> *The mountains are young fold mountains formed in the Alpine era and are composed in this region of a red Tertiary sandstone. Trace fossils can be found, wormlike fossils. Settlement consists of small peasant holdings distributed all over the hills and rather more concentrated in the valleys. The villages themselves never consist of nucleated settlements but of numbers of houses scattered within a radius of several kilometres. Pastoral farming is predominant, but farms are small and fairly self-contained. Most farms grow some corn (maize). Every farmer has several cows of a red breed very frequent in Poland. Also, goats, chickens, ducks and geese are common.*
>
> *The deciduous trees mingle with natural coniferous growth at the lower valley levels. This changes to coniferous forest and, eventually, bare rock on the highest mountain in this area, Babia Góra, at 1,725 metres.*

Instead of square fields surrounded by hedges, as I am used to in Britain, here the landscape is filled with long, narrow strips. Each house in the village has a small patch of garden and orchard behind it, and beyond that its own land is cultivated in long, narrow strips. The range of different crops makes a colourful striped pattern on the landscape.

I know that among the socialist countries of Eastern Europe, Poland has managed to avoid enforced collectivisation of the farms. It remains a land of independent farmers.

As I come closer to the mountains on the skyline, the rolling foothills are replaced by small, pointed hills with square-shaped fields, green pastures, dotted with trees and woodlands.

Rambling along, I daydream about my own future. The countryside reminds me of my childhood home around Hay-on-Wye on the Welsh borders. My diary:

> *All morning I'd been building up images of a little place I shall have in the country, somewhere near Hay, with a cow and a horse and a barn for all my friends to stay in at weekends. Maybe that will always be my dream.*

Pangs of homesickness overtake me again, and I begin to imagine just getting on a train and going straight back home. In these days, despite the new freedoms of society, the push for a young woman like me to catch her man and get married is still strong. I feel a failure. My younger sister is married, and some of my friends are heading in the same direction. Whereas I, unattached, and in this state of mind, am feeling pulled between the urge to establish a home with a man who loves me beyond all others, and the call of adventure. It had hit me in Berlin and is striking again.

But the countryside is healing, fresh and warm, and I soon cheer up. I follow little tracks between one village and another and sit by a stream for a while. While there, a Polish woman sees me.

"*Skąd Pani jest?*" Where are you from, madam? She asks the usual question, shyly.

"*Proszę Pani do mojego domu,*" she says, inviting me into her farmhouse. It is easy to understand that *domu* means house, and I am well used to *proszę* for please. By now I can have a basic conversation about family and food. She gives me bread and butter and fruit and makes coffee.

Her mother, her children and the grandchildren are all together in this summertime, ages ranging from a child of about three to a teenage girl. There are three boys and five girls, all thin, brown, healthy-looking and barefoot: eight children, who surely must be required to help with the tasks of the farm and yet free to run around in-between times. It seems an enviable life.

It is corn harvest season in the hills, and as I leave them, I wander through little fields with stooks of corn in tidy rows. The people are loading them onto carts pulled by their strong, long-legged horses and wave as I go by. The hay has already been cut and is stacked to dry on picturesque cone-shaped stands among the clover.

Wooden houses, with the flowers rampaging along the garden paths, are unlike any I have seen so far in Poland. There are beehives on wooden stilts in some of the paddocks, roofed and brightly painted. The hives are among the fruit trees in the cottage gardens, sometimes with the family's calves grazing among them, and surrounded by neat, wooded palings. I am bewitched by this lovely scenery.

There is little or no motor transport along the tiny country roads, and it is a pleasure to walk along without thinking about getting lifts. I am heading for the youth hostel at Wiśniowa, and the next day my plan is to continue to the one at Rabka.

I now begin to understand the reason for the extensive network of youth hostels in Poland. In the summer, village schools are converted for the use of group visits to the countryside. And what a sensible idea I think that is. I knock at the door of the house next to the school with the youth hostel sign in Wiśniowa. The young man, probably the school's teacher, looks surprised but welcomes me and shows me in. Unexpected visitors seem unusual, but the rules of the International Youth Hostel Federation allow for individual travellers like me to turn up.

The bunk beds are in rows in the classroom with the children's school desks stacked at the side. I am pleased to be given a set of pans in the school kitchen so that I can prepare myself an evening meal. It turns out that indeed he is the school's teacher. I guess that groups of children are his usual summer clientele.

In the morning, he and his assistant teacher invite me for coffee, and their kindness helps me overcome my homesickness. We can't have much conversation beyond the basic standard sentences, but their smiles and good manners help me overcome my faltering courage. My diary:

> *The products which create my happiness have come all together here. A feeling of purpose, a mileage which had to be walked, lovely scenery in which I felt at home, good weather and food and, most important, friendly people that I liked.*

For two full days I follow tracks and minor roads in the rolling hills until I arrive at a more populated valley with big lorries rattling by. The weather has turned rainy. After getting lost and discouraged, I end up at my destination of Rabka where the youth hostel is once again in a school.

Next day, I take a local train to the town of Maków and, from there, a bus to a village called Zawoja. This place, everyone tells me, is a true mountain village.

I haven't yet worked out where I will spend the night. I sit in a café in Zawoja to keep out of the rain, and I occupy myself by answering letters. I send a note to Tom and the *zbereżniki*. As I plan to meet them later, they provide some kind of certainty in my unfocused life. An English-speaking Polish woman and I start chatting.

"There is an Englishman staying in Zawoja," she says. "Would you like to meet him?"

Of course, I agree. We go to a little wooden house where he is staying. I am enraptured. The house is completely made of wood, built onto a stone foundation. A porch with clambering plants extends into the roof with a dormer window. The windows are painted white, and the roof is of grey slate. The long, wooden beams of the walls meet each other in criss-cross fashion at the corners. Behind the house is a building which is much older, perhaps either a former dilapidated house or a barn, with a steeply sloping roof of wooden tiles extending almost to the ground. My Polish companion knocks on the door, and the Englishman appears.

"What are you doing here?" I ask him.

"I can say the same to you," he says. Neither of us expected to meet someone from England in this remote village.

Frank is undertaking his PhD on the rocks here in the Polish Carpathians. "And you?"

"I am wandering around to see what I can learn. I'm going to be a geography teacher."

"Probably you can stay here too," he suggests and introduces me to his hostess and her aged mother.

"*Tak, tak Pani,*" they say. Yes, yes, of course, madam. And they show me the bedroom.

My bed has clean cotton sheets. This is better than the narrow standard sheet sleeping bag which, like all hostellers, I have been using for the last two nights. I sink into the comfy feather mattress on my first night in blissful contentment. But then I begin to feel something. Am I imagining it? I am tired enough to drop off to sleep. Next morning, the red blobs around my midriff are the evidence. I have had company during the night. When I mention my suspicions to Frank, he says blithely: "You get used to it."

For the next couple of days, he and I go for walks in gaps between the worst of the rain. We chat about his geological studies, based at the Jagiellonian University in Kraków, and his girlfriend Barbara in England. The rain is certainly severe, and I have plenty of practice in saying: *deszcz pada*. Forestry is important in Zawoja. Piles of wood are waiting to be collected and sold, and the wooden houses, fences and barns are in evidence all through the village which straggles for several kilometres along the road. The highest mountain to the south, Babia Góra, is usually hidden in the rain clouds. Beyond that is the unknown land of Czechoslovakia.

In Zawoja, I am able to buy some black-and-white postcards. I stick these in my diary at night, and being in superb detail, they are a good record of the 1966 Zawoja landscape while tourism is still minimal.

After two more nights of insect company, I realise it is time to leave. I count seventy-three bites around my abdomen, and they itch furiously. I pay my hostess what I owe and look through my rucksack for something else I can give her. I pull out a pair of nylon stockings. These are a luxury item in Poland, and I don't know when, if ever, I'd wear them myself. For her aged mother, I donate my set of needles in a pretty plastic flowered pack. Her smile spreads across her wrinkled face.

I leave on a Sunday, walking down the valley, the sun shining now and the mountains on the frontier of Czechoslovakia peeping through the clouds. Sunday still has special meaning in this mountain valley, and everyone is dressed in their best, some of the old women wearing coloured scarves and shawls on their way to church. I walk and hitch in the general direction of Oświęcim, to the next youth hostel along my route. I've learned a little about the green Carpathian foothills, but now I am heading for grimmer regions. And here I'll learn how pathetic, immoral almost, was my own self-pity of the last few days.

OŚWIĘCIM

A Polish name for a Polish town, Oświęcim. But it has another name, and a certain reputation. A little to the west of the town is the concentration camp better known by its German name of Auschwitz.

I find myself in a comfortable hotel in the town centre. Although my handbook tells me there is a youth hostel in town, I don't find it. Consequently, I spend forty zlotys on a room with a shower, and I have a tasty omelette for my supper. And for me, with horrible imagery in my mind of what had happened there, to be resting in comfort seems a travesty. Yet there I am.

Next day, I join a Polish group at the site. Walking around with them, I understand little of the guides' explanation. But I see the thousands of pairs of glasses, the millions of shoes, mugshots of some of the prisoners, mounds of human hair, suitcases in which the unknowing victims carried their belongings and canisters of the Zyklon B pellets which were the source of the poison gas. Our group is taken across the open area towards the notorious entrance to Auschwitz II with its gateway, above which is written *ARBEIT MACHT FREI*. I can only guess what those words mean.

Most of the barracks behind the gateway have been taken down. The brick buildings that are left are dark and dour. More than a million people. Each one with a story, a family. The gas chambers and the crematoriums. It is too much to comprehend. Too fearsome to grasp.

I find it hard to write adequately about this place in my diary. At twenty-two years of age, I am naive and have been protected from horror all my life. The best I can do is this:

It was a dreadful place. I found it so difficult to understand how people can be so cruel to other human beings. It must be terrible ever to truly learn the meaning of hate. I felt sure everyone thought I was German as the party walked around.

One thing I realised is that this camp is preserved to keep the fear and wickedness of war alive in people's minds, to keep people alert to the danger of Nazism and also to preserve anti-German feeling in Poland so that the Poles will look on the Soviet Union as the liberator.

I cut out the following extract in French from a tourism leaflet and stick it in my diary:

C'est à Oświęcim et dans la localité voisine de Brzezinka que les hitlériens avaient crée au cours de la dernière guerre des camps de concentration où périrent dans les chambres à gaz et les fours crématoires plus de 4 millions de personnes de diverses nationalités. Il ne faut pas manquer la visite du Musée de la Martyrologie.

It is at Oświęcim, and nearby at Brzezinka, that the Hitlerians created, in the course of the last war, the concentration camps, where perished in the gas chambers and the ovens of the crematoriums more than four million people of various nationalities. It is important to visit the Museum of Martyrology.

From this time onwards, I find myself looking at Polish people of my parents' generation and wondering what they know, what they have seen, what they suffered or what they have done. In this sunny August weather, in peacetime, it is all incomprehensible.

The smoky Silesian coalfields

My family had moved to the north-east of England when I was eleven years of age, and so I am accustomed to coalfield cities where all the buildings are blackened with coal smoke. I know about colliery towns, pit heaps, belching steam trains and billowing chimneys. I hold in my memory the smell of coal smoke which, in damp weather, hangs in the atmosphere so that one takes it in at every breath. Now, as I enter into the Silesian coalfield area of Poland, it feels familiar.

I sit on a road bridge over a railway and draw a pen portrait in the centre of this area, between Mysłowice and Katowice. My diary:

Since leaving Oświęcim at midday, travelling in the direction of Katowice, the area has become more and more industrialised. It is very flat here, but several low ridges and many spoil dumps enable extensive views from certain points. In fact, this is the valley-plain region of the river Vistula and tributaries with their source in the Carpathian Mountains, which flow through Warsaw and Gdańsk to the Baltic Sea.

From where I'm sitting, a panorama of industry can be seen in every direction. Four of the old wheel shafts of coal pits are within five minutes' walk, and several more are further away in the smoky haze. The skyline is one of the most fascinating I have ever seen, and what a contrast to the mountains only a few miles away.

Standing out in the haze most conspicuously are literally hundreds of factory chimneys, mostly long and thin, and many coughing up black smoke. There are pylons too, tall, insect-like constructions stretching their lines across the whole landscape. Many tall buildings stand out, and church spires of old, blackened red bricks are plentiful.

Between the mass of buildings, factories obviously in full production and dirty, tumbledown-looking houses, are large areas of derelict land, spoil heaps, slag heaps and old coal sites now overgrown with weeds and grass, much of it flooded or marshy. Some of them have been given back to the farmers, and a man and horse are cutting hay behind me. A large area of land, however, remains useless.

A network of railway lines obviously deals with most of the heavy transport, but there are more lorries here than anywhere else in Poland that I've seen. Trains and lorries are chugging around all the time, and although they are all old-fashioned, they're nevertheless working hard to justify their existence.

The villages seem to straggle in and out of the industrial sites, being as dirty and poverty-stricken as any English pit village. Despite the raggedy children and soot-covered houses, I feel there is no real poverty and, as in England, the insides of those houses are probably sparkling clean.

The sun is shining and it's a hot day. From here, all around every chimney-poked horizon, the sun beams hazily through the smoke, and the air must be quite unhealthy. This is the area of Polish extractive industry. I have several miles to walk before I reach Katowice, and the panorama looks as though it will be the same all the way.

I know that taking photographs of industrial enterprises is forbidden. Even though I don't know how my amateurish attempts might threaten the mighty socialist state, I do sneak one or two snaps. I am a little nervous in case I am being spied on by someone wondering: *Why would she want to take a picture of that? Who is*

she going to show it to? Then they might tell the police who could confiscate my film.

I take a photo from the railway bridge showing a cart pulled by horses being passed by a couple of lorries, black smoke billowing from chimneys behind. Another is of two pithead winding wheels which would look quite at home in the north-east coalfields. The sign on the closer shaft, which probably named the pithead, was later scratched off before I collected the photos. Who would do that? Someone in the photographer's shop wanting to fight this dangerous enemy of socialism?

While resting in a pit village near Mysłowice, two fair-haired little boys sit with me on the grass, one barefoot. The straight road lined with houses behind us bears hardly a vehicle or a person.

Arriving at Katowice, the largest city in the area, I discover once again that the hostel is closed, and so I hitch onwards to Bytom. Here, fortunately, the hostel in the school is open, and I have a room all to myself for a handful of zlotys. My diary:

My window looks out over roofs, chimneys and city lights. Sounds from the roaring of buses and cars to the squeaking of pram wheels and voices of people all carry up to my room. The next morning I fill with wandering around Bytom. It is a typical type of industrial town, tram wires, sooty buildings, cobbled streets. The old women of this region wear an interesting costume: long black skirts, pastel-coloured tops, apron and headscarf.

Postcards are not easy to find in Poland, but I am able to buy two in Bytom. One shows soot-encrusted, old-fashioned, six-storey buildings overlooking a park with a round fountain in the middle. The back of the card reveals the name of the park, *Plac Feliksa Dzierżyńskiego*, with the name also in English, French and Russian, but not German, despite the town having been part of Germany before the war.

I know Felix Dzerzhinsky to be a wicked man who headed the Soviet state's secret police. Yet here, in 1966 Poland, the square is named after him. Surely only hard-line Stalinists would see him as worthy of this honour. The postcard is, I hope, a relic of an earlier oppressive epoch. Yet I feel the faint shadow of fear hanging over Poland from the past.

The cost of posting a card like that is sixty groszy. I buy two stamps showing pride in Poland's industrial development. One shows the Lenin steelworks at Kraków and the other a gigantic power station at Turoszów.

I buy another card, a watercolour in pinks, greys and browns. It shows a town called Wałbrzych, a townscape with factory chimneys and housing set against the background of a rounded mountain. It could have been a picture from the Welsh valleys or the Durham coalfield.

Being sociable in Wrocław

"Hello, English girl," says the tall young man at the roadside. He is holding up his Autostop card and has seen my Union Jack. "Where you going?"

I tell him I am going to Wrocław, and we agree to go together. His name is Stanisław. He is from Gdańsk and, like so many young people, spending his summer holiday hitchhiking around Poland.

A lorry stops, and the driver invites us to clamber up. Yes, he is going to Wrocław. It is a hot, sticky day, and after picking up several more hitchhikers, the driver pulls up beside a pool made from a blocked stream. Here everyone strips down to the basics, me putting on my swimsuit discreetly, and we all have a swim. The driver benefits from quite a few Autostop stamps that day.

Once at Wrocław, fair-haired Cesary, one of the other hitchhikers, invites Stanisław and me to stay with his family in their flat. His mother seems unsurprised at him turning up with unexpected visitors. We are given food, and the use of the bathroom, and then sit and watch Polish television all evening with the family until bedtime. Just like that!

As visitors, packed into the tiny flat, Stanisław and I are accommodated in the same room as Cesary, the teenage son.

I do find that odd, but no one turns a hair. At bedtime, Cesary is practising on his guitar; Stanisław is looking at his English grammar book; and I am writing in my diary.

"*Komm, essen,*" Cesary's mother says in the morning. She thinks I'd understand her German better than Polish. She puts out bread, jam, butter and lots of black tea, watched by her two daughters. In the course of conversation with Stanisław, who is able to translate, she explains that their family had come from the east of Poland. Like many Polish people in Wrocław, as I will learn, they were deported from the eastern sector of Poland, which was taken over by the Soviet Union after the war, and rehabilitated in the western part, taken from Germany. They were like hundreds of thousands of others included as part of the great move westwards of the boundaries of Poland. The Soviet Union has moved its area of influence westwards.

Gypsies in Wrocław

"Hey, boy, what are you doing?" Cesary is accompanying Stanisław and me as far as Wrocław centre. We are crossing a

wasteland between his apartment block and the city, and he calls
out to a boy he knew among the gypsies camped there. My diary:

*There must have been at least eight wooden caravans in a wide
circle, and we soon had a crowd around us. The children were a
lively, good-looking bunch with their dark, curly hair and dark
eyes, though there were other colourings. Their clothes were really
gay, many of the girls wearing long chiffon dresses with frills. I
had no trouble getting them to queue to have their photo taken,
and the huge ear-ringed father joined the scene. I found them
quite as interesting as they found me, and it was a relief to be able
to stare openly, as they did. Some of the children had scabs and
skin infections, which was a shame as they were so pretty.*

*I showed them a few things from my rucksack, and they
all wanted my compass. I managed to hold on to that but did
sacrifice a few safety pins.*

*One of the boys was unbelievably handsome, with dark,
curly hair, curling
eyebrows and lashes
and deep black eyes.
They were a saucy lot,
though. The children's
friendly farewell was
to throw stones at us as
they laughed, and the
girls danced. This was
received by roars and
threats from the older
boys.*

As we leave, I am glad to
learn that there are still
some gypsies in Poland

and that not all perished in the Holocaust. They are so sparkling in comparison with the calmer, dignified Poles.

Eastern bloc young people in Wrocław

Stanisław is going to find his girlfriend in Wrocław, and I am heading to meet the *zbereżniki*. My diary:

> *When I got near their street I heard that Polish wolf whistle I know so well, and a minute later Dionysus came rushing out, followed by Tom. I was so pleased to see them. I was promenaded into Tom's house, while Dionysus fetched Julo and Marian.*

Tom's mother makes me a delicious meal of scrambled eggs, tea and bread and butter. He has already told her about me, and she accepts my arrival with equanimity.

Then we all go to look around the town. The full horrors of the siege of Wrocław are revealed to me by Stanisław. He gives me a booklet in black and white, showing pictures of the destroyed city in 1945 and the current reconstructions. My diary:

> *Wrocław still has many bomb sites and burnt-out buildings which I believe the Germans did to their own city when the Russians came in from the east. Much has been rebuilt however, judging from photographs which are available. We climbed a church tower from which we could see the city, which has acres of new, flat buildings all around it.*

There are few cars and virtually no advertising. My companions don't refer to the German origin of Wrocław, with its name of Breslau. As young people, they've grown up seeing it as a Polish city. Like me, born at the end of the war or soon afterwards, they've known it only as Wrocław. It has always been Polish as far as they

are concerned. For Tom and Marian, Julo and Dionysus, Stanisław and Cesary, this is their reality in 1966.

Yet it feels as though we are tiptoeing still through the relics of war. All the parents of these boys have been through its traumas, in close, stark reality. Any of them could have told many an unhappy story about the past if I'd had the language to understand.

As we wander along by the banks of the *Odra*, past his university, I comment to Tom: "It is so peaceful here. No advertising. Hardly any cars."

But Tom has a different point of view. "For me, I would like to try it. I would like to have a car. This is not possible for me in Poland. If I had a car, I could go wherever I want. I would feel free."

And of course, he is quite right. It is easy for me to say what I did as I have a choice, and he does not.

Marian and Tom accompany me to the youth hostel in the evening where I'd said I'd meet Stanisław. My diary:

There was a Polish boy there who speaks a little English and wants to hitchhike with me. I said I would go with him after two days. He's the rough, tough, beat-poet type, handsome, attractive and intelligent. But the other boys didn't like him, and they instilled doubts in my mind.

I have the address of a very nice Yugoslav boy too. I speak enough Polish now not to be a complete dumb mute, and bits of English, French and German are mixed in with the conversation. I haven't exactly decided what I'll do when I leave Wrocław.

"*Belgrade est une belle ville. Tu dois aller là-bas. Je t'aide trouver accommodation,*" Dushko, the boy from Yugoslavia, tells me. Belgrade is a beautiful city. You must go there. I can help you find accommodation. Our mutual language is a little French. As I have a vague idea of being in Israel by Christmas, the idea of finding help to stay along the way sounds appealing.

Dushko is an enthusiastic Communist Party member, a student group at Belgrade's university. He is the first admitted Communist that I've met, but this causes no apparent friction within the company.

The young Poles and he speak to each other in their own languages, his Serbo-Croat and their Polish being apparently mutually comprehensible. They all know some Russian, but they much prefer to try their English with me as intermediary.

At Tom's house, his mother has organised a bed for me in the living room of their apartment. Like all such dwellings that I've been in, each room has multiple uses. Sofa beds are normal and used, as in my case, for guests. Mine has clean, white cotton sheets, and a frilly pink nightdress is laid out on the pillow.

I write a letter to my family in England:

Tom's mother is fairly old, fiftyish. She gives me heaps of food, including fried potatoes you eat with sugar and jam, sausage-shaped items made of cheese, flour and potato covered with spices. I can't get used to sugar and cream cheese together. They put sugar on almost everything and they think I'm very odd when I put salt on the same things.

Tom's father is very kind too. Like most adult Polish people, he speaks German as they were forced to learn it when the Germans were here. And like most Polish people, he automatically showers me with a kind of pidgin German, so I'm learning some of that language too.

THE RUSSIAN CEMETERY

"We'll take you to see our Russian friends!" says Tom ironically, early next day. "Dionysus's brother Lutek will be coming too."

There are two great Red Army tanks at the entrance to the Soviet Army Officers' Cemetery. The boys translate the plaque:

DEDICATED TO ALL THE RUSSIAN SOLDIER HEROES WHO DIED FIGHTING GERMAN FASCISM

Then Tom and Lutek start to clamber up to the top of one of the tanks.

"Hey, don't do that," I cry out. "There might be someone with guns around." This could be seen as a defiant political statement rather than youthful high spirits. But all remains calm, and I take a photograph.

"Look who's coming!" Tom says. Walking down the paved pathway from the pillared monument in our direction is a smartly dressed soldier.

"Can you speak to him?" I ask. This is not a chance to be missed, to meet a soldier from our Cold War enemy, the Soviet Union.

These boys with their easy command of Russian engage him in conversation. They tell him I am from England. What does he know about that? What rumours and horror stories about my capitalist country might he have learned? I look at him with as much curiosity as he looks at me.

Why is he wandering around this cemetery in his smart dress uniform, his cap with the red hammer and sickle emblem, medals on his tightly belted jacket and knee-length black boots? I find out later that he is wearing the uniform of a Soviet army major. We look at each other, but the mysteries are more than the explanations. He must suspect that the young Polish men dislike the presence of the Soviet army in Poland. However, this is a casual encounter. No officers who are senior to him are around, and he writes down his name and address in Cyrillic capital letters for me.

"May I take a photograph?" I ask, and the three young men stand smartly to attention.

I note in my diary that 'we said *Do swidania* instead of the Polish *Do widzenia* when we said goodbye'. How alike and yet how different we all are.

"He was not very well educated, you know," comments Tom, once our new acquaintance is well out of sight. He and Lutek chuckle as they mimic the way he spoke Russian as if it were a crude local dialect.

"He could only print his name in clumsy capital letters," adds Lutek. We look at what he wrote on the scrap of paper I had provided. But I suspect that, although they were friendly and polite to him in front of me, the element of fear is not entirely absent. The Red Army overshadows their lives in ways I cannot fully understand.

We wander around looking at the neatly coiffured tombs of the officer cemetery, all the same size, bearing the date of the 6th of May 1945 and a simple red star. These men had died when I was a baby in my mother's arms.

One photo of a tomb has survived in my diary. It bears the surname of Osipov, and the date is the 6th of May 1945. I am thinking that this lost soldier was a man just like the young Russian officer we met. In times of war, such young men can become involved in brutal battles of extraordinary violence, unimaginable on a peaceful summer day like this. And who is to say it will never happen again, here in a country like Poland on the borderlands of Europe?

We have more Russian culture one evening when off we go to the glamorous pillared opera house for a performance of Borodin's Prince Igor. Andrzej, one of Tom's friends, comes with us and turns up impressively in full evening dress. This being a socialist country, high-culture opera is available for the masses. It is not essential to dress smartly, and I see cloth caps and T-shirts, jackets and sandals. In any case, for me it is a choice of my denim skirt or my best red dress, so I wear the latter with my flip-flops.

My diary reveals that I go to sleep a couple of times, even though the performance is doubtless first class. I can't understand the Polish dialogue, and I find the music heavy going. However, I wake up brightly for the splendid dancing sequence, which my diary records as 'hurly-burly, hurtle scurtle, terrific leaps and twists and bounds, wild and fiery music'.

At another time, at Andrzej's house, we have a different kind of music session. He is the musical one among Tom's friends, and I am always keen to learn more folk tunes or play around on different instruments.

"Bridget, you must try this accordion," he says. My diary:

The manipulation of not being able to see the button on the left hand, playing a tune with the right and pulling at the same time, also reading the music, it was fantastically complicated. I know what to do, but trying to do so many things at once is too much for me. Still, we had a good time with Andrzej. He was playing on the piano and clarinet. I decided of course that the man I marry must be musical.

As we walk home, Dionysus and Julo share plums and apples they have stolen.

That evening, Tom is telling me about Poland in Stalin's time and how glad everyone was when the dictator died in 1953, thirteen years ago, when he was a child. He says twenty-five thousand Polish people are still living in a camp somewhere in the eastern Soviet Union, people who disappeared in the war and in Stalin's time. No one can know its whereabouts. No one can go east of Moscow.

The subject of Germany comes up. My diary:

The West Germans in the eyes of these people are a danger to their future even now. They are being allowed to rearm; they are a wealthy capitalistic people; they want Silesia and Western Poland back for Germany.

Marian could only say: "West German bad fascist."

Of course, these young people in Wrocław are worried. If West Germany wants back the area of Poland in which they live, what would happen to them all?

In the course of my travels in Poland, I've twice encountered individual German girls from the DDR. Each time, I noted that they were friendly but not communicative, and my diary mentions my feeling that there is little laughter in their lives. It can't have been easy answering the inevitable question: where are you from? I've certainly learned that it was diplomatic for me to show that I am not German while I am in Poland.

Churches

In the course of my weeks here, I have paid no attention to churches other than looking at them from the outside. Although I know Poland is mainly Catholic, the young friends I've made never drew my attention, one way or another, to churches.

But one day, Andrzej says: "You must come and see this special church," and we go with Tom and Julo. This is the first time I have ever been in an eastern Orthodox church, and I note in my diary what I see and what my friends explain to me:

Most of the Eastern European countries, that is Bulgaria, Russia and parts of Hungary and Poland, have adopted the branch of Christianity which spread from Constantinople as distinct from Roman Catholicism. The texts are written in Old Slavonic language, similar to Russian. The service is also in this language.

The church music was sung by a mixed choir, in four parts. It was written as normal but had no time notation. The words were in Old Slavonic, and the music dates from the fifth to sixth centuries.

> *The priest was a spectacular figure. He entered the church when everything was ready for the service in his black robes and his Archbishop Makarios-shaped headdress. He had hair as long as a beatnik's, a thick beard and glassy eyes. He conducted the whole service in an automatic way, as though he himself was doing nothing, his mind removed from his body which was a shell performing a function. The whole service was a scene of a thousand years ago, what with incense, symbolic signs, heaving bells donging at crucial points in the service.*

The church had been Catholic when Wrocław was German. One corner was reserved for a Catholic chapel, Andrzej tells me. A priest who has no church in Wrocław asked for a little corner for himself, and he was allowed to have this.

I am given a twenty-four-page booklet which is written in Russian, and from this I can see that this is the permitted Polish branch of the Orthodox church, with its headquarters in Warsaw.

Andrzej presents me with a page of beautifully handwritten, Cyrillic text on squared schoolbook paper, from the *Kodeks Marianski, Mateusz XXl*, in the Old Slavonic language. From this visit, I realise that the Communist government is permitting this form of worship in Wrocław in 1966. My *zbereżniki* friends are clearly interested in this church, but whether it is because of the beauty of the liturgy, or that they are true believers, or just want to show me something different, I don't know.

KODEKS MARIAŃSKI

(Mateusz XXI)

[18] ЮТРО ЖЕ ВЪЗВРАШТЪ СА ВЪ ГРАДЪ ВЪЗАЛКА.

[19] I ОУЗЬРѢВЪ СМОКОВЬНИЦЯ ЕДИНЯ ПРИ ПѦТИ.
ПРИДЕ КЪ НЕИ. I НИЧЬСОЖЕ НЕ ОБРѢТЕ НА НЕ
ТЪКМО ЛИСТВЬЕ ЕДИНО. I Г(ЛАГО)ЛА ЕИ. ДА
НИКОЛИЖЕ ПЛОДА ОТЪ ТЕБЕ НЕ БѦДЕТЪ
ВЪ ВѢКЪ. I АБЬЕ ИСЪШЕ СМОКОВЬНИЦА.

[20] I ВИДѢВЪШЕ ОУЧЕНИЦИ ДИВИША СА ГЛ(АГОЛ)Ю
КАКО АБЬЕ ОУСЪШЕ СМОКОВЬНІЦА.

[21] ОТЪВѢЩАВЪ ЖЕ И(СОУ)СЪ РЕЧЕ ИМЪ. АМИНЬ
Г(ЛАГО)ЛЬѦ ВАМЪ. АЩЕ ИМАТЕ ВѢРѦ И НЕ
ОУСѦМЬНИТЕ СА НЕ ТКМО СМОКОВЬНИЧЬНОЕ
СЪТВОРИТЕ. НЪ АШТЕ И ГОРѢ СЕИ РЕЧЕТЕ

ORTHODOX CHURCH

'The Orthodox Church conducted religious activities by permission of Communist authorities in Poland, but its church hierarchy was totally infiltrated by secret agents. Almost all bishops were, for example, the covert agents of SB (the Polish version of KGB). They should be totally loyal to the Communist government. Most of the Orthodox practising people live in Eastern Poland (now about 150–200,000), but many were removed after the Second World War to new post-German lands, including Wrocław'.

Janusz Zaręba, personal communication, January 2021

GOING SHOPPING

All the time I have been in Poland, there has been no difficulty in buying what I need. My food needs are simple: bread, cheese, butter, eggs, tomatoes, cucumber, all easily obtainable.

There is food in the shops. Virtually all of them are state shops, with a limited choice of goods, poorly displayed and indifferently served. I find a postcard of a *Dom Towarowy*, a shop selling a variety of goods in the town of Cybinka. Such a shop is sufficiently novel to be celebrated with a postcard. It shows that the customers either walk there or cycle, parking their bikes in racks on the pavement. If they come by motorbike, they park on the street. There is not a car in sight.

Certainly, I frequently see queues. In a Wrocław street, as I pass by, a shop has had a delivery of glassware. Women with prams and smartly dressed young men line up patiently. There are often queues for meat.

In a letter to my friends in England, I tell them about the cost of clothes:

Mary – the old sweater you gave me from the Oxfam box is really admired here as it is the height of fashion. [It is a brown, fluffy mohair buttoned cardigan.] Everyone tries to touch it.

Clothes here are fantastically expensive. Both ready-made outfits and material cost far more than in England. An average decent sweater costing about £2 in Marks & Spencer here would cost £10 to £11. And it would be much poorer quality.

I need to go on a shopping spree as my legally allowable time in Poland is drawing to an end. My remaining zlotys are of no value outside the country, and anyway it is illegal to take them out. The question is how best to use the money.

Tom and Andrzej help. They know the odd hidden little private places where I might buy things of interest for souvenirs. I buy two crocheted collars for dresses; a pair of hand-made leather shoes for a baby; carved wooden brooches for my friends from college; a set of coloured art postcards for my father; and Polish songbooks for my mother and me. My final treasure, which uses up nearly all my remaining zlotys, is a little girl's traditional Polish costume. It consists of a white blouse with red ribbons threaded through the neck and sleeves, a red cotton skirt with coloured stripes stitched around, a black waistcoat with coloured patterns of sequins and a nifty white apron. It costs the equivalent of £5. I don't know exactly where this will end up, or if I'd ever have a little daughter, but it is a good way to use up my remaining zlotys and is probably a good sale for a hard-working dressmaker.

Now it all has to be packaged up and posted. I can hardly carry all these items around with me in my rucksack during my onwards march towards Yugoslavia and Israel. So, once it is all neatly packed up with the help of Tom's mother, the patient boys escort me to the queues at the post office. Unfortunately, the customs restrictions are onerous and ridiculously expensive. I am cross but decide not to send the parcel. I'll have to take the gifts, which fortunately are not bulky, out of Poland with me and send them home from West Germany.

TIME TO LEAVE

It is Tuesday the 6th of September, nearly time for the expiry of my visa.

That evening, Dionysus whips me upstairs to his house where they are having a party to commemorate my leaving with Marian, Tom and Julo, his family, girls and parents and children. I feel real affection for the *zbereżniki* and sad to be leaving them behind. I am obliged to drink a couple of glasses of vodka and am wrapped in the warmth of their friendliness and their charming, slightly tipsy selves.

Next day, Wednesday the 7th of September, I must leave Wrocław. I hand Tom my illicit copy of *Doctor Zhivago*. He and Julo come with me on the tram to the edge of the city. Tom is laughing and joking as usual, and Julo's handsome face is nearby. The moment we get down from the tram onto the roadside, a car stops. A quick farewell, and they help me with my bags into the car. I am whipped away.

This must be a moment of truth for Tom and Julo. I am leaving, but they are not free to leave. The barrier is implacable. This is surely the thought in their minds as the car carries me away.

To the frontier

The lift takes me to one small town, after which I walk for a while and then get a lift to another. I am crossing the slightly rolling farmlands that had once been in Germany and then added to the west of Poland at the end of the war. I find a farm where I can stay in the village of Krosno, about twenty-five miles from Kunowice station. Where my Polish journey started is where it will end. I am due to catch the train out of Poland the next day.

The farmer is kind, but he takes my passport overnight. This rather shocks me, but he is probably a little worried about who I am and what I am doing in this frontier district where smugglers, escapees and illegal migrants might be moving around. Otherwise, my plans are working like clockwork. My diary:

The next day, Thursday the 8th of September, I left the farm early and got a lift straight to Słubice, close to Kunowice station. Słubice is the small Polish frontier town on the opposite side of the river Oder from Frankfurt. I had quite a surprise when I arrived and was deposited by the main road crossing, where the traffic from the DDR passes through into Poland.

On the other side of the river from where I'm now sitting is a haunted-looking series of dockside industries and trading establishments. There are some barges bearing the black, red and yellow flag of the DDR, piles of coal, chimneys tall and thin. The twin towers of a church point sadly and grimly into the sky.

Although Frankfurt is obviously a busy trading centre, noises of machines and engines boom at different pitches and echo across the water, that feeling of emptiness, of a deserted, unloved city, carries over to me here. Although I've been sitting here for well over an hour, not a car has passed between the two towns, the main road between Moscow and the West.

The water is wide and deep, flowing steadily northwards to the Baltic Sea. Even the river is divided, red flags marking the narrow German stretch off from the wider Polish stretch which is not navigated. Although figures can be seen working on the dockside, never a voice is raised.

The Polish side of the river was probably one of the bourgeois areas of Frankfurt before the war. Tall tenement houses overlook the river. Not many people are around, although some have time to wander down to the waterside and sit in the sun.

Słubice itself is quite a happy little town but seems quieter than the average Polish village. I can't imagine many Polish people who were moved here after the war would have wanted to be so close to the hated Germans.

Now here I am, lying on the grass beside the Odra, in Poland, and looking over into one of the most dangerous and tricky countries to get to know in Europe. Tomorrow I'll be going through it, not stopping until Berlin, and then hitching through the other side of East Germany and into the West again. That is, I am if all goes according to plan.

I'm leaving Poland. Today I'm behind the Iron Curtain. Tomorrow I won't be.

I have time to write the above and ruminate on my four weeks in Poland. Three fair-haired little Polish boys join me, curious about my Union Jack which I have stuck in the ground. They are wearing woolly tights under their shorts, and one with a round hand-knitted cap on his head is holding an important cardboard box. The photo I have of them shows the weeds on the riverbank and the road bridge between the two countries behind.

The *Odra*/Oder river is a significant boundary. And yet the movement between the two countries, as reflected by the road traffic, seems minimal. It still feels like enmity, a remainder of

wartime animosity. I am looking over the DDR, an unfriendly land which separates the people of Poland from the West. Even though both countries are within the Soviet-dominated Eastern bloc, and under strict Communist regimes, there are still tensions. Movement is not straightforward.

I came to Poland with little knowledge and am leaving with only a little more. If I'd come as part of a coach tour group, I would have had much more Polish history explained to me. I'd have visited palaces and great churches and cathedrals and had fairly comfortable accommodation in hotels. If I'd come with a socialist friendship group, I'd have been given a politically biased tour. But I had done none of those things.

I am not a great deal wiser about Polish history and have learned only a little more of the great and melancholy dramas of the twentieth century. My encounters with people were as a guest and, in that sense, superficial. They haven't regaled me with their problems or their stories of past miseries. And there has been the lack of language. How much have I understood of what I was seeing? I've been lucky in that I have not clashed with any fearsome authorities with their rules and regulations.

What I have done is to share a summer interlude with the *zbereżniki* and their friends. I will not be here to see the reality of their daily lives once summer is over. But in these August days which we've spent together, I've shared their conversations and their pleasures, and I can see that all is not morbid. The main difference between their lives and mine, as students, seems to be that I am free, even though with some difficulty, to travel in their country, but they are not free to travel in mine.

I've managed to spend a month in Poland on the limited budget of £30, which in fact is more than enough according to my normal hitchhiking lifestyle of staying in barns, farms and youth hostels. I've had left over money to spend on a shopping spree which included a little girl's traditional costume.

As for the countryside and the landscape, I've seen the lake district, the mountains of the Carpathians and the coal and steel belt of the area around Katowice. I've had glimpses of Warsaw and Gdańsk and spent a week in Wrocław with friends who took me to places of unusual interest. My knowledge of Polish has developed sufficiently to manage everyday situations, and I've looked in the face of a Soviet army soldier.

My journey has not been like that of an ace journalist or a university academic who would have interesting reports of wider concern in the West. Mine is humbler. I've been engaged with the everyday lives of people, quietly, moving around from place to place according to my own priorities. My story doesn't reflect great insights. I have simply gained a feeling about the country. And now, later in the day, I am leaving, without any certainty that I'll ever return.

That is, I'll be leaving if all goes to plan, which it does not.

ON THE TRAIN AND OFF AGAIN

The grassy bank at Słubice upon which I was meditating is just a few kilometres from Kunowice station where I arrive in good time for the evening train. Near the station is a little snack kiosk, and I have three hours to wait. It makes sense to spend my last handful of zlotys on supplies of food. My diary:

> *There was a man sitting whose papers were somehow wrong, and he had waited seven hours without any money, so I bought him tea and biscuits. Little did I guess the tables were soon to be turned. The great train came a-roaring in, and after being duly examined and stamped, I climbed on. Then, a minute later, I was chased off again by a uniformed border guard, and the train left without me.*

What on earth has happened? It takes time to understand my situation, but eventually I work out that it is something like this. The available thirty days of my visa ended on the 9th of September. I am leaving on the 8th of September. Surely that is acceptable? But what I had got wrong was that because I'd arrived in Poland on the 8th of August, I am now trying to leave on the 32nd day since then. In other words, I should have registered with the police two days earlier.

How could I possibly have understood that explanation while I was on the great train waiting to steam out of Poland, from officious border guards speaking sternly to me in Polish and everybody looking at me? I was told to go to the police station in Słubice. That much I do understand.

So there I am, deposited on Kunowice station platform, with no Polish money, no place to stay the night, and the next day my visa will expire. What possible advantage the security of the Polish state could gain by throwing me off the train is a mystery. They make it hard enough to come into their country with their visa

73

system, and now they are making it hard for me to get out. And as my visa is due to run out the next day, I can imagine the costs and bureaucracy of trying to sort that out. My diary:

> *However, trying to be philosophical and laughing at my own rage, I set out to solve my problems. By very good fortune, the first farm I asked if I could stay at proved very hospitable. I will be eternally grateful for the way they accepted me without any question. I left my bags with them and set out for Słubice as night was falling.*
>
> *There was a beautiful sunset, but I was a bit scared of this precarious border region at night and didn't like hitching. As I was picked up by two French boys, I was all right, but my next pleasure was to discover that the police station could not help me until tomorrow. I'd walked all the way in the dark for nothing and missed the morning train into the bargain. I quaked back between the gloomy deserted fields and woods and imagined all sorts of noises and spy-traps that I might fall into. Of course, I got back safely and sat talking to the family, with their two friendly daughters, for an hour before dropping asleep in a cuddly feather bed.*
>
> *I say 'talking', but really I am struggling through conversation in Polish, using the few words I know. It's a pity for me that I'm leaving Poland. Polish is a difficult language to say the least, and so entirely different from English. I can now understand a little and speak back a sentence or two. It's not much to have learned in a month, but I'm getting a hold onto the way to say things, and now I'm leaving. I'll have to struggle with Deutsche next.*

Next day I do manage to get to Słubice and sort out the registration with the police. I am back at the farm by midday. Hence I am able to lend a hand with some raking in the hayfield, my train not leaving until the evening.

I have some time to write some observations in my diary too, which I called 'Towns and Farms in the Western Region of Poland, Formerly Germany':

The buildings are almost without exception old German buildings. The whole scene is a mixture between old German formal building and town layout and the poorer, less organised but gayer Polish atmosphere. Even the old Germanic cottages are overflowing with weeds and flowers in the gardens.

The land is farmed differently from the other parts of Poland I've seen. Although this area has been resettled by Poles, large open fields predominate. Most other Polish field patterns are of long, narrow strips.

However Polish horses, carts and haystacks are still to be seen. Today I was out haymaking, and the large fields are inconspicuously divided into peasant plots. The farmer's wife said to me: "Much work, little money," and it is true that Polish farming is uneconomic. The field in question was fifteen minutes' journey from the farmhouse.

A type of haystack here is interesting. The movable roof supported by four poles forms a shelter for the hay. This type I've seen in larger versions in Holland.

The villages around here seem to have a characteristic pattern. Small, square-shaped detached houses line the roadside. Each has a series of barns and buildings forming a square yard behind. At a T-angle, a small road goes off, also lined with houses. All the houses appear to be peasant farms. The village is nucleated, with fields for each farmer divided round about. Every farmer seems to have a few cows, pigs and poultry and is, to some degree, self-sufficient. The houses themselves look certainly twentieth century, although many of the half-timbered barns are old. Possibly these are planned villages.

The land around here is very sandy and infertile. In some places, piles of sand dunes can be seen, which bear only scanty grass covering. Peasants dig sand and pile it into their carts. Many exposed sand quarries can be seen.

These observations include what I'd seen the day before as I hitchhiked from Wrocław. If I hadn't had a day's delay owing to the saga of the errant visa, neither would I have shared the haymaking with this kind family, nor had time to write all this in my diary.

Leaving Poland

"*Do widzenia.*" Goodbye. The two girls from the farm wave me off onto the evening train. I feel bitterly sad to be going. My diary:

But this was not the end. The train puffed out of the station, stopped and puffed back in again. Each time, the train was thoroughly searched by Polish soldiers.

Fortunately, my bits and pieces are in order this time; who knows what they are looking for. I am reminded, once again, of the danger and paranoia at border crossings, even within the Communist countries themselves. The train crosses the Oder into the DDR and stops yet once more. My diary:

> *We were searched again as we entered the grey Deutsche Demokratische Republik: passports, visa, currency declaration etc. My visa wasn't alright. I don't know why. So, they took from me all my German money for a new one. Oh, this business of getting through Communist frontiers! We eventually arrived in East Berlin, riding through that ghostly city at night. The horrifying no man's land between the two parts of Berlin is even worse at night. I could only imagine the terrors anyone goes through who tries to escape.*
>
> *West Berlin at last, full of noise and clamour and colour. Having no money, and it being midnight or thereabouts, I was in a pretty pickle. Eventually I found a mission where I was given a clean bed and, despite the noise of trains rumbling overhead, I slept like a log.*

Next day, I get a lift in a Dutch lorry right across the DDR and through the border controls. The date is Saturday the 10th of September 1966. I've traversed the Iron Curtain, leaving behind all those people whom I have met and consider friends behind its barrier, whereas I can go where I want. And I do. By Friday the 16th of September, I am in the southern part of West Germany, in Munich, and I have a job.

POLAND CHRONOLOGY

1939	Nazi Soviet pact, division of Poland
1939	Germany invades Poland, start of the Second World War
1939–1945	Nazi government rules Poland, Soviet army invades
1943	Tehran conference, east Poland to stay in USSR
1944	Nazis abandon Oświęcim/Auschwitz
1944	Warsaw uprising. Retreating Nazis destroy Warsaw
1945	Siege of Wrocław, city bombarded to ruin
1945	The 8th of May Germany surrendered to Allies
1947	Communist state established in Poland
1953	Death of Stalin
1956	Khrushchev's speech denounces crimes of Stalin, followed by 'Thaw'
1956	Protests and riots in Poznań, Gomułka becomes new 'moderate' leader of Poland
1960s	**Easing of hardship, author's visit to Poland**
1970s	Gomułka replaced by Gierek
1980s	Hardship, strikes centred on Gdańsk shipyards led by Lech Wałęsa, rise of trade union Solidarity
1981–1983	General Jaruzelski declares martial law
1980s	Gorbachev in USSR encourages hopes of relaxation
1989	Round Table talks between Solidarity and government
1989	Berlin Wall comes down; Eastern European Communist regimes quickly tumble
1989–1990	Poland's first free elections
2004	Poland joins EU
2014–2022	Cold War confrontations erupting between Russia, Ukraine and NATO

3

Peeping over the Iron Curtain

Munich, September 1966

From the West looking East

I am looking out of the window of my new accommodation in Munich, the workers' hostel of the Agfa photographic factory where I have found a job. In order to continue my travels, I must earn some money. Everyone like me, loose-footed and floating around in Europe at the time, tends to head for the Federal Republic of Germany, the larger western part of the country, where work can be found. My diary:

> *I'm on the sixth floor, so I have an expansive view of the huge building of the Agfa works, backed by a non-spectacular skyline which includes a tall chimney, two floodlamps from the football pitch and one church spire. There is a golden line of sunset which is turning red as the sky darkens. The neon sign in red and blue from the sports field has become my starlight. I sit here eating my supper as night falls. It is a crispy clear autumn evening, making me long for the country.*

When I arrived in Munich, I headed straight for the *Arbeitsamt*, the employment bureau. They promptly sent me to the Agfa factory where I was offered work for £45 per month. From this, a mere £5 would be deducted for my lodging in the *Wohnheim*, the factory hostel. I plan that I might save £60 in two months, enough to keep me going for the next stage of my travels.

My accommodation is comfortable. I share a room with a German girl called Trudi, who is often away staying with her *Mann*, her husband. There's a kitchen and small bathroom with hot water. Everything is provided except for cooking utensils, but someone has lent me a saucepan so I can boil water for tea.

But oh dear, the work! I am a most unamenable employee. Every day, I sit in front of a machine mounting the small transparencies which must be cut and fixed firmly between the two parts of their plastic slide holders. The same four movements are repeated hundreds of times every day. The room is filled with lines of these machines, in two rows facing each other. They are all operated by women, and our floor manager, Herr Fiedler, a stout short man in a white coat, marches around keeping an eye on things.

Work starts at 7am, and goes on until 4pm. At 9am, the machines are paused, and we all troop down to the cafeteria for our *Zweite Frühstück*, our Second Breakfast. During these fifteen minutes, I can munch a tasty apple strudel and drink a cup of tea. At 11am, the moving elevator band amid the rows of machines comes to a halt. A woman employee stands on the belt. We all do exercises under her benign command. We rotate our heads, wriggle our shoulders, lift our arms, bend our waists, all to instructions in German. Of course, this is all very sensible, designed to alleviate stresses from the motions of our work. The steady German women employees take it very seriously. But I and the three Irish girls, Loreen, Marie and Betty, who also work the machines, find it hilarious. We are just not so biddable; we are too young and immature to appreciate the benefits. We'd rather go out for a cigarette, but there is no chance of that.

The work is tedious. Awful. I try all kinds of tricks to help the hours go by. After six days, I am developing tricks. My diary:

Today I was fairly happy at my boring job. I have invented a thousand ways to make the time go more excitingly, little excuses for walks, opening windows, drawing curtains, and I sing my entire repertoire of songs. I sustain the minimum of concentration necessary to make sure I keep an eye on what I'm doing, and the rest of the time I'm barely conscious of where I am. I go off into little dream worlds.

My attempts at singing annoy my neighbours and earn me a scolding from Herr Fiedler. A few days later, my diary records an experiment:

Today I have begun a scheme to try to ignore time. As the work is so repetitive, one hour is exactly like two, if you don't have a clock. Therefore, by not knowing the time, thus cancelling it from being the worst bugbear of all, I'm trying to eliminate the seeming endlessness of the work. Only difficulty is that the clock always stares me in the face and it's hard not to see it. Still, I think this theory is worth working on.

But really, I am an ungrateful person. I have clean, comfortable accommodation, and my work is enabling me to earn money. The pages I waste in my diary writing about how much I dislike this work, and my complaints about the dullness of the German people around me, are the rantings of an immature young woman. When I describe them in a letter to my mother, who is aged forty-five, she replies with a quote by Madame Merle, in Henry James's *Portrait of a Lady*:

'One can't judge till one is forty; before that we are too eager, too hard, too cruel, and in addition too ignorant. I am

*sorry for you – it will be a long time before you are forty. But
every gain is a loss of some kind. I often think that after forty,
one can't really feel – the freshness, the quickness have gone.
You will keep them longer than most people. It will be a great
satisfaction to me to see you some years hence. One thing is
certain – it can't spoil you. It may pull you about horribly –
but I defy it to break you up'.*

Two kinds of Wohnheim

The workers at the Agfa factory are mainly German and, in my
department, all are women. However, there is a sprinkling of *Ausländer*,
foreigners. As well as me, there are the sprightly Irish girls and some
young Portuguese women with dark hair and eyes. One day I visit my
new Portuguese friends, and I am surprised to find how differently
they are accommodated. Irish workers must be on the same northern
European value scale as Germans and me, the *Engländerin*, the English
girl. We all have spacious accommodation in the *Wohnheim*, sharing
a room for three with single beds. But some rule-makers, somewhere,
have decided that southern Europeans don't need such comfort. The
room of the Portuguese girls is smaller than the one which I share
with Trudi. In theirs, three double bunks are fitted tightly in so that
six people can share together. Similarly, my new friend, delicate, fair-
haired Svetlana, from Ljubljana in Yugoslavia, is staying in a room
crowded together with five others. The accommodation is decent, but
clearly these people are second-class citizens.

Looking towards the gloomy East

The weekends are free. Autostop in Germany is fairly easy, and there
is a lot to explore in Bavaria within an easy distance from Munich.
One youth hostel, north of the city, in the village of Hohenberg,
is close to the Iron Curtain, and this is where I plan to go on the

weekend of the 7th, 8th and 9th of October. I am fascinated by the thought that, through the veil, the mist, between West and East, there must be hundreds of lanes being cut off across the boundary, stopping abruptly amid woods and fields. And how about streams – do they flow across the Iron Curtain, or might they even be part of it? This quiet frontier in the countryside is much less known than the Berlin Wall. My diary:

> *I am heading for a corner of north-eastern Bavaria, where West and East Germany are split, and Czechoslovakia converges on the two zones. The iron thread positioned and patrolled by the East is as carefully patrolled by the West.*

I get lifts from one small country town to another, passing through villages with tiny churches and statues of what I call 'a sorrowing Jesus', sitting down with his head on his hand, elbows on knee, on the way to his crucifixion. At Tirschenreuth, I take a very quiet road which heads towards the frontier with Czechoslovakia. At the pleasant village of Mähring, I stop for lunch. I am only five kilometres from the border. I stop to make a sketch of the farmhouses which form the village street. My diary:

> *The big square buildings have archways through the middle, through which the farmers drive their tractors and animals to the fields. The cultivation is in long strips. This time of year, potatoes, turnips and mangolds are being harvested, and the land is being ploughed up and reseeded. Red and white mottled cattle, pigs and poultry are all common. The landscape is gentle rolling hills. The village is very reliant on wood for building and fuel. All the houses have neat woodpiles. Sawmills are outside the village, and forest is all around. The village obviously began as a hilltop settlement in a clearing in the forest. The simple domed church is in the central position, with a 'sorrowing Jesus'.*

I note in my diary that the place names round here – *Reuth, Ried* and *Rodin* on the end of words – mean 'clearing in the forest'.

When I walk on, I have a lift from two men on a tractor and a cart. I rattle along on the cart behind the men in their Bavarian hats. Near Neualbenreuth, I stop to chat with a man and a woman who are ploughing with a pair of oxen.

"*Grüß Gott*," I say in my best Bavarian German. (I haven't yet realised that these words mean Greetings from God, visualising them as 'Grew Scott'.) They smile and reply. They work their way along their long strip of land, she leading the oxen at the front, and he steering the plough behind. The horned oxen are reddish-brown with white faces, strong and docile. The field of turnips has not long been harvested and will soon be reseeded.

Behind them a rolling forest reaches to the skyline, and amid the forest is a clearing.

"*Tschechoslowakei*," they tell me. Czechoslovakia. They indicate towards the forest and the open area among the trees. "*Soldaten*." Soldiers. I will later learn the meaning of that ominous clearing.

I walk on through a forest before two German men offer me a lift. They decide they'll be my guides. Because they speak English quite well, I will learn more about what I am about to see. They drive me along a road which stops at the Czech frontier where stones mark the boundaries. I find this all so exciting that I make mental notes and think about writing an article for *The Journal*, North East England's regional newspaper. It is published later, and here are some extracts which continue the story:

Walk along a forest road in this corner of Bavaria and you may suddenly find yourself in a clearing with the white markers crossing it. Beyond lies Czechoslovakia, and you may be tempted to step behind the posts for an instant to be able to say you've been a yard or two inside Communist territory, but

*don't! There are soldiers – young boys with machine guns – in
the innocent-looking woods beyond.*

The men take me to a formal observation tower where we purchase
an *Eintrittskarte*, entry ticket, costing fifty pfennigs. I am visitor
number 001872. From there we can see into Czechoslovakia. I
write what I see from the tower in my article:

*Mount the tower, and you can see, five kilometres away,
white concrete posts and wires stretching into the distance.
Three rows of wires there are, all electrified. Touch them, and
you may suffer instant death.*

*Fragile wooden guard towers are positioned along the line,
close enough together for each to be visible from the next. The
soldiers manning them are armed with machine guns.*

*Now and again an old tractor can be seen turning over
the earth beside the wires. Why? An escaping man must
stumble or fall on the soft, clinging surface if he runs. And
even if he doesn't, he must leave a trail of footprints which
the ever-ready guards will follow, guns primed.*

*Even the guards themselves are guarded in case they
should try to cross the border. Friends are not stationed
together – only strangers. They patrol in pairs, and the pairs
are changed every three weeks.*

*Farmers in the West can be seen ploughing right up
to the frontier posts of Czechoslovakia, but they are not
allowed to fraternise with their neighbours across the border.
That is why the Communists have declared an area of
land, five kilometres wide, a 'no man's land'. No villages in
Czechoslovakia, no farmhouses or barns, are nearer to the
German frontier than this.*

*Along a boundary of about 150 miles is an area of almost
wasted land, cut off from a poverty-stricken nation. One*

wonders what the Czechs think about this – if they dare to think at all.

From the German side you can see into the Czech town of Cheb, with the aid of field glasses. Here are high, white, skyscraper-type buildings and smoking chimneys. It is a disturbing thought that the people in these factories and houses are prisoners of their environment.

Except for three closely controlled frontier road passes between Czechoslovakia and Germany, local contact between the two countries has been completely severed.

The men drive me to two more places where there are country roads which had once passed between the two countries. They are now cut in two, forbidden and overgrown, with simple red and white barriers at the boundary. I am now facing towards the deadly military zone which winds through the countryside. We note a farm track between the cultivated strips on the western side, with a sign beside it:

ATTENTION
50 METERS TO
CZECH BORDER

My kind guides take me to Hohenberg, my destination for the night. My diary:

What a lovely surprise it was to arrive in this village on a hilltop to the chorus of evening bells from the church, a quiet square with old men sitting around, the sun beginning to set in a scarlet sky over the forested hills.

I discovered the hostel in a fairy tale castle, surrounded by a deep, dried-up moat in an enclosed courtyard and three round towers. In the centre of the courtyard is a big deep well. From

the round towers you can see into Czechoslovakia. I leaned
from the castle window and thought, Rapunzel, Rapunzel, let
down your golden hair. Everything was idyllically lovely.

The Lutheran pastor of the village took me to a family
who are acting as hostel wardens. Here I was given a bed, a
lovely supper and sat with the family awhile. They charged
nothing because they thought it was so funny me only having
one mark and twenty pfennigs left.

The friendliness of the drivers in the car and the people in the
village of Hohenberg are improving my attitude. I still have a lot to
learn about Germany.

Hohenberg has some postcards which I buy to put in my
diary. One is a view from the air. It shows me what I have come
to see for myself, the fearsome line, the boundary lands between
East and West. The river Eger meanders through the land, its tree-
lined course clearly showing from the air. Such an innocent little
river here bears the political burden of being the line of the Iron
Curtain. On the nearside of the view is the hilltop village and castle
of Hohenberg. The background shows the bleak, bare ploughed
strip and, behind it, the boundary forest. The view may have been
deliberately taken to show the eastern borderlands. Tomorrow I
shall look for myself. The postcard also shows a mill in a curve of
the river Eger, and I take a photograph.

When the fog-shrouded Sunday morning arrives, my kind hosts
feed me with coffee, bread and honey and give me a little pot of the
latter to set me on my way. My diary:

I called in at the attractive Lutheran church. Here on the
wall was a picture of a fat Martin Luther with his Bible.
This simple little Protestant church, with its purple cross on
a white background, is very charming, repaired since it was
damaged during the war.

I walk out of the village, down the hill to the river Eger. Here it is the boundary between Germany and Czechoslovakia, the town of Cheb only a few forbidden kilometres downstream, an impermeable barrier. On the bridge is a stone figure of a bagpiper. The river is small but large enough for a still-functioning watermill. I look back at it, but as it is Sunday, I feel unwilling to interrupt the day of rest. I resolve to return another time.

Hohenberg as a refuge for Sudeten Germans

Many Germans were expelled from the Czechoslovakian Sudetenland after 1945 and moved to rural parts of Bavaria, mainly because it was closest to their original homes and they still hoped to be able to move back again. The former castle at Hohenberg was chosen as the office for the Sudeten German Social Welfare Association because it had views over to the Egerland, the area of Czechoslovakia from which many had been expelled. This way they kept a link with their homeland.

Although the castle dates from the Middle Ages, pre-1945 it had been used to house forestry workers and as a school hostel. In 1955 the State of Bavaria, which owns the castle, leased it to the Sudeten German Social Welfare Association which, attracted by its location close to the Czech border, used it as a support centre for displaced Sudeten Germans, organising clothing packages for refugees from the East and offering short-term accommodation and medical care, particularly for young people who were malnourished or had learning difficulties.

Links were established with other European youth organisations, and seminars on cross-border cooperation were organised. Work started on converting the prison tower into a youth hostel in 1956 and it was expanded in 1966/67 to include washing facilities and increase capacity from twenty to thirty-six places. It continued to operate as a youth hostel until 2014 when it was closed due to high costs of maintenance and renovation. In 2019 the state of Bavaria agreed to finance the renovation. Provided the work remains on schedule, the youth hostel should reopen in 2022.

Research by Diane Milburn, 2021

THE IRON CURTAIN IN THE COUNTRYSIDE

I continue along my way, close to the Iron Curtain. My diary:

The road here runs right along the Czech border. I stepped into Czechoslovakia quickly, then out again, for there was no one around. Then I was a bit scared of soldiers appearing to take me behind this invisible Iron Curtain, especially when a blackbird squawked an alarm call from the woods above me. I picked some rose hips growing in Czechoslovakia, leaning over the roadside and also some frozen early morning apples, which I love. The granite cliffs loomed above me, grown around with trees penetrating the tor-like cracks in the rocks.

Having had a glimpse of the Iron Curtain along the border between Czechoslovakia and Germany, my next intention is to look over into the Soviet Zone of the *Deutsche Demokratische Republik*, the DDR. I hitch and walk northwards in the newly appearing sunshine, towards small villages on the frontier. My diary:

A farmer dropped me off in the middle of a rolling hillside in the middle of nowhere. The road was untarred and bumpy. He pointed to a village in a valley. This was Nentschau, my destination. His wife gave me an apple, and I set off down the stony track through the granite hills. Nentschau was very pretty, lanes going up and down banks, with ponds and golden chestnut trees. An accordion was sounding through a cottage window of a Protestant hymn I know. But I climbed out of the village and walked towards the Grenze, the frontier. Here there was a military policeman sitting under a chestnut tree on guard duty.

He had a young Alsatian dog tied to a tree, who leapt at me barking ferociously. The policeman lent me his field glasses. I could see the village of Posseck in the East Zone, only half a kilometre away, children playing and horses running around in a field. The black church spire looked over the village. The policeman said that Posseck is in Saxony, and we are in Frankenland, and both are Protestant lands. The East Germans have been allowed to have church services now for five years.

Between us and this innocent-looking village of Posseck was a double-track of barbed wire with a mined zone in-between, keeping Posseck as good as a thousand miles away. The policeman said that East Zone soldiers were in those pretty woods and that sometimes you could see them. All I could see were three farmers ploughing up the large communal fields.

I record the next episode in my article for *The Journal*:

The scene looks harmless enough, but it is not. The East German population are prevented from joining their Western relations by a stretch of mined lane fifty metres wide. As I gaze in astonishment an armoured car drives out of the woodlands, and some East German soldiers climb out. Then another in a distinctive uniform, a Russian.

Together they check the fencing, but we in our impetuosity must wave to them. One soldier sees us and waves back surreptitiously with a slight movement of his hand. The other soldiers apparently don't see him do this.

It is not long before the soldiers are driving away in their armoured car, and a heavy silence seems to descend on Posseck.

The Western border policeman with his dog is surprisingly friendly, and as we chat, an enormous armoured car arrives. Two young military policemen jump out, and they smile at the novelty of a young English girl taking an interest in their daily routine. They are certainly not like the forbidding guards I'd encountered going into East Berlin and let me take a photograph of them. Then I pluck up my courage.

"*Wo gehen Sie?*" I try my best German.

They say something like "*Grenzepatrolle,*" and so I ask "*Kann ich komm?*" and they say "*Ja.*"

Thus, I go on frontier patrol with the policemen with their machine guns. We bump over the rugged terrain in their armoured car until we come to a wood. Here I follow the two young soldiers, creeping through the crunchy beech leaves, until suddenly we are almost on the eastern mined zone and looking over the village of Posseck from a high vantage point. Binoculars come out, and we gaze around. Nothing to be seen. They obligingly allow me to take their photograph beside a sign in the lane which warns that we are fifty metres from the Soviet Zone. The lane runs as far as the barrier, the bare mined zone behind and the rooftops of Posseck beyond.

How quiet East Germany seems. No soldiers are in the Posseck observation tower. Where must they all be hidden? So, we creep out of the woods, back to the patrol car, radio to HQ in Bayreuth and bump away again. Now it is lunchtime, and I eat with them in a restaurant in the village of Nentschau.

These soldiers, like most young Germans, speak good English, so I ask lots of questions. I am able to report what they tell me in my article for *The Journal*:

> *Many of the older people of Nentschau once lived in Posseck, and some have married sons and daughters living there. Immediately after the war, restrictions between the two villages were fairly flexible.*
>
> *For a small bribe, the Russians, and later the East German soldiers, would allow the villagers free passage and would maybe even share a drink with them. Gradually, restrictions tightened, and border crossings came to a standstill.*

Then the mined zone was laid out, hiding a massive trench through which no car could drive. German began to spy on German, and the only means of contact was by letter or parcel. Even these were strictly controlled. Parcels were often opened by customs men.

Yet Nentschau mothers can still see their sons farming in the communal fields, and children can see their unknown cousins playing only a little distance from them – cousins they may never know.

After leaving the soldiers, I spend the rest of the day ambling, hitchhiking, south towards Munich. I pass Hof and other little cotton mill towns, Bayreuth, and then through limestone hills where the rocks stand out like white tors on hilltops, and there are famous caves. One driver takes me to Nuremberg, and when he drops me off on the Autobahn, I meet two Scottish hitchhikers going round the world with a guitar and one pfennig, so they tell me. They'd been waiting for a lift for three hours. I have a lift within ten minutes. Hitchhiking is so much easier for women.

Arriving back in Munich, I take a tram to the Agfa factory. To the tidy German passengers, I look like a tramp as I've lost my hairbrush and have been through hedges and woodlands during the adventures of the day. Once at the *Wohnheim*, I rush to tell all the stories to my Irish friends. Then I get on with writing up my diary while everything is fresh in my mind. Tomorrow is Monday. *Morgen – arbeiten.* Work!

In the next day or two, in my room at the Agfa factory, I get out pen, ink and a notepad and write up my story of what I have seen over the weekend. I have been looking from the West into the East. I will remind the readers that the Iron Curtain is not just the Berlin Wall but extends right through Germany from north to south and borders Czechoslovakia too. The article will be a useful source of money for me, as well as relating my unusual experiences.

I post my story to my father in Newcastle, asking him to send it to *The Journal*. Although I don't find out until much later, the editor accepts the article, offers payment and asks my father to supply a photo of me.

The editor created the headline as 'A wasteland that cuts off sons from mothers', used a smiling photo of me, and then printed every word of my story.

Thus, on the 23rd of December 1966, casual readers back home in England, opening their newspaper at the breakfast table or sitting by their coal fires, could read about this strange frontier. For many of them, East Germany and Czechoslovakia are distant, remote places across Europe, and they will barely understand that the Iron Curtain also cuts through the countryside. A wandering girl from Newcastle has a story to tell.

THE SIGNIFICANT POST – MUNICH

The post in Munich links me with the life I have left behind, the life I would be having if I had become a teacher. My friends from college are beginning to face the hard reality of working to earn their living. Several of them have taken teaching jobs in Birmingham. When I was in my insecure, despondent phase in Berlin, I had sent a letter there to Jenny, my philosophical friend. Her reply expresses the tug of war that affects us all: the pressure to become a teacher and then to marry the man of our dreams on the one hand, and the pull of travel and freedom on the other. She wrote a letter including a little poem:

> *Stick with it – even if it does get lonely, all our thoughts are here with you, and there is only one chance in a lifetime.*

> *When you're wandering through the world*
> *Against many walls you will be hurled*

But remember your friends
And you'll see it through to the end.

We had to find somewhere to stay in Birmingham and found a flat above a dressmakers' shop which means after shop hours we have it to ourselves. Next door is a deaf lady. And we have a little strip of a garden. It has a lounge, a double bedroom, single bedroom, kitchen and small bathroom. £2.10 all in, including heating.

Hitched back home from Brum. English lorry drivers – ugh, they can be awkward. But I met a really fabulous one too. We really fell for each other. He was cute. Had all his fishing equipment to go fishing in the Thames and brewed us both some coffee on a paraffin stove.

Len sent a letter from Morocco. But it is a good job that he has gone because I would have scared him off with 'marrying ideas'. Times change, and so do I. Don't you go and do anything drastic like that Bridget. It's very tempting, I know, when you're out there by yourself, but wait until later to settle down.

I reckon it is going to be hard trying to settle down to hard work for all of us.

The London lads are thinking of giving up their jobs and working their way towards Libya where they say there is an oilfield where they can get jobs of some kind. Len and Harris went as far as the south of Spain, but Gar couldn't get his passport in time, so they went without him.

I'm realising that before long we'll all be older and stiffer and not wanting to do and see things, so we must do them before it's too late. This philosophical note is intended to encourage you if you are feeling at all despondent.

Another letter, which was posted a little later, had some bad news. The friends moved into the Birmingham flat, but overnight stays from young males are not allowed:

The landlady, the dressmaker below, is worried about her trade. She came in one morning and found Len and Mary doing the washing up. So! We have to leave. It is a pity because it is a beautiful little flat. So don't give anyone our address here unless they come in the daytime and don't expect to stay the night.

As for the teaching job:

I have a class of forty-two children. Tonie has a class of immigrant children, with only five white. Mary has the smallest class of thirty-two. All the children in my class have Irish names, O'Leary, O'Connor etc. My favourite is a beautiful little Irish boy. He's a tiny, sincere little character with fair hair, a squarish face and close-cropped hair.

Another friend Jean is teaching in Wiltshire.

My class of twenty-three seven- to eight-year-olds is fairly well behaved. I hitchhiked to the south of France and then to a work camp in Portugal. Here in Britain, I must be careful what I do, say and where I go. You know what village life is like.

I feel that in all I don't want to settle down in teaching before I have travelled a lot. But when I qualify from my first probationary year, I shall make up my mind. I shall get my grey hair either teaching or hitchhiking.

Some of the letters describe our common method of travel. Mary tells me about hitchhiking in Scandinavia:

I'd been hitching with a gorgeous American called Keith. In Copenhagen, he went to some lecture on the welfare state. I went walking along the pedestrian street. Numerous hitchers from all over the world were down there trying to make some money. I chatted to two who came from Meknes in Morocco. It was the day we won the Cup Final, so some English boys, horrible and bawdy, were making fools of themselves.

I sailed with Keith on a boat for Sweden in brilliant sunshine, on the top deck, completely wrapped up in our mad holiday love.

Advantages of hitchhiking: to meet and speak to hundreds of men who are interested in you and not necessarily in making ze love.

Disadvantages: funny and unfunny situations need someone to share them with. I really missed having someone to laugh with.

In Finland, I did the usual things. Saw loads of reindeer. Visited timber yards, watching the whole process from water to stacked timber. But no one could understand a word I said when I asked questions. Later, in a restaurant, I ordered reindeer stew.

My brother had been hitchhiking through France and had had really bad luck. He waited hours for lifts, and his record day was no more than thirty kilometres. He is about to start his A levels at the local technical college. My sister Rosie has returned from Germany and is getting ready to start college in Newcastle. My father hadn't obtained the job he had applied for as beekeeping officer in Aberystwyth:

There are too many good beekeeping blokes about and not enough senior jobs. I expect I am stuck in Northumberland now.

My mother has become confused about where I am:

> *I thought you were settled in Munich in Germany. Please write back at once if you get this because it makes me feel quite desperate not knowing what country you are in.*

She sends me several letters while I am in Munich. Separated from my father for a couple of years now, she is working as a cleaner and housekeeper for a well-to-do family. At the same time, she has passed the necessary exams and is now in a three-year college course training to be a teacher. My parents' experience gives me an object lesson in some of life's more uneasy outcomes. Marriage isn't always a blessing.

However, my younger sister Helen has started on this route. Her letter:

> *I don't know if you're in Timbuktu or anywhere. Our news here is good. Michael and I expect to hear the patter of tiny feet around the place next year, and you will be Aunty Bridget. I am glad I have not got to become a hearty career woman but an enthusiastic mum. I have already taught myself to knit – 1½ cardigans and four mittens so far, and three sweet little nighties. It is all an enthralling subject for me; as yet, I have no visible bump. So don't stay away too long but come and meet your first niece/nephew, March/April.*
>
> *I have just been out to get myself a job to qualify for some maternity benefits. In a sandwich bar, 7am to 2pm.*

Letters also arrive for me from Poland. Tom sends me a neatly written letter in English with a Polish folk song, and Andrzej too sends an affectionate note. Frank has sent me a card and a Polish song from Zawoja.

Theo, with whom I'd spent time in Poland, wrote from Amsterdam. He had been travelling quietly, inconspicuously, through Poland at the same time as me and been welcomed 'as some wonder of the world'. While hitching south to Kraków, he was helped by a policeman, 'who stopped several cars, asking the drivers where they were going, and gave me in this manner a good lift to Kraków'. A helpful Polish policeman!

Other letters are very significant in decisions I must make for my future travels.

I had written to the embassy of the Soviet Union in Munich, thinking that they might be able to help me get visas for ongoing travel through countries I might visit on my way to Israel. One can't just randomly go to these countries behind the Iron Curtain. I receive a typewritten letter:

> *Dear Bridget Ashton!*
>
> *In reply to your letter, we tell you that we have nothing to do with the questions concerning the visit of Hungary, Bulgaria and Romania. In West Germany, the Embassy of the Soviet Union represents only the USSR. To get visas for visiting Hungary, Bulgaria and Romania, you should address the embassies of above mentioned countries which are situated in Ost Berlin (the German Democratic Republic).*

It is rather a compliment that the Soviet Embassy sent me such a special signed letter, even though I couldn't read the signature. It feels almost friendly.

Family friends who had been refugees and who now live in Israel invite me warmly to their kibbutz. My beloved grandmother writes:

> *I learn that your next address will be in Israel. This is a happy surprise.*

Her letter, like several others, is sent by airmail. These letters are written on special lightweight paper and envelopes. Airmail is quicker than ordinary land mail but is paid for by weight and more expensive.

On Monday the 25th of October, I receive a parcel from my sister Rosie with shampoo, tea and luxurious hand cream.

I still have unformed ideas about moving south through Yugoslavia to Israel after the winter is over and post a package of my summer clothes to a Poste Restante address in Greece. Dushko, the Serbian student I'd met in Wrocław, lures me onwards. He writes from Belgrade, in his best French:

Il est joli rencontre à nouveau, à l'autre place et en autre pays, une jeune fille très simpatique comme toi, et j'espere que nous rencontrons et que je pourrai montrer à toi notre capitale, Belgrade.

It is pleasing to meet again, in another place and country, a young friendly girl like you, and I hope that we will meet and that I may show you our capital city Belgrade.

My most important plan is to go to Hungary, which is on the way to Yugoslavia, and I have a strong family link there. In 1956, my family had hosted a refugee from the Hungarian Revolution. His name is Imre Gulyás. We know him by his anglicised name of Henry. Now, ten years later, I am hoping to visit his family, and so I write a letter to them in early October. I receive wonderful affirmative replies, the first from Henry's sister Marika who has learned some English:

Mezőberény, 24 Oct. 1966

Dear Bridget,
    We was very glad to get your letter. I know you, we don't

forget your mother and we have a photo where you are a little girl.

I'm Henry's sister. I'm twenty-six years old I have husband, and we are living at home with my mother and father. I don't know can you read in Germany, so I write, the second letter is an invitacion to you. We are very glad to meet with you. I'm in this we can understand each other.

Dear Bridget, ask for you write me early when you will come here, then I shall to do some program to you. I need to write you, we are living in a village, from Budapest 180km.

We wait for you with heaps of love.

Yours sincerely,

Marika Kiss

Marika's mother and mine had always communicated in German. She handwrote in perfect German a most warm and welcoming letter. Here is the translation:

Dear Bridget,

I have received your kind letter. I am very pleased that you are in Germany. We're waiting for you with a great deal of love and joy. Please come to Hungary soon. I hope that you will enjoy being in our home country and in Mezőberény. My daughter Marika and my son-in-law Sandor completed their studies last year at the University of Technology in Budapest. They are now working in Békéscsaba as engineers. Their flat is here with us in Mezőberény. My son Henry is in The Hague with his wife and their charming little girl Marika.

Dear Bridget, please write and let us know when you're coming! Bye-bye, with lots of love and kisses.

Mrs Gulyás

I reply with grateful thanks and say that I hope to arrive there before Christmas. Ideas of Israel are being pushed further away in the future.

It takes me many hours of writing to reply to all these letters, a pleasurable and essential task. The post is fundamentally important for keeping me within my network. Like those families who are separated between Posseck and Nentschau, or Cheb and Hohenberg, we keep in touch by post. The national and international postal services in 1966 are the way people who are physically separated from each other maintain their links. It is amazing how well it works.

WEEKEND VISITS AND MAKING MAPS

I continue working during October, November and early December at the Agfa factory. I am learning what it is like to earn one's living beside a machine in a factory. One's personal whims and feelings must be kept down, controlled. Every minute and hour and day are spent tied to the machine, while the crushing boredom must be coped with. All this tedium is accepted by the workers because the money which is earned enables them to have the lifestyle of their choice. My mother calls it 'healthy discipline', but at twenty-two years of age, I am very bad at it. As I need the money to continue my travels, I must submit, and even accept overtime when it is offered.

On one of my roving weekends, I damage one of my flip-flops. The rubber thong breaks. These have been my footwear through all the summer, and I am making them last until I need to wear my winter bootees. I am able to replace the broken thong with a piece of binder twine, making a satisfactory repair. But when I wear it to work next day, the infuriated Herr Fiedler is more than usually angry with me and calls me a *Gammler*, which I later learn means a layabout or dropout.

When I first arrived in Munich, I'd been impressed by the *Oktoberfest* with its wonderful, costumed parades, but I am also aware of the beerhalls' association with Adolf Hitler. One day, my Irish friends and I visit Dachau. Having just come from Poland where the memory of the war with Germany is still raw, and after visiting Auschwitz, I am tense. My diary:

The fact that the camp is in Germany, the guilty nation, proclaiming its own guilty past to the world, is why its horrors feel even more alive. I think these places must be kept alive if only as a reminder of the powers of cruelty latent in every human being, as much as the powers of unselfishness are the opposite… I feel every human being must accept guilt for the actions of others, for how can we know if we are blameless now or in the future and that we are not capable of doing atrocious acts… The sad pity of the continued existence of the concentration camps is that it tends to keep a bit of anti-German feeling alive. The Fascist camps are supposed to have been the cruellest places in the history of mankind, and yet they existed through my parents' lifetime, and until visiting Auschwitz, I knew hardly anything about them. The real life lessons of awareness of the possibilities of human nature are everywhere to be seen, but how easy it is to go around with ears and eyes closed.

I want to make maps and draw up what I learn for my diary. I still expect one day to be a geography teacher in England. In the evenings, I often go to the Institute of Geography where I am permitted to use the library and given free access to the maps. This is West Germany! Such a request in East Germany would have been met with horror. Why on earth would I want to see maps, unless I am a spy for the militant capitalists?

I acquire a grey woollen shift dress and sew one of my white lace collars from Poland on it. This makes an adequate dress for evenings at the international folk dancing sessions in the University Student Club where I go with my Portuguese girl friends from Agfa. Here I meet Reiner, Reinhardt and Tony. They all of course speak perfect English, better than we natives, and Tony, with his light hair and cheerful demeanour, likes to correct my English. I don't pronounce the 'a' sound properly. I say 'Frannce' rather than 'Frahnce', and he says this is not the correct pronunciation. I argue. What is wrong with my short vowel, from my northern English origin? No one has ever said that to me before.

Winter is coming

November is passing; Christmas is approaching; and I give in my notice at the factory. My diary entry includes an episode of silliness:

> *11 Nov – gave notice. Irish girls and I singing and playing mouth organs at Zweites Frühstück, Second Breakfast. This made a German woman fly at me with her claws out and left me bleeding. Herr Fiedler reported me to the boss, but he didn't seem very angry and just asked me to try to stay out of trouble.*

As it is autumn, there are fewer and fewer sets of holiday slides to be processed. We workers are diverted to checking through the empty cassette containers. We must feel inside them to remove the paper instructions and then sort the cassettes into different boxes according to their material and colour. This is even more mindless work than mounting the slides, but the compensation is that it is possible to chat and sing during the work. And the Irish girls and I take advantage of this. My diary records that 'the dust from the tins blocks my nose and makes me sneeze, so I tie a blue headscarf around my nose like an Arab veil'. This causes Herr Fiedler to shake his head and mutter at me in annoyance.

Friday the 18th of November is my last day of work. The German women who don't like me are glad I'm leaving. My diary:

> *In their eyes I'm lazy, deliberately irritating, causing others to be likewise, a filthy little Gammler and blatantly conceited and amused by myself and life in general. I see their point of view.*
>
> *The only way I survived that work was by not allowing it to dominate me. I must either absorb myself in song, in conversation with Loreen, listening to Betty and Marie imitating actresses, talking German and Yugoslav with Svetlana, anything as long as I wasn't thinking about what I was doing.*

I must acquire clothes for my winter travels. Under the kind guidance of Marie, my Irish friend, I am completing knitting a warm sweater in maroon wool with a thick double rib pattern. On the 14th of October:

> *I've already been given a pair of black bootees, some black slingback heeled shoes; I've bought some dark blue tights, and what with my knitting, I'm coming on fine.*

Trudi, my roommate, then supplies me with a brown, suede coat. And my mother, to my delight, posts me some sheepskin gloves. My diary:

> *My Christmas present from Mother had arrived. Oh, wrapped beautifully in gay paper with an ivy leaf were a delicious woolly pair of sheepskin mitts, soft and downy and lovely around my hands.*

I write to her:

Dear Mother,

I can hardly wait to thank you for those simply fabulous gloves. They are so gorgeous. I am vegetarian only in spirit now – what with my fur hat (artificial), my suede coat and my sheepskin gloves. I'm admirably bedecked for winter.

I ask her, and all my other correspondents, to reply to Poste Restante, *Wien, Österreich* so that the letters arrive before the 7th of December. Thus, my plans have firmed up sufficiently. I am aiming to pass through Austria so that I will arrive in Hungary with the Gulyás family for Christmas.

In the last days before I leave, Tony and I have many conversations. We talk about English literature, of which he knows much more than me, and he tries to educate me. "You must learn to speak well if you are going to be a teacher."

"Like you?" I reply. He does play on my feelings of insecurity. I am a little bit lost in this world which is not mine.

We talk about the German way of life. I tell him that the women I meet are consumed with tidiness and keeping their windowsills dusted. Those I encounter in the factory are obsessed with saving to buy *things*, material goods, to furnish their neat houses. "But that is sensible," he says. I demur. I can't imagine being so concerned about dust and furniture. I am certainly not ready to consider being a German *Hausfrau*.

It is definitely time to leave. I must travel through Austria to get to Hungary, and in Vienna I have arranged to meet a friend. She will introduce me to a suspicious underground world: the black market across the Iron Curtain.

GERMANY CHRONOLOGY

1933	Hitler becomes chancellor of Germany
1933	Dachau established as a camp to control political dissidents
1939	Germany invades Poland, start of the Second World War
1939–1945	Second World War
1945	Germany unconditionally surrenders
1949	Two German states formalised, Federal Republic of Germany (West) and German Democratic Republic (East)
1950s–80s	Build-up of militarised zone between East and West, Baltic to the Black Sea
1953	Death of Stalin
1961	Berlin Wall constructed
1966–1967	**Author's visit to Germany**
1980s	Gorbachev in USSR encourages hopes of relaxation
1989	Berlin Wall comes down and Iron Curtain across Europe collapses
1990	Two German nations unite
2014–2022	Cold War confrontations erupting between Russia, Ukraine and NATO

4

Girl Smugglers across the Border

BRATISLAVA, DECEMBER 1966

DUBIOUS COMPANY IN VIENNA

I am climbing up the stairs to the fifth floor of a tenement in Vienna, and I knock at a certain door. A Polish man opens it and seems to be vaguely expecting me. I am seated, waiting, making loose conversation in a mixture of my German and Polish. I am tired because I've had a long day hitching from Munich. The lorry driver who gave me a lift bought me lunch and drove to the factory where his load of steel was lifted off by a crane. After this he drove around looking for Große Sperlgasse until, after many enquiries, he managed to find the street on the other side of the canal.

So here I am, waiting and wondering. Before too long, Isobel arrives. We embrace each other with relief. She is the Scottish girl I had spent time with in Kraków, and she is very glad to see me because she is undertaking some rather dubious activities. She would like my support, although I don't at first understand exactly what she is up to.

She is a slightly built middle-class Scottish girl, attached to her Polish boyfriend who lives in Warsaw. When I met her in August in Kraków, she and he were together for her summer holiday. Shortly after returning to her university studies in Dundee, her Polish grandmother in Warsaw died, and she had returned there with her mother for the funeral. Then she decided she would drop her social studies degree for a year and stay in the eastern world. Her mother returned to Scotland without her. Like me, she has to earn money to support herself, and links between Warsaw and Vienna have brought her here.

My diary, the 7th of December:

I sensed the strange activities in the atmosphere. She hinted a little, and it'll probably all emerge later. She soon left. She is off to Venice shortly and is coming back in a few days. The Polish men are very nice, and I was excited and thrilled by my new adventures, to be staying alone in this flat with these unknown men, so courteous and immaculately mannered. The life of the smuggling, high-living unknown world of these Poles is all so different from the hard-working life of my last few months.

Isobel seems to be a runner for these men, slipping through frontiers in apparent innocent youthfulness. Three Polish men, Isobel and I share a meal of Polish soup, Italian wine, Austrian bread and margarine. We listen to American music and smoke German cigarettes. It feels very cosmopolitan. Later the same afternoon, Isobel disappears, hitchhiking to Venice all by herself.

I have a few important things to do in this city. The next day, I go out into the cold, frosty morning through the gaily decorated Christmas streets. First, I collect my post, and then I make my way to the Hungarian consulate. It is surprisingly easy to obtain and pay for my visa. There must be frequent journeys between the Communist and capitalist countries, between Budapest and Vienna, and the process has been smoothed.

I wander through the streets of Vienna, lit with its wintry lights, walking into the massive Gothic cathedral of Saint Stephen. I am thinking of the life in Germany and my friends there whom I've left behind, missing them and definitely feeling a little lonesome. I walk down to the Danube river, fast, wide, deep and greenish-brown. There are three coal barges coming in from Budapest. The two cities are connected by this river, and yet there is an invisible political barrier cutting through the waters between them.

OVER THE GLOOMY BORDER TO BRATISLAVA

I am not sure how Isobel has persuaded me to go with her. She returned from Venice the next day, her unaccompanied journey there and back having been successful. I am not naturally attracted to illicit smuggling activities, and nor under normal circumstances would I have thought that she was either. But here we are, hitching out of Vienna on a cold, bleak winter morning, on the 9th of December, along the main road east. We get out of our lift at a junction in a small town called Gattendorf. From here, a local road leads towards the *Staatsgrenze*, the state frontier, into the Slovakian part of Czechoslovakia.

I look at Isobel, standing beside the road sign to Bratislava. She is wearing a white, fluffy hat, a knee-length coat showing her stockinged knees, black boots, and she looks perfectly cheerful. On the ground beside her is a holdall containing Italian woollen shirts hidden beneath her own clothing. A rucksack on her back contains more, a total of thirty shirts altogether. My usual idea of contraband is of brandy, diamonds or gold, but it seems that the shirts are valuable items in Czechoslovakia.

I take a photograph of her. It shows a wintry, foggy day with spindly leafless trees and a smattering of snow on the ground. We soon get a lift along the winding minor road to the frontier control post. Leaving the Austrian side is straightforward, and then the car drives the short distance across the usual no man's land to the Czechoslovakian side.

Perhaps we looked like simple, innocent students on a holiday visit. The guards wave the car through after looking cursorily at our passports and don't look in our bags. But let's just stop and think for a moment. Supposing they had? What would happen to us if they found the forbidden shirts? Vague ideas about Communist gaols float around in my mind. This is surely a foolish enterprise. Nevertheless, the car we are in passes the frontier, crosses the Danube, and suddenly we are in Bratislava.

The very name of this city is mysterious and thrilling. Bratislava. It rings of foreign places, Eastern lands, Slavic lands, the unknown. It is the capital of Slovakia, the poorer of the two small nations of Czechoslovakia.

Our lift puts us down in the centre of the city amid a snowstorm. The streets are wet and slushy. We must get our bearings and find somewhere to stay. Isobel is paying all our expenses, but she has borrowed some money from me in order to do it. She will pay me back from her profits. My diary records a first look around the square:

> *I was immediately surprised by the apparent wealth of everyone compared to Poland. Most people had gaily coloured winter clothes and furry boots and hats. There were plenty of cars, possibly not as many as in Austria, but still plenty. There were cars from Western Europe too, French and Italian. The street lighting was inferior, and the clearing-away of snow practically non-existent. Otherwise, everything seemed fairly normal. The shop windows were brightly and gaily decorated, showing ample variety in goods, in great contrast with Poland. Every shop is part of a state concern here, however.*

The smaller, cheaper hotels seem to be full, and not one to deny herself, Isobel decides that we must stay at the Carlton, the top hotel of Bratislava. I am most unaccustomed to staying in such places, but she is the decision-maker. The vast hotel occupies a complete block overlooking one of the main squares. She books us in for two nights, and we enter our names in the visitors' book. Celebrated guests in the past have included Franz Liszt, Johannes Brahms, Thomas Edison and Allen Ginsberg. During the war, the hotel hosted Nazi officers, and at the end of the war, the Red Army. Now, the clientele is a trickle of tourist groups and shady characters, including two rather disreputable British girls. We make our way to the fifth floor.

The room feels very *ancien régime*. A large, high double bed takes pride of place, and at its foot, fixed at right angles, is a shallow single bed. The big bed is for the well-to-do occupiers of the room, and the lower one for the serving maid. Isobel naturally occupies the larger and I the smaller. We love the room with its antiquated but working bathroom of which we are in great need. The view from the window looks down over the huge square and over rooftops to a high castle on a hill.

We need to eat, and the Slovakian equivalent of the Polish bar *mleczny* is the place to go. The state-run eating place is smarter, cleaner and has a better range of food than the ones I'd known in Poland. My diary:

> *While Isobel was off on her dangerous selling/investigating jobs, I walked up to the castle and around the quieter portions of the town. The castle, square and ugly, was fortified by a series of walls now falling to bits. The interior of this huge building was bare and grotesquely plain, high, dark and forbidding, especially in the grey, snowy weather. However, it commanded a view over the whole city and along the Danube for several miles.*
>
> *Then I was walking in the poorer parts of the town, and here I saw that not everywhere was there relative wealth. Many houses were propped up with wooden poles. Old women were walking along leaning on sticks and bent double sweeping away the snow from their paths or patches of pavement.*
>
> *I explored the outer regions of the old town. This part is dropping into decay, and it looks like the Communist state is not doing anything about it. All the money in that town seems to be going to the rehousing schemes in the new suburban areas.*

I draw a sketch map of what I interpret as the town development of Bratislava for my diary and list five areas:

1. The clifftop castle next to the Danube, the original defensive site.

2. Development of medieval fortified town, now largely derelict in slum conditions.
3. The baroque town, expanding during the administration of the Austro-Hungarian empire. This becomes more prosperous and less derelict as it leaves the old town area and merges into:
4. The administrative and shopping centre of the town, mainly later baroque, nineteenth-century monster buildings and early twentieth-century development.
5. The post-war socialist development schemes, large area of flats and factories, ugly, almost devoid of shops, but where most of the people live. Reminds me of East Berlin.

An interesting comparison between this and a Western town is that the older parts seem entirely neglected at the expense of the new development. The town centre is not the old town but has moved away from it.

BRATISLAVA NIGHTLIFE

Meeting again at the hotel, Isobel informs me that she needs to meet some people and wants me to come too. Her contacts have been supplied by the Polish men in Vienna. She has an appointment at a nightclub. Dressed in my best grey wool dress with the white lace collar, I make the effort to smarten myself up, having little idea of what to expect. My diary:

> We had to go to this crummy nightclub to wait for a contact
> of Isobel's and to look for others. It was a ghastly place, ugly
> though not tumbledown, just plain ugly with awful music
> and badly dressed people. Two chaps, one an old soldier,
> the other a crude, woman-hungry youngster, attached
> themselves to us. The soldier who spoke English promised to

help us with our selling. The sordidness of this selling business
was getting Isobel down, and me too.

What on earth am I doing in a place like this? I quietly observe the
grotesque scene. My diary:

The attempt at sex appeal everywhere repulsed me, the
smoochy music, the tight dresses and painted faces of the
females, the clutchy clingy dance, the poor but coloured
lighting, the bad-quality plush seats.

It grows worse when a smarmy Austrian makes overtures to
Isobel. He begins to handle her improperly, and because she needs
to build up her selling routine, she doesn't resist as strongly as I'd
have liked. This is really annoying me, and I leave in a bad temper,
making my way back to our luxury hotel room and my serving-
maid status.

During the next afternoon, I follow Isobel around with her
holdall of shirts. She goes behind the scenes in small, shop-like
establishments, leaving me in the doorways. We traipse around
from place to place in the cold gloom of the day, slopping in the
snow. She has some success I gather but keeps the details from
me.

In the course of the day, we become acquainted with Victor
and Vlado, two Slovakian students who improve things mightily.

"You like music?" says Vlado. "We'll take you somewhere that
you'll like."

Anything would be better than that awful club of last night, so
I am glad to agree. They have a car and drive us to a place on the
outskirts of the town. My diary:

The wine, first white, then red, was warm and sweetened.
It was served in china jugs and china pottery mugs, and it

was utterly delicious. But the music – oh it was marvellous, a gypsy band. There was a lead and a second violin, a bass and, of all things, a cimbalom! I had never before encountered this stringed instrument which is played with little hammers. The music, that sliding, coaxing, sensual violin, the gentle plonk of the cimbalom, was sheer ecstasy. We danced, waltzes, whirling round and round even to the familiar 'Blue Danube'.

Music like this is totally unknown to me. The gypsy violinist wanders over to the different tables where people are sitting, looks us in the eye as he discerns what we like and then produces it. Easily. Any tune you want – you hum it; they know it. I am bewitched and grateful to Victor and Vlado. This is much better than last night. They return us to our hotel, where I drop off to sleep in our warm room, the music ringing through my dreams.

THE COUNTRYSIDE AND THE PARTING

Isobel has decided that she is unlikely to sell any more shirts. After breakfasting in the great arched dining area of the Carlton Hotel, we meet Vlado and Victor with their car. They are taking us into the countryside because they know that I am interested in farming and the land. I write about what I see in my diary:

A distinctive feature of the land near Bratislava is the large areas given over to the townspeople for allotments, which all have little wooden huts.

The collective farms are also evident. The fields are large and undivided into peasant strips of any kind. The farm buildings are new, in the centre of the land which they serve. The collective farms we saw were mainly tomato farms, plus mixed general arable. The people who farm here live in villages, old villages. The particular village we visited was composed of small, individual cottages where the families live. Gardens, vegetable growing and rearing of fowls give the village a normal appearance. The standards seem higher in dress, housing and roads than in Polish villages.

We have only just met Vlado and Victor, and we like them, but there will be no chance to get to know them better. Bratislava is only fifty miles from Vienna, but it is in a different world, on the other side of that line, the Iron Curtain. We may walk out, but they must stay in. My diary:

I was sorry to be leaving them so abruptly. How awful it was as we passed the guard lines where the electric wires are, the boys impotent in their trap of a country, mutely left behind. How free we are by comparison. We walk by, chat gleefully to the heavily armed guards and wave to the boys from the other side. The electric lines here are so deceitfully inconspicuous. If I had never seen what they are like away from the tourist through-routes, in the backwoods of Germany, I'm sure I wouldn't have noticed them. Isobel never had, though she'd been six times through this frontier.

We smuggled the remainder of the shirts back out, and Isobel had wads of notes inside her boots. The guards were all rather merry, it being Sunday, and we got through with no bother.

I am hugely relieved to have finished with my first taste of smuggling. We hitchhike back to Vienna, where in the Poles' flat there is a gathering of low-life people. Isobel is sorting out the money, exchanging her wads of one currency for another out of sight in the kitchen, and she repays me what she owes. One of the Poles comes in with a monster bottle of cognac. Some sordid scenes follow, and I know I need to escape.

I've had a glimpse into the wintry greyness of Bratislava and the small-scale activities of the black market. It is time to head for the country with the mysterious, magnetic name I used to see in my childhood stamp collections, *Magyarország*, Hungary.

5

Warmth amid the Winter Chills

HUNGARY, DECEMBER 1966

ACROSS THE DREARY BORDERLAND BY AUTOSTOP

I am very cosy in my winter outfit, artificial fur hat, brown suede coat, skirt, blue tights and black bootees and appreciate more than anything my mother's Christmas present of sheepskin gloves. Rucksack on my back, Union Jack in hand, I find my way to the N10 autobahn out of Vienna which leads to Budapest.

I am walking eastwards, towards Hungary, with a visa for three weeks stamped in my passport. With only the vaguest ideas of what lies ahead, I sense the fearsome barrier in front of me, the line between two worlds of the West and the East. All I know about Hungary at this time can be summed up in one paragraph:

There was a revolution in 1956, and after some excitement and success, Russian tanks invaded and shot the people. There were black-and-white photographs in the newspapers. My family took in one, then another, Hungarian refugee student. Tihamer Kover came first, followed by Imre Gulyás, who stayed for a couple of years and to whose family home I am now heading. Imre, who we knew as Henry, was a slim, sophisticated student who learned English from nothing in four months and gained a place at Kings College, the university in Newcastle. He was dark haired with a goatee beard, played our piano brilliantly and bought my sisters and brothers and me lovely Christmas presents. My idea of young Hungarian men is thus that they are clever, studious and musical and have been sadly wronged by the Soviet Union.

And that is the limit of my knowledge.

A driver stops for me in a big, fast car going all the way to Budapest. As we leave Austria and approach the Hungarian frontier, the road narrows; hills fold in around the valley; and my English-speaking driver tells me: "Those hills form the gateway to central Europe. Through that gap came invasion after invasion on the Germanic lands, the Huns, the Turks."

I am a guest in his car, and I am not confident enough to ask about invasions going in the other direction. I note in my diary that the villages in this eastern part of Austria are different from the Germanic nucleated type. The pattern is one which I am to see frequently in the future. Houses in the streets are joined by walls, facing each other to form courtyards, all on a grid pattern. The people look poorer, more like peasants in dress and manner.

Once again, having crossed the Iron Curtain into and out of East Germany on my way to Poland, then to Slovakia, I am now to be entering the closed land of Hungary. I am safe in this experienced German traveller's car, and my passport is stamped with its visa. Yet the world beyond is dark and mysterious, and soon I will be alone, heading all the way across this land with not a word of the language. At the Hungarian border crossing, my diary records:

*Communist guards, heavily armed, seemed to be everywhere.
The barely noticeable mined zone of red earth surrounded
the buildings, and there were the inevitable observation
towers. We eventually got away from the customs after going
through a rigorous system of control.*

My driver is taking me along the primary national route of
Hungary which links Vienna to Budapest. After we pass the border
crossing, the road goes through small towns. The driver helps me
to interpret what I am seeing. My diary:

*Every few kilometres along the main road were two soldiers
marching on patrol, heavily armed. Within an area of five
kilometres from the frontier, nobody except soldiers on
duty and resident village people were allowed to pass. We
saw several peasants get off bicycles to show their passes to
the patrolling soldiers. We also saw Russian soldiers, and
since the revolution they are forbidden to have any contact
whatsoever with the Hungarians. Great areas of land are
given over to training for Russian tanks. We saw a statue
of a 'liberating soldier', a memorial to the first Russian who
entered Hungary after the war.*

*In the villages, conditions seemed rather bad. The
people were not very well dressed; cars were exceptional
and horses the average farmer's means of transport. The
roads and pavements were covered with mud because of
recent rain. Shops looked dowdy, and there were not many.
The buses were ancient and covered with mud, and there
was a general air of depression and desolation everywhere.*

The middle of winter is not the best time to see scenery generally,
and here the mud and greyness isn't helping. I note that the flat land
is unrelieved by hedge or wood or hill, looking gloomy and uncared

for. There are no peasant strips, just the large brown fields of the collective farms. Often the fields are flooded and badly drained.

As we drive further towards Budapest, passing Mosonmagyaróvár and Győr, the bleak, bare spaces of the frontier zone change. My diary:

We pass through an industrial region where there were coal mines and cement works. The whole landscape was filthy with black, belching smoke. This must have resembled a Black Country scene of a hundred years ago.

HENRY'S ESCAPE AFTER THE 1956 REVOLUTION – HOW HE CAME TO NEWCASTLE

Just a few miles south of the border crossing and the road in which I was travelling is the city of Sopron. This is where Henry was in university at the time of the revolution. I did not know this story as I travelled into Hungary, and he wrote this to me in spring 2021.

"Before the revolution, every university was assigned a specific arm of the armed forces, and ours was artillery. I had already been promoted to sergeant. When the revolution broke out, I was in Sopron, going through my third year of university studies.

"The revolutionary committee made me responsible for assuring that the town had enough bread, cooking oil and fat and other basics. I was so successful in this that I was sent to Budapest with two truckfuls of bread flour for the army, the unit under General Paul Maleter, who was executed after the revolution.

"The artillery regiment near Sopron supplied us with arms and 120mm howitzers, which we knew how to handle, being trained artillery officer cadets. We set up the guns to close the approach to Sopron, waiting for the Russians to arrive. When the first Russian tank appeared and saw the guns, it stopped. I was ordered to fire with the first gun. Nothing happened. The ignition pin had been removed from the guns. Fortunately, the Russians retreated, but we knew they'd come back, and the game was up.

"Sixty or so of us from the school of mining decided to leave. We trudged through the snow over the hills into Austria, where the border guards welcomed us and housed us in some barracks. A few days later, some of us were transported to St Wolfgang by the Sea, and while there we were offered help of many kinds. I accepted an offer to study in the UK, and soon we were taken by plane to Newcastle airport. Once there, we went to the National Coal Board's residential training centre to learn English. Four months later, I passed the university entrance exam and gained admittance to the School of Mining Engineering at Kings College, in Newcastle."

We arrive in Budapest where I notice the first signs of cheerfulness. On the outskirts are several blocks of new flats. My driver drops me off in the centre of the city, but I waste no time. I head for the road out of the city in the direction of Szolnok. I am aiming for the little town of Mezőberény, on the extreme opposite side of Hungary from where I'd entered. I pass through towns with the unpronounceable names of Törökszentmiklós, Mezőtúr and Gyomaendrőd. By 4pm, I have a long way to go but really hope to get there tonight. Otherwise, where will I stay? I write my diary a few days later, but here is the story:

My first lifts were a joke. It was dark; I was in a hurry and of course could not say a word to anyone in Hungarian. The night drew in; lifts were getting slower and slower as

the roads grew smaller and narrower towards Mezőberény.
It really seemed to be in the middle of nowhere. I have
memories of being squashed in between piles of men in
noisy crawling lorries, men who said that England must be
marvellous in comparison with this dreary land and that,
with Communism, it was all work and no money.

Eventually, when I am about thirty kilometres from Mezőberény, waiting by the roadside at about 8pm, some young Hungarian men approach me. They take me to the station, and I am glad to take a train for the last few miles. Everyone on the train treats me as if I've just come down from the moon.

At last, the train arrives at Mezőberény, the village where our Hungarian student came from. I am muddy, uncombed, with a sore throat and cold; my rucksack weighs heavily, and I am worn out from my long day. Now I must find Henry's house. At just the right moment, along comes a postman. He looks at me curiously and of course knows the address I have copied from Mrs Gulyás's letter. He leads me along the dark, muddy streets. My diary:

The postman stops outside a tall, wooden gateway in the
side of the building, and we go into a kind of farm courtyard,
buildings all around, balconies of wood and creeping vines
visible in the darkness. It looks so much nicer from the
inside.

It is about 10pm; the lights are out; and the family must be settled down for the night. The postman knocks on the inside door, and I wait uncertainly.

THE FAMILY OPENS ITS ARMS

"Who can be knocking on the door at this time of night?" the mother of the house must have said to her sleepy husband. He has just sunk comfortably into his feather bed. She goes to the door, and there I am. Untidy. Tired. Unsure.

She opens her arms. "It is Bridget! Imre, come, quickly – it is Bridget."

I drop my bag and fall into her warm embrace. Never mind how untidy or raggedy or sniffly with my cold I am. She hugs me and cuddles me and draws me inside. The kitchen is warm, the big stove giving off welcome heat.

I am overwhelmed with a feeling of kindness. She is not at all as I imagined, a tall, slim lady like a female version of Henry. Middle aged, as of course I should have realised, with greying hair, a little plump. Her husband, Imre, tumbles himself out of bed, comes into the kitchen and beams at me, opening his arms and addressing me with kind tones in Hungarian. He is more like Henry; I absorb this while I am being seated at the table.

"Hast du Hunger?" Are you hungry? Mutti, as I learn to call her, speaks to me in German. And those words I understand. While she rattles the pots around, under the single light bulb hanging from a wire over the table, Henry's sister Marika comes in smiling and welcomes me in English.

"Bridget, we don't know you are coming today," she says. All the family has now been roused out of bed. Shoni comes in. He is Marika's husband. I will later learn to spell his name correctly, but that is what it sounds like.

Imre Bácsi, Uncle Imre, as I learn to call Henry's father, shows me to the outside toilet in the yard. I am given a bowl of warm water for a quick wash. Mutti has discovered quickly that I am a vegetarian and won't eat her delicious sausage. She mixes up some eggs and makes me an omelette which she puts on the table with bread, butter, cheese and tea. I've hardly eaten a thing all day, and I am ravenous.

Surrounded by their affection, their smiles and the warmth of the kitchen, I do justice to this food. What happiness after the long, cold day! And my bed is ready. They knew I was coming at some date around now although not exactly when. My bed is like the maid's bed at the Carlton hotel in Bratislava. It is along the foot of Mutti and Imre Bácsi's double bed. I sink into its feather mattress, soft and cosy. The warmth is beyond expectation.

THE HOUSE AND VILLAGE OF MEZŐBERÉNY

Marika and Shoni have left the house for their work in the nearby town of Békéscsaba when I wake up.

Mutti embraces me hugely. "*Guten Morgen liebe Bridget. Komm an den Tisch und frühstücke,*" she says. Good morning. Come to the table, dear Bridget, and have some breakfast. At this rate, I shall be improving my German, and indeed I am ready for lots of tea and breakfast.

First, I must look outside where I can see Imre Bácsi. I stand on the wooden balcony. In front of me is a structure of a splendid T shape. What can it be? What is he doing? A tall, sturdy wooden pole with a forked top is erected in the yard. The two parts of the fork are connected by a piece of wood. Across this, a beam is balancing horizontally. From one end of the beam, a heavy stone is hanging, and at the other end hangs a bucket on a thin, wooden pole. The whole thing is carefully balanced so that when Imre Bácsi pulls the thin, wooden pole upwards, the horizontal beam swings downwards. Then he lowers the bucket into the well and fills it. Next, he pours the water into another bucket which can be carried away, ready for use.

"*Jó reggelt kívánok, Putzin Bridget,*" he says with a broad smile. Good morning, little Bridget. I learn this is my nickname.

"What is this?" I indicate the well. He answers with the Hungarian word: *geemeeshkoot*. I have been observing the workings of a balance beam well, and later I learn the correct spelling, *gémeskút*, which means 'tree trunk well'.

Hens are pecking around the well on the earthy yard, and dried red peppers are hanging in strings from the balcony. A pig is grunting off to the side, a Christmas pig, although I don't know it yet. I am already beginning to think that Hungary is

unlike any place I have seen before.

After breakfast of eggs and home-made bread, which is my favourite food, I go out through the great wooden gate into *Arpad Utca*, Arpad Street.

The gable ends of houses face onto the street, high walls connecting the properties. The road is surfaced with hard, frozen earth. Running parallel on each side of the road are ditches, next to them a grassy line with small trees, and then the pavements which reach to the walls of the houses.

As I look, two horses come along pulling a high-seated cart. It is driven by a statuesque, moustachioed man wearing a tall, black, woolly hat and a sleeveless sheepskin jacket. A Hungarian horseman! The horses clip clop along the street. Mezőberény is full of surprises. I spend the morning exploring the town. Men are driving horses and carts, and women with shopping bags make their way to a state-run shop. I learn that the street pattern of *Arpad Utca* is standard and that the whole town centre is constructed this way on a grid pattern. The trees are there to provide shade in the summer. The ditches are for rainwater, and little stone bridges cross them here and there. Following *Arpad Utca*, I come to a square in the town centre where there is a church of simple design with a dome and a little further away another with a small, pointed tower.

Marika and Shoni, whose name I shall now spell correctly as Sanyi, come home from work in the darkness of the evening. They are surveyors and work in a little office in the neighbouring town of Békéscsaba. Mutti provides the evening meal.

If there is one word to summarise the attitude of this family to me, it is kindness. They spread their love around and through me, and if any of my attitudes, or ignorance of the correct way to behave in Hungary, is annoying, they wouldn't dream of showing it. Marika smiles down at me, her chin lowered a little, as she expresses herself in English. Her working day is long. She and Sanyi walk to the station every morning along the cold streets, wait in a draughty station for the steam train, and on arrival they have another long walk to their office. In the cold winter days, this is tiring. But she never complains

to me. She smiles and looks after my welfare. She and Sanyi have plans to entertain me, and I am thrilled and excited. When they are at work, I walk around this village-town, write in my diary and attend to my post. Mutti feeds me and Imre Bácsi jokes with me. I am content.

The Turks were here

"Tomorrow is Saturday, and I propose that we visit Gyula," Marika suggests. This involves a lengthy journey of two train rides each way. The town of Gyula amazes me. There is a gigantic castle made of brick three metres thick. We have plenty of castles in Northumberland, and I am used to them, but this something quite different. What is the purpose of such a great castle here on the extreme eastern boundary of Hungary?

"The Turks were here," explains Marika. "Gyula was on the battleground." Turks? Here in Hungary? All I know about Turks is the pink and white confectionery coated with icing sugar called Turkish delight, and sometimes a pub sign of a turbaned man outside the Turk's Head. It is hard to picture the Turks battling in a European country like Hungary, while I am with Western-minded people like Marika and Sanyi. And yet it was so. The great plains of Hungary drew in the Ottoman invaders, as far as Budapest and on towards Vienna. Now I understand the 'Torok' part of the village names as I'd hitchhiked to Mezőberény. The Turks had been there. Here in Gyula, the Turks had been masters for 129 years, between 1566 and 1694. Hungary was on the boundary of Europe then, just as it is now. My diary:

We visited the only castle in this part of Hungary, strategic in the battles between the Turks and the Hungarians. It was grim, red brick. This part of the world must have been as unfortunate then as it is now, a continual battleground of ideology, with the Hungarians often getting the worse of the bargain, marshy, badly drained, full of lakes and swamps.

Gyula town on this wintry December day is wet, snowy and slushy, but it doesn't depress our spirits. Marika and Sanyi find a teashop where we enjoy scrumptious food, mine consisting of tea with lemon, delicious cheese omelette and jam pancakes, finishing off with sweet chestnuts and whipped cream. My diary:

We visited a tiny little Turkish sweetshop where I was bought an enormous lump of 'Turkish honey', very similar to our cinder toffee. There was an old Turk behind the counter, sitting on guard over the women workers.

This seems an extraordinary relic of those ancient conquests, a Turkish family descended from those warlike times still living in present-day Gyula.

We had come to Gyula on two steam trains, changing in Békéscsaba, the same way Marika and Sanyi travel to work. My diary:

There is something gloomily fascinating about trains in this Communist land. There are policemen hanging around, quietly in the shadows. It is strictly forbidden to take photographs. The stations are so primitive. There's no such thing as platforms. We are on the same level as the rails, which means climbing high up into the carriages. There is mud and snow everywhere, poor people in peasant clothes patiently waiting for trains that are so often late. In the evening, the huge, roaring steam engines shunt in and out, guards yelling and running. Through this thread of communication which stretches from Russia out to its victim satellites, one senses the most indomitable power of Communism, the filth and inefficiency, treating the railway system as though it is a deadly secret to be guarded. Here one can sense the contrasting silent menace of the police, the bossiness of the station officials who have power on their side, with the patient, uncomplaining but long-suffering crowds who use the railway service. Their patience is also learned from years of bitter experience. And the pity of it is that every person in sight, with all their own individual life stories and experiences, are but puppets in the hands of Almighty Russia. People of Hungary hardly have the right of ownership of their own souls. But it is not expected to remain forever this way.

Such writing is based on my perceptions but also my immaturity and lack of understanding. People such as Marika and her family very much have ownership of their own souls, and our conversations reveal this as the days go on.

A FEW DAYS BEFORE CHRISTMAS

Marika is far too self-respecting to complain or apologise about her country. A few of us are sitting round the table. I ask how it feels being confined in Hungary by soldiers and mines.

"I'm afraid the Government doesn't trust the people," she replies. "But things are getting better for us all now in Hungary. I'm sorry my brother has left us."

We discuss the standard of living. "Yes, life is hard, and we are poor," Marika says. "But it doesn't matter if we don't have a car and a fine house. Everyone else is poor too."

One of the younger friends has visited England. "Money isn't everything," she says. "People here are kind and care for each other. Socialist life may mean that nobody now is rich, but the peasants have more than they ever had before. Now everybody has equal opportunity."

These are sentiments with which I can sympathise.

Yet it was not easy for Marika when her brother left the country. She is four years older than me but has only just completed her three years of higher education. At first, she was seen as a 'class enemy' because her brother had fled the country and, despite being qualified, was denied university entrance. For three years she took work on a collective farm near Mezőberény. Her excellent record there resulted in a change of attitude by the authorities, and she was allowed to enter university in Budapest. But she does not tell me this. I find it out years later. Marika does not look for sympathy.

The family have planned exactly the sort of programme for me that I appreciate. They introduce me to people of interest, like this group of youngsters with whom we are chatting. They take me to meet a family friend, Gittanéni, an older lady of great character. She is a widow, the wife of a wealthy businessman, has travelled considerably and speaks flawless English. Now she lives alone in a tiny cottage. The conversation moves between German, English and Hungarian, and even sometimes a little French. I learn that she had lived in Budapest and that her house had been commandeered by the Communists. There are others in Mezőberény living in similar circumstances.

"They took everything from me," she says. "But they could not take my education. That is why each young person should take every opportunity to learn. It is the only thing that remains theirs for as long as they live." These words strike me. I have a rather unappreciative attitude to my own education. I am impressed by how well educated these people are.

A medical student receiving free state education gives me his views. "I'd give ten years of my life in Hungary for one month in Las Vegas," he says.

A little later, I write these conversations into an article for *The Journal*, but I should have been more prudent. Such conversations in the paranoia of Communism can lead to troubles with the political police, and even among friendly seeming neighbours there can be informers.

At the time, I am reading an English language book by a young Russian poet, Yevgeny Yevtushenko, called *Precocious*

Autobiography. I have brought it with me in my rucksack from Germany. The cover of my copy shows a good-looking young man, broadly smiling, and with a cigarette hanging stylishly from his lips. All fashionable young people smoke in these days. It is of special interest to me because it reveals the thinking of a young person brought up in a Communist society, and I write extracts from his book in my diary. He writes about how the Russian people have suffered throughout their history as perhaps none other, and how this might be expected to blunt and degrade the human spirit and destroy its capacity for belief in anything. Yet he writes that just the opposite seems to be the truth, that it is the prosperous nations of today, those favoured by their geographical position and historical circumstances, which seem to show a weaker hold on moral values. Neither does he call those nations happy, and he would include mine in this. Even though he is from an officially atheist country, he quotes the Biblical saying: 'Man does not live by bread alone'.

He writes of his new standard by which to measure intellectuals, that a person's intelligence is not the sum of what they know but the soundness of their judgement and power to understand and to help others; that some of the most educated people he knows are less cultured than soldiers, peasants, workers and even criminals. For him, true aristocracy is not made up of those who can spend hours quoting from Plato to Kafka and Joyce, but of those whose hearts are open to others. From his own experience, those whose education makes them worse scoundrels are the rabble.

I think about these things while talking with Marika and her Mezőberény friends, whose intelligence and humanity impress me greatly and who are obliged to tolerate insufferable officialdom. I compare it with young people from my own country. My diary:

I have noticed our wealth of dissatisfied beatniks, rebels of all kinds, gammlers, among students. Too much easy living

produces juvenile delinquents, the fights between the 'mods'
and the 'rockers'. But here in Hungary, the fight is for survival.

One evening, Sanyi and Marika decide to take me to the village inn where the gypsies will be performing. We enter a narrow room with a few tables along one side, and I am bought some red Hungarian wine. This to me is wonderland. The gypsy music enchants me. The violins weave their magic spells and tinkle-tinkle goes the cimbalom. The lead gypsy approaches our table, knowing that here is a stranger. Marika doesn't want to dance but sits smiling, encouraging Sanyi to get me up. He whirls me around to the waltzes and polkas and introduces me to the *csárdás*, a wild Hungarian dance. I am in ecstasy. This is like nothing I've ever known before, except for that one time in Bratislava. Gypsy music! In the winter in deepest Hungary! Who would ever have thought this could be me?

EDUCATION AND LANGUAGES

Almost everyone I meet is multilingual. As well as their own Hungarian language, all the young people have learned Russian in school, and many learn English too. Those of the older generation who know German often keep this knowledge hidden. I learn to call Marika's mother Mutti. She speaks High German, and I am learning from her. When the children were growing up, the language was banned in the house. Those were dangerous times for German speakers. I find out that her uncles were both deported to Siberia after the war, that one died there and the other returned a broken man. Married to a Hungarian, she escaped the deportations.

For me, Hungarian is a very difficult language. I had learned a few basic Polish phrases and made some effort at German. I'll always try French if I get the chance, and Spanish too, although there is little likelihood of needing that here. But Hungarian is entirely different from almost all other European languages. No one expects me to speak it, but I try a few words.

I learn to say *cursenem saypen* for 'thank you', which unfathomably is written *Köszönöm szépen*, and *Jó napot kívánok* for 'good day'.

One day, a slim, gypsy-like man comes into the family kitchen. He greets the family: "*Chocolom.*" Now that is an easy word for me, with its similarity to chocolate. Next time he comes to the house, I address him with *Chocolom*, and everyone's face bursts into smiles. What is so funny? They explain politely that I have kissed his hand! (The word correctly in Hungarian is spelled *Csókolom*.)

On two occasions, my hosts take me to visit a local school. Having 1,900 pupils, they must come from a range of villages around. My diary:

> *There is little in the way of equipment, an entire lack of free methods, and everything is very formal and yet friendly. The classrooms appear dowdy and old-fashioned. The standards of learning seem high, the keenness of the children, especially the fourteen-year-olds, is inspiring. Every ounce of energy goes into learning, and those children know a great deal. Although I think teaching is more enjoyable for both teacher and pupil by our freer methods, I think of how little I actually know, and hence how little I shall be able to teach the children in my future classes so that they know too. In England I was a professed follower of the new methods of learning, by my desire to enjoy teaching so that it wasn't too much like work. I had not a little scorn for the old ways. But here I'm forced to see a different point of view.*

Marika also arranged for me to meet her in Békéscsaba where we would go to the high school. I manage to miss the morning train but, undeterred, set out to hitchhike the eighteen kilometres. My diary:

It's quite an event for a girl to hitchhike here. A lorry picked me up. In Békés, we were stopped by traffic police. A plain-clothes policeman decided to interview me and spent ages examining my passport which of course was in perfect order. Then I was sent to the police station, where there was a reasonable policeman who spoke German to me and laughed it all off. It was nothing but fuss and bother and wasted an hour for no purpose.

I eventually meet Marika and her young friend Sophie, and we go off to the school. I participate in the English language class with an impressive, enthusiastic group. Once again, I admire the fluency and willingness of the students to speak in English.

I am asked a question. "Why does the singer say 'I can't get *no* satisfaction!'? Shouldn't it be 'I can't get *any* satisfaction!'?" This is the era of The Rolling Stones and The Beatles. The young people are learning good English grammar. I can only say that this is pop music language and blame American influence.

A map on the wall is pointed out to me. It shows Greater Hungary, with its boundaries before the First World War, and present-day Hungary isolated in the middle. The country has lost over three million people and two thirds of its territory which are now in surrounding countries, a reality which is impressed upon the young people.

THE PEOPLE OF THE ALFÖLD

The Great Hungarian plain, the Alföld, wide and open to the skies, flat as far as the eye can see in every direction, has been trampled over throughout history.

At the Battle of Mohács in 1526, the Hungarians were routed by the Turks. Suleiman the Magnificent crossed the plains with his armies as he advanced northwards towards Budapest during 1526, burning villages and taking slaves.

For around two hundred years, the Ottomans held the plains of Hungary. Villagers collected in towns for safety. Able-bodied members of the families would camp out on their fields in the season, remote from the towns, cultivating their crops, leaving the aged and young at home. The isolated farms, known as tanyas, with their T-shaped wells, would become icons of the Hungarian landscape.

Large village-towns like Kecskemét, Debrecen, Szabadka (now Subotica in Serbia) and Szeged expanded, as did smaller places like Mezőberény and Békéscsaba. To this day, the map shows these large village-towns with wide, open spaces between them.

Eventually, the Turks were driven back, and the devastated plains needed to be resettled. Empress Maria Theresa, sovereign of Austria and Hungary from 1740–1780, encouraged settlers, in particular from Germany and Slovakia.

Henry Gulyás's mother's antecedents came to Mezőberény from Germany. His father's ancestors moved there from other parts of Hungary.

After the Treaty of Trianon in 1919, and the break-up of the Austro-Hungarian empire, great expanses of this plain were lost to other nations. The population of the new state of Hungary was less than half of the old kingdom, reduced from twenty million to eight million. To the north, lands went to Slovakia; to the east, to Romania; to the south, to Yugoslavia. Mezőberény and Békéscsaba became part of the remote south-eastern corner of Hungary.

THE SIGNIFICANT POST – MEZŐBERÉNY

Here in Mezőberény, I am still in touch with my network of friends and family. The post to Hungary has been perfectly reliable.

My sister Rosie, now aged eighteen, tells me she is working as an apprentice catering manager in a Newcastle hospital. She is enjoying the Christmas lights, and 'there is a canny lad at work called Vic who I like. One half of me likes the lad next door; the other half loves the lad a few hundred miles away. Oh, I don't know at all'.

Friends from college send me stories about their boyfriends. Mary is now enamoured with Damien; Jenny is threatening to finish with Len not very emphatically; and Jean is trying to get away from Geoff. It is all about boys, and love, at our age.

My mother reports that my youngest brother Stephen only got twenty-five out of a hundred for his maths exam, and that Rosie and Stephen are the only ones at home who will need Christmas stockings now. She feels 'quite sad at the carol service in church. They had a little procession of children coming up the aisle, singing and carrying little candles, just as you used to'. She sends a pretty hand-drawn card of my cat looking out of the window.

Rosie writes that my article in *The Journal* from the Iron Curtain across rural Germany has been printed and that I have earned a nice sum of money for that. My grandmother sends me a letter on lightweight airmail paper, saying 'how kind of Mrs Gulyás and her family to offer you this wonderful hospitality'.

Theo, the Dutch student with whom I'd spent some time in Warsaw, reminds me that it is not only the Communist lands that try to exercise thought control:

I annoy for days at events in Nederlands. People are arrested for they say that they don't agree with the American intervenience in Vietnam; people are arrested when they say they don't agree with such arrestings; people are not allowed to show photographs of real state in Vietnam; people are not allowed to say they do not agree with that etc. It is not funny to live in Holland. I hope you come and see this wonderful country yet!

When I met you in Poland, Bridget, you did not know

much about politics, about people of Europe. You only had
a small book. My impression was you lived in England in
a relatively small domain. Yet you were not satisfied and
wanted to find out by yourself, didn't you, what was going
on around you, what was going on in the world. I was much
impressed by that, for it does not happen often. Most people
are lazy and stay at home. I hardly can believe you are doing
it so to tell it the children in school when you are back again.
Don't you find it very amazing to see new people every
month? I for myself cannot answer this problem.

I am remembered, and the post links me to my past. I reply to
everyone with a forwarding address in Belgrade, Yugoslavia, care
of Dushko.

PIG KILLING AND FAMILY FEASTINGS

I am drowsing in my cosy feather bed at 8am one morning when I
hear the unusual sound of many chattering voices in the kitchen.
Who can be there so early?

Probably, Mutti and Imre Bácsi are glad that I've slept this
late. Knowing that I am a vegetarian, they may well have hoped to
get the worst of things over before I wake up. I learn that the pig,
which I now call the Christmas pig, is now in porcine heaven. All
the action took place while I was contentedly asleep. And truly I
am relieved to have known nothing about it.

All the family are in action. I am fascinated and repelled at the
same time. My diary:

The meat was minced up and put into a huge wooden bath,
covered with paprika, mixed up, and then put into the
machine to make sausages, the skins being the freshly cleaned
intestines of the pig.

The whole day was a kind of work celebration. I didn't watch the proceedings exactly, me being vegetarian, but I was amazed at the variety of things they made from one pig. Piles of sausages and salted hams. The smell of blood and fat, and the smoky melting fat, was not appealing to me. At midday dinner time, there was a huge meal, presumably of quickly decaying meats and those which were not suitable for conservation. Everyone was very merry, drinking and eating enormous helpings of freshly killed and cooked meat.

I found it very barbaric, somewhat fascinating, to see such meat-hungry people. By supper time, another enormous meal was ready, and everybody tucked in again. It was just like a feast, the amount and variety of dishes that disappeared. There was a lot of work to be done all the time, and it was not finished until well into the night.

Next day, huge joints of meat were covered in salt. Various other concoctions were made from the fat, and the smell lingered. This amount of meat, however, largely sustains the family for a year. And in a land where meat is very expensive, sometimes not even available, the pig killing is a necessary luxury.

This kind family thus continue their own essential activities, coping with a rather reluctant vegetarian in the background. I am fascinated by how much of their food they supply from their own resources and look at the shelves in the larder:

The degree of self-sufficiency of food production in this family is amazing and is probably typical of most peasant and ordinary country people. Firstly, they produce most of their own meat and eggs. Then the garden, which is not very large, supplies the following: apples, cherries and pears which are preserved in enormous rows of bottles; apricots made both into preserves and delicious jam; grapes which are stored in quantity until Christmas. From them are made a delicious home-made wine, poppy seeds which make special sweet-meat delicacies, an enormous variety of herbs dried and hanging in bags, paprikas of several varieties pickled in colourful jars with cabbage etc, enormous gherkins and cucumber-like vegetables, tomato sauce preserve, not to mention countless bottles of sauces and pickles.

This is a whole year's supply of much of the family's food. In addition, from the uncle's house in the country comes quantities of walnuts, hazelnuts and honey. Mutti makes her own cottage cheese with onions and paprika, although she buys the milk. In effect almost the only food that has to be bought is bread – although Mutti sometimes makes this too – flour, salt, butter and margarine, and occasional meat for a change from the pig, tea, coffee and sugar.

Two days before Christmas, more kitchen wonders seduce me:

Walnuts were ground and put in little dishes. Hazelnuts were crushed. Egg whites were beaten into a stiff mixture with sugar, and nuts added. Poppy seeds were ground into a black, oily pulp and mixed with sugar. Chocolate paste was being beaten until stiff. Much of what went on I didn't see but it is clear that these country people feast on the food of kings. I'm longing for Christmas day. At least one great pile of sweets and pies has emerged, and an enormous cake made mostly of egg whites coated in chocolate and nuts is standing temptingly in the kitchen.

CHRISTMAS SUCH AS I HAVE NEVER KNOWN IT

Happiness, wonder and sadness are all combined in these days in Mezőberény. Marika and Sanyi must work on the morning of Christmas Eve but are home after midday. Mutti has been organising spring cleaning the house in the morning. Marika and I decorate the tree. This is a house with German influence where the tree is truly traditional. I have bought tiny odds and ends from Vienna which I put on the tree. I wrap a tiny seal for Marika with his little furry head and black eyes peeping out of the paper, and she screams when she sees it, thinking it is a mouse. My diary:

> *There is no mention of churchgoing either tonight or on Christmas Day. At supper time, Mutti laid out a candlelit spread. A special food made of round, ball-like biscuits, soaked in hot water and mixed up with ground poppy seeds and sugar was served. It was delicious. There was a chocolate and walnut cake, more cream than cake, a huge, golden, home-made sweet loaf, other sausage-shaped rolled cakes containing ground poppy seeds and sugar. What with drinking home-made wine, we almost burst by the time we finished.*

Now it is time to do something which will pull our heartstrings. Mutti works as a telephonist at the local telephone exchange. Because of this, she is able to organise phone connections with her son Henry. It is because of him that I am here at all, and I am kindly invited to share this family occasion.

We walk through the cold, wintry streets in the dark. In the telephone exchange, Mutti arranges for each of us to have a set of earphones. Henry is connected, and they exchange greetings. How hard it must be to say anything other than how much they miss each other. Everyone has a word with him. I didn't expect to speak, but they put me on too.

"Bridget, what are you doing in Mezőberény with my family?" he asks me in a strained voice. These are words I will remember for my lifetime.

We all walk home through the cold, thinking of the distance which separates members of this close and loving family. It is ten years since Henry had last been with them. Ten long years, and so many miles, with a great, impenetrable barrier between them.

But what is to be done? We return to the warm, wooden house.

We are all chased out of the room. Then Imre Bácsi rings a little bell, and we go in to see the tree lit up in all its glory. While everyone admires the tree, Marika and I play '*Stille Nacht, Heilige Nacht*', she on the piano and me on my little pipe, and it echoes through the silence of the candlelit room.

Henry, you are so far away. The thought is on everyone's mind.

Presents are distributed. I am thrilled with mine. Sanyi and Marika, worried about me freezing to death in my thin suede coat, have bought me a warm quilted lining for it. Mutti likewise supplies me with a pair of bottle-green tights. Imre Bácsi gives me a box of chocolates from Budapest with pictures on, and Marika and Sanyi present me with a hand-carved wooden Hungarian pipe.

The next day, the 25th of December, is passed quietly, after Mutti's celebration breakfast of eggs, titbits from the Christmas pig and fried onions. I am allowed to play with Imre Bácsi's violin and make sufficient screeching noises to please myself although certainly no one else. We read and write letters.

In the evening, I am taken to a local dance, not with Marika and her family but with their young friend Sophie. She tells me that I will surely find it old-fashioned, and the band plays music that sounds ten years out of date, but I am not critical. My diary:

All the local girls and chaps were there, with rows of mothers sitting on the seats around the edge to keep an eye on their precious daughters and to guard them on the dangerous route home.

We go home in the crispy moonlight, and I write about it in my letter home:

The nights are so lovely. There's clear moonlight now, and the silhouettes of the trees, buildings and wells suddenly become graceful and charming. It is so clean smelling, I am filled with health and vigour, and I feel I could walk for hours. We come into a small, cosy wooden house, every room warm, and we drop into snuggly feather beds and curl up cosy until the pale sunlight of morning and cockerels crowing wakes us up. This is really one of my favourite places in the world.

I am seduced by this winter land. But I am a mere visitor. There are very hard realities here, some of which concern the farmland.

THE OPEN BLEAK FARMLANDS

As I travel with Marika and Sanyi to Békéscsaba and Gyula, or on my walks on the outskirts of Mezőberény, I am aware of the bleakness of the countryside. The land is completely flat, stretching off in all directions, only varied by the long, high banks keeping out the flood waters of the great rivers. All is brown, grey, muddy and bare. Leftover stalks from crops that were harvested are bent by the wind. There is hardly a building, with only a rare, isolated farmhouse to be seen. Patches of watery bogland are left uncultivated. When I discuss this at the family home, Imre Bácsi tells me that because the land is collectivised, no one cares to do anything about it.

One day, I visit a collective farm. The long, low buildings for the animals are surrounded by mud and manure, frozen hard. The wind is piercingly strong, and I go into the communal office where the workers are sitting around on broken chairs, shivering, conversing sparsely with each other. They offer me a mug of some kind of coffee. I have no Hungarian with which to ask questions, so despite their friendliness, I soon say: "*Viszontlátásra.*" Goodbye. I make my way back to the village-town along the hard, frozen mud tracks.

I know that the farmlands of these Eastern European countries under the Soviet yoke were enforcedly collectivised from the late 1940s onwards, Poland being an exception where small farms are still being cultivated in long strips by individual families. But here, in this vast, open land of south-eastern Hungary, the farming families had been unable to prevent collectivisation. It had been a cruel and terrible process.

FARM COLLECTIVISATION

In spring 2021, Henry Gulyás told me the story.

"During the collectivisation process, wholescale barbarities were committed against the farmers. A small farmer lives and dies by his land. It is not a possession, but the very part of his being. Many understood that they could not resist the gruesome monolith. Others resisted. Truckloads of Communist Party cadres were sent around the countryside to beat with pickaxe handles and chains the farmers and their families, including the children, until the man signed away his land, or died. There always was a doctor with them who issued the Certificate of Death from natural causes.

"In 1949, when I was thirteen years old, and my father working in another part of Hungary, the family's small area of land was demanded 'voluntarily' during the collectivisation process.

"My father refused. He was far away in Trans-Danubia, working. Thus, it fell to Mother and me, aged thirteen, to bike the ten-kilometre ride and till the land all day with hand hoes. By the time the sun set, our bodies being unaccustomed to hard physical work, facing the bike ride home filled us with horror. Arriving at home on our last legs, all we wanted was to wash and collapse in bed. My little sister Marika, aged nine, awaited us with a full meal, which she had cooked after working all day.

"In the end, it was clear that the state would take the land anyway.

"So finally, Mother wrote to my father saying: 'We have no option...' The only thing that was left was the little acacia forest my father had given to his brother, as a birthday present, once, long ago. The trees were cut down during the Kadar years, when they were beautifully mature and tall.

"Until 1949, the year of total Communist takeover, the Hungarian countryside had been a veritable mosaic of cottages and homesteads, sprinkled by quite a few castles. The confiscation of the land by the Communists led to the demolition of the country cottages and the destruction of a way of life which had provided independence to its inhabitants for centuries."

VISIT TO BUDAPEST

The family are ensuring that I see the best of their country. I am to be taken to Budapest for a four-day visit, and I am not allowed to pay a penny of the cost. It seems that the hospitality shown by my parents to their son Henry is to be repaid a hundred times.

Our early morning train from Mezőberény station once again crosses those wide, flat expanses, the *Alföld*, the Hungarian name for the great plain. Such spaces and such openings for the imagination. We stop at Gyomaendrőd, Mezőtúr, Törökszentmiklós, Szolnok, Cegléd and arrive at Keleti station by midday.

All has been planned. "We'll go first to the National Gallery," Marika says. Under the dull, misty skies, we make our way along the streets of Pest as far as the Danube with its bridges in both directions. Everything, trams and people, seem to be in shades of brown and grey, but nothing dampens my spirits. We cross by the Chain Bridge and climb up the hill to the palace of Buda which holds the National Gallery.

In the wing which contains the nineteenth-century Hungarian painters, Marika wants to show me one painting which she really loves. It is a group of young people lounging on the grass having a picnic, and the woman in the pink dress makes a strong impact. The artist is Pál Szinyei Merse, and he painted it in an impressionist style. With my interest in the Hungarian landscape, I pay attention to the landscapes of artists like Munkácsy Mihály and Géza Mészöly which show villagers and houses of the plains. "We must take you to the Munkácsy museum in Békéscsaba," Marika tells me.

We stay in lodgings with a widow who lets rooms in her flat. Next day, we visit a student couple, friends of Marika and Sanyi. They live with their little daughter, not in a flat but in a corridor. On the way to see them, we find a man who is selling bananas in the street. Bananas? In Hungary in winter? This is something unusual. We buy one and give it to the young couple for their daughter. While the four friends exchange all their news in Hungarian, I am thinking that this beloved little girl is as happy as any princess. Even if she lives in a corridor, to her parents she is priceless, and a banana is as good as Christmas.

In the evenings, we have delicious meals while I am entertained by gypsy bands. And after one such meal, Marika and Sanyi take me to the Hungarian State Opera House for a performance of Verdi's *Simon Boccanegra*. Amid the glittering golden interior of the opera house, I partly snooze and partly enjoy it. I am a bit of a barbarian compared to my cultured friends.

TIME TO LEAVE

I must leave Mezőberény. My visa is for three weeks only, and as I had crossed into Hungary on the 17th of December, I must leave

147

by the 3rd of January. While I am still drowsing in my feather-bed cosiness, Marika and Sanyi bid me farewell as they leave for work. Marika, so beautiful and wise, and Sanyi, so kind and equable.

Mutti and Imre Bácsi come to the bus stop with me. They won't dream of letting me hitchhike and insist on paying my fare. We are standing in the cold, and the bus hasn't come. We wait for half an hour, an hour, and still it hasn't come. We stamp our feet, exchange a few courtesies with the other passengers and can do nothing but wait. Conversation is difficult. I am filled with thoughts of how they have enclosed me in their love for these two weeks, and I am now leaving them with the hard reality of their lives. Cold and uncomplaining, they wait. One and a half hours pass, and then finally, after two hours, the bus approaches.

"*Viszontlátásra, Puţzin Bridget.*" Goodbye, little Bridget. Imre Bácsi smiles and hugs me, and Mutti does the same. I pile onto the bus with the other people, and when I find my seat, I can see Mutti's gentle, proud face, smiling a little sadly, her white hair and green scarf a blur through the grimy steamed window. As the bus leaves, I am trying hard not to cry.

HENRY AND LITTLE SALOMON

Henry told me the following story in spring 2021.

"My first experience of evil came at the age of eight. My father was sent by the government of the day to search for oil or gas in the region of Hungary near the Ukrainian border. He took me with him in the summer school holidays. The house where my father lived was that of a Jewish widow, who had six children. The youngest was Salomon, my age, who became my pal. I had got a toy car for Christmas that year, a beautiful blue convertible, about a foot long. We played with the car all summer.

"One day I could not find either Salomon or his mother,

Aunty Hanna. I went around asking where they were. Someone told me to go to the railroad station. The road was closed by Hungarian gendarmes. I went around through the woods and hid in the bushes, where I could see the station platform. A long train of cattle wagons stood there, without a locomotive. My little buddy Salomon holding Aunty Hanna's hand, and clutching the blue car in the other, was in the door of one of the cattle cars, surrounded by weeping men and women. The entire Jewish population of the village was on that train.

"When I asked, my father would not give me a straight answer. But later, my mother told me they were taken away to be killed. To this day, I feel the pain and helplessness of a little boy, as well as the hatred of any political system where the fate of people is decided by political cliques."

AUTHOR'S NOTE

Most of the Hungarian Jews were taken to Auschwitz, to Oświęcim, where they were killed by the tens of thousands. Primo Levi was there when Salomon, with Henry's little blue car, arrived at the camp. In his book *If This Is a Man*, Primo Levi wrote: 'Throughout the spring of 1944, convoys arrived from Hungary; one prisoner in two was Hungarian, and Hungarian had become the second language in the camp after Yiddish'.

When Henry was eight years old, I was a new baby in the England of 1944.

HUNGARY CHRONOLOGY

1920	Treaty of Trianon, Hungary loses two-thirds of its lands to Slovakia, Romania and Yugoslavia
1940s	Hungary sides with Axis powers at first
1944	Hitler invades Hungary
1945–1948	End of the Second World War. Communist Party establishes power under Soviet control
1949	Rakosi imposed totalitarian rule on Hungary
1953	Death of Stalin. Rakosi replaced by Imre Nagy
1956	Khrushchev's speech denounces crimes of Stalin. Imre Nagy's New Course eases some restrictions. Hungarian revolution. 4 November invasion by Soviet army
1958	Imre Nagy executed. Kadar regime imposed; some liberal policies gradually implemented
1966–1967	**Author visits Hungary**
1960-1980	Kadar's limited political liberalisation
1989	Berlin Wall comes down 9 November
1998	Viktor Orbán's Fidesz Party wins election
2004	Hungary joins European Union
2014–2022	Cold War confrontations erupting between Russia, Ukraine and NATO

Yugoslavia, Golubac.
Castle on the Danube

Yugoslavia,
Donji Milanovac.
Village market

Hungary, Hortobágy.
Long-horned cattle at
the collective farm well

Yugoslavia, Novi Sad. Country women shopping

Hungary, Hortobágy. Pig herders

Hungary, Hortobágy.
Collective farm goose woman

Hungary, Hortobágy.
Collective farm women hoeing peppers

Romania, Deta.
Piglet for sale at the market

Romania, Făgăraş mountains.
The shepherds spend all summer in the hills

Romania, Făgăraş mountains.
Laundry for the mountain hostel

Romania, Sâmbăta de Jos. Laundry by the village stream

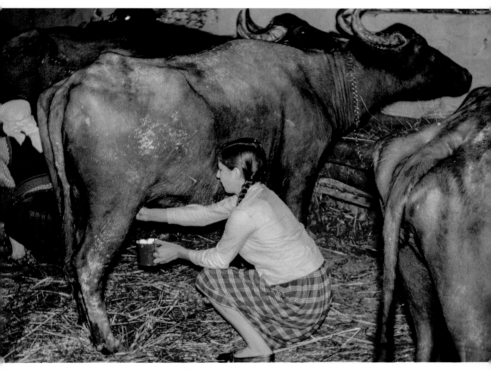

Romania, Sâmbăta de Jos. Milking the buffalo cows

Bulgaria, Varna.
Celebration of Bulgaria's liberation by Soviet army, 9 September 1944

Bulgaria, Varna. Men dancing to bagpipe music

Bulgaria, Elhovo.
President Tudor Zhivkov overlooks the gateway to the collective pig farm

Bulgaria, Elhovo. The five-year plan for the collective pig farm

*Bulgaria, Elhovo.
Women collective
farm workers
harvesting peppers
and tomatoes*

*Bulgaria, Elhovo.
Village women
spinning fleece*

*Bulgaria, Elhovo.
Gypsy girls washing
clothes at the village
fountain*

6

Students in the World of Tito

Belgrade, January 1967

"Why don't you sit with us?" a young man suggests to me. I am in a cafeteria in the southern Hungarian city of Szeged, on my way to Yugoslavia. The border is only a few kilometres away, and my plan is to hitchhike to the capital city of Belgrade the same day. My friend Dushko is expecting me and will be organising somewhere for me to stay.

We sit over some tea in this little Hungarian café and chat. They both speak English reasonably fluently. Michi is Hungarian and Silvester is Serbian. We are all heading south across the border into Yugoslavia which we expect to cross with ease.

The conversation turns to music. I discover that they like Elvis Presley! How absurd! That kind of music has been scorned by my own friends and acquaintances for years. I was obsessed with Elvis when I was sixteen, but that is six years ago. The world has moved on, and now it is the era of The Beatles and The Rolling Stones. I can't believe that here, in Hungary, in the 1960s world of Communism, anyone can still admire American rock 'n' roll.

The three of us travel by bus the sixteen kilometres to the border. This is an internal frontier between two Communist countries, Hungary and Yugoslavia. I have learned that citizens of the Eastern European lands dominated by the Soviet Union can travel, seemingly easily enough, between one and another. My visa is in order, and the Hungarian guards let me pass through without more than a cursory look. Michi has his passport, but Silvester discovers, to his consternation, that his is lost. Somehow, he has left it in Szeged. Quickly, we make plans. Michi and I will go on to Subotica, their home town just a little further into Yugoslavia, while Silvy returns to seek his passport. He scribbles his address on a scrap of paper.

"Go to my house, Bridget. My parents will welcome you, and you can wait for me there." I agree. Michi will come with me and explain the situation to his parents. There is no pressure on me to go immediately to Belgrade.

In Subotica

I end up staying with Silvy's family for a few days. It is one of those houses which I've seen in the village-towns of the plains in Hungary. It is a long, low, four-roomed building, facing the street, with walls enclosing a substantial yard and garden. Poultry peck about in the yard, and there are outbuildings, workshops, a balance beam well and fruit trees, leafless at this time of year.

Silvy's mother is a good-looking, straight-featured woman, head-scarved and aproned as she goes about her tasks. Over the next few days, I learn that his father was in Tito's partisan army, so he definitely is of Communist sympathies. They are the same generation as my parents, but I reflect on what a different experience of the war they have had. His father will have known cruelty, death and hunger, whereas my father, a conscientious objector, waited at home for the slaughter to end. Silvy translates our conversations. His brother Petro lives there too in his own private room at one end of the house. He is reserved, occupying himself with his books, already a married and divorced man in his mid-twenties. Both brothers had higher education, although Silvy did not complete his degree. He is presently earning some money by framing pictures and selling them at local markets.

The town of Subotica was formerly known by its Hungarian name of Szabadka. Silvy and his parents tell me stories of how the Hungarians massacred Serbian people when they invaded the city during the war. These old wounds are not easily forgotten. To me, the town looks like those I have seen in Hungary, like Gyula, Békéscsaba and Mezőberény. There are impressive churches, a synagogue and civic buildings. It is the side streets I like most. They are similar to those in Mezőberény with their parallel lines of trees and ditches, in the grid pattern of the Hungarian plains. The roads are often not hard surfaced which gives them a country feeling. There is a farmyard smell of pigs and horses. Cockerels are crowing and hens clucking. Every house has a dog tied to its kennel. Horsemen sit on their high perches as they drive the carts along the soft, muddy roads with their loads of logs or straw. Behind the high walls are families like Silvy's with their animals and gardens, workshops and kitchens.

BAJMOK MARKET

There are crowds of country people, women in skirts and headscarves, men wearing the local high sheepskin hats, handsome as well as warm, and lots of animals. The colourful scene is dotted with the bright red cardigans of the women, many of whom are guiding their free-walking pigs with sticks. The pigs must be used to this and don't try to run away. A white, fluffy goat on a straw-filled cart is bargained over by a group of men, who think it is hilariously funny that I should want to take their photograph. Calves, goats, sheep and the sellers and buyers create a colourful picture on this winter day. The weather is sunny, and the first hint of spring is in the air. Country life here is obviously thriving, and these villagers are practising private enterprise in this Communist land.

I leave Silvy selling his cheap reproductions of religious pictures and wander off. No one pays much attention to me. A group of gypsy men is squatting on the ground, clustered around some game of chance. They are healthy looking, with glossy, black hair, and they don't wear the sheepskin hats of the other men in the market.

I then come across the strangest phenomenon. Sticking out from the ground inconspicuously are lots of upstanding narrow stones. They are regularly spaced, some no more than a foot or so high, others up to about three feet. Curiously, a few are topped with what looks like an oriental turban. A tired-looking pony is tied next to them, and a few piglets are rummaging around. There is no explanation to be seen, and obviously they have no value. They are just there, some old, abandoned stones. What can they be? I conclude that I am looking at the remnant of an old Ottoman village cemetery, a relic of former days when this land had been ruled by Turks and now is in Serbia, one of the republics of Yugoslavia. These sad little gravestones are left abandoned, lying along the edge of Bajmok's village market.

To the capital

Dushko, the young man I'd met in Wrocław, is expecting me at some unspecified date around now. The road between Subotica and Belgrade is open to me. And so, on the 10th of January, in the cold, clear air of the winter morning, I walk out of town, towards a new and unknown city, Belgrade, the capital of Serbia and Yugoslavia.

I find my way to his address in Kod Bajic Street. Dushko is just the kind of companion I appreciate, humorous and kindly and competent.

"Bridget, *tu es venu!*" he says, smiling and surprised. You have come! Yes, I really have. He brings me my post, and then off we go to the hostel of the political high school, at Jove Ilića 165. He has a little influence as he is a Communist Party member. And thus, I am safely installed, for the fee of £3 a month. I have a bed in a room for three, *soba 26*, room 26.

Nazan Arapi and Hurema Berisha are my roommates. They are Albanians from Prizren in Kosovo. I have never met any Albanians. We get to know each other using their half dozen words of English, but mostly by signs and smiles. Nazan points to herself and says, "*Torok.*" Turk. They describe themselves as *Shiptar*, too, which I learn is the Serbian word for Albanians.

YOUNG PEOPLE AND HOW I SPEND MY TIME

I have a little red camping cooker which is easily filled at any petrol station for a few pence. On this, my new friends show me how to make Serbian coffee, very strong and very sweet. I put the ground coffee in a little metal jug with a handle and top it up with water. Once on the cooker, it soon comes to the boil, and then I turn it down, add some sugar, stir and let the grounds settle down. We drink it with *locum*, pink or white jelly sweets which in the UK we would call Turkish delight. But here, it really is Turkish, denser and chewier and coated with icing sugar.

The students here are from all the six corners of Yugoslavia.

"Ibrahim, your coffee, sir," I say one day to a new friend whose room is not far from ours. He is pleased to receive his morning stimulant. Together we smoke his strong cigarettes and drink the heavily sweetened brew. Healthy considerations don't exist.

Ibrahim likes to say that he is one-eighth Turkish. I tell my mother about him in one of my letters:

His grandfather was one of the Ottoman Turks. He has inherited the Muslim religion, yet he is seven-eighths Slav. He doesn't speak Turkish, even though he has cousins living in Istanbul. He is completely European in thought, word and deed.

He comes from Bijelo Polje, a small town in Montenegro, and shows me a postcard of a little town among the hills, with a fine, slim minaret of a mosque among the houses. I am fascinated by his exotic background. He is tall, clever and lively, with curly, fair hair and engaging eyes. He is studying French literature, which seems an extraordinary world away from his home town.

Dushko is Serbian, and both of us have a little French. His name is the diminutive form of Dušan, a famous Serbian medieval king. When I met him in Poland, he and the young people there could understand each other's first languages to some extent. Ibrahim has learned some English. Nazan and Hurema from Kosovo speak Albanian and Serbian. Among other friends, Ildico is a Hungarian Yugoslav. She and Gordana, who is Serbian, are studying languages and are fluent in English. Another young man is from the north of the country near the Italian border and looks and behaves like an Italian. The multinational, multilingual country of Tito's Yugoslavia is well represented. If there is a common language, it is Serbian, but they all like to try their English.

YUGOSLAVIA

Yugoslavia at this time comprises six separate republics: Slovenia, Croatia, Bosnia-Herzegovina, Serbia, Montenegro and Macedonia. Belgrade in Serbia is the capital city of Yugoslavia. There are two autonomous provinces within Serbia, Vojvodina and Kosovo. Subotica, Silvy's family town, is the second largest in Vojvodina and stretches to the Hungarian border. Prizren, Nazan and Hurema's town is in Kosovo, in the south of Serbia.

From what I can gather most of my new friends are committed to socialism. Young people from less privileged backgrounds are given priority education in the new Yugoslavia. Every one of them will have parents and families who saw, and perhaps took part in, inter-ethnic horrors during the Second World War. Now they are studying together in what seems to me an atmosphere of tolerance and enthusiasm.

One night, it is Hurema's birthday, and a group of young people, girls and boys, crowd into our room to celebrate. The room is just about big enough for three beds, with a few cupboards, a desk and a couple of chairs. The smoking, drinking and conversation go on well into the early hours. One student from Belgium is studying in Moscow, here on a visit, and is a committed Communist. I tell my father about him in one of my letters.

> *He is super-intelligent and super-fanatical, the type that I dread to think of in power because of his simple aim to make Communism a world faith. And he was so clever. A student only. Today I talked to Dushko, my friend here. He is a Yugoslavian Communist, far more moderate and normal but nevertheless convinced that the future of Yugoslavia is dependent on Communism. Yugoslavia is the best country in Europe to experience the contrast of Communist/capitalist life. It is so moderate, experimental, not tied to strict dogma as is Russia and satellite countries. All the people I listen to here assert proudly that there is no one poor in Yugoslavia if they are willing to work. Although far from perfect, this is a very inspiring little country. It's a shame that so many visitors neglect it en route to Greece.*

During conversations with the students, I usually understand only a little of what is said. Still, I gather that they are committed to playing their part in building a new society. At one time, they tell me about the earthquake at Skopje in 1963 and how the young people had voluntarily gone to help clear up the rubble and serve as best they could. They want me to have a good impression of their country.

I still have with me my copy of Yevtuskenko's A *Precocious Autobiography*. Born in 1933, this Russian poet is not too far in age and experience from the students I am meeting, and I find them in touch with the sort of sentiments he expresses. He writes that a Communist is not merely someone who belongs to the Party and pays his dues, but a person who puts the common good above his or her own interests. He says that he is ashamed that Stalin distrusted the people who believed in Communism and destroyed so many of them.

In Belgrade, I feel no personal sense of oppression, and the students express themselves freely, and increasingly loudly, as the nights go on. Yugoslavia is a much more relaxed country than Hungary or Poland. President Tito is not far away from where we are chatting. One of his several residences is in a suburb of Belgrade. Milovan Djilas, one of the founders of Yugoslavia with Tito, but who later fell out with the regime, has just been released from prison and is now living in the city.

Living now as I am, among students from all backgrounds, I report my views in a letter to my friends in England:

This country is a hotbed of cultural differences for historical reasons. It's also a prime example of how to get rid of them. Their method is socialism and equality. In this direction, if no other, Yugoslavian socialism has made a great step forward. I'm not idealising. People don't forget ancient differences quickly. But it's an interesting and humane experiment, and vive la Tito for his efforts. He is idealised by his people, and it's easy to see why. He's a charismatic leader. What happens when he goes out of action will be something interesting.

In the daytime, I take the noisy, rattling trams from the hostel into the centre of Belgrade. I have learned to locate the Serbian equivalent of the *bar mleczny* where food is cheap and tasty. This is where I buy freshly baked *burek*. Huge trays of flaky pastry filled with cheese are cut into squares. It is hot, inviting, not good for the figure but a tasty early morning breakfast food.

In the letter to my friends in England, I describe a visit to a café with Dushko and the delicious food:

> *Here there are the most fabulous Turkish cafés. Coffee is thick, sweet, black and strong – delicious once you get a taste for it. The cakes, sweet, dripping with syrup, golden and soft, filled with nuts, raisins, honey, fruit. And you can have real Turkish delight, honeycomb-cinder toffee. These are one of the best remains of the Ottoman empire.*

Belgrade itself was largely destroyed during the Second World War and mostly is filled with big, block-like buildings including our student hostel. But I am not in a mood to miss historic old places. I find my way to the British Council because I hope they will be able to advise me about finding work here – I need to build up my finances. They have a library of books in English, and so I go there regularly. The library has 'yearbooks' giving statistics about economics and details about politics of the different countries I am visiting. Thus, I learn indirectly about collectivisation, how the small plots of land given to the peasants after their lands were taken away from them have resulted in around fifty per cent of food in these nations being produced from five per cent of the land. Yugoslavia and Poland are different, the collectivisation plans there having collapsed, and small farms still exist.

Importantly, I find a book called *The Eastern Marchlands of Europe*, by Harriet Wanklyn. A Cambridge geographer, she researched and wrote the book during the 1930s and published it in 1941. As the war was still ongoing, she was not to know how it would end. Hitler's war could have triumphed in the long term. As I plan to head for Czechoslovakia, I see maps in her book which show the mysterious region of Ruthenia on its eastern fringe which is not on my modern maps. I'll see if I can go that way.

I also take out books to read in English for pleasure. I note in my diary that I am reading *Kenilworth* by Sir Walter Scott, Somerset Maughan's *The Casuarina Tree*, plays by Tennessee Williams, *The Canterbury Tales* and Doris Lessing's *Martha Quest*.

At the library, I have a peaceful corner in which to read, write and think. I have British newspapers at hand, and from them I pick up information about current affairs. My diary records what I make of some of the news of 1967:

At last it seems as though a real movement in the right direction is happening. Soviet Communism has failed to keep down nationalist tendencies in the Eastern European states, and now it seems that they're spreading their fingers outwards. Romania is establishing diplomatic relations with Bonn, and it's believed that Hungary and Bulgaria are inclined that way. Ulbricht's regime in East Germany is threatened if the satellite countries become too friendly with the West. Only Poland and Czechoslovakia have a fear of the territorial claims of a powerful West Germany. Russia is too busy with Chinese problems to concentrate too heavily on the satellites. Mr Kosygin is visiting Harold Wilson and presumably wants to establish good relations.

The English economy is looking a little steadier, but the Conservatives are accusing Wilson of almost socialist dictatorship. There are whispers of some kind of end or let-up in Vietnam. It almost seems like peace is on its way to the world, except China! Refugees are still flooding into Russia – into Russia!

I know I am very lucky to have cheap accommodation in the room I share with Nazan and Hurema. My two roommates are hospitable and kindly. I do sometimes find the small spaces and lack of privacy wearisome. Often at nights, other students congregate in our room, and the talking goes on for hours. I am impatient and want to go to sleep. Without being rude, it is hard to end the sessions. Thus, it is a great blessing having a library to retreat to, where I can read, consolidate my thoughts, prepare for my English classes and write my articles for *The Journal* back home in Newcastle.

THE LANGUAGE AND THE CULTURE

I have bought myself *Teach Yourself Serbo-Croat*, a large book with an orange cover, written for English speakers like me. From this I learn that Serbian and Croatian are virtually the same language, but Serbian is written in the Cyrillic script like Russian, while Croatian is in our familiar Latin script. I'd come across Cyrillic writing in the Old Slavonic church at Wrocław in Poland, but here it is everywhere. This fascinates me: the shop signs, the newspapers, books and street names, all at first indecipherable. I learn that Serbians are mainly Orthodox Christians, whereas Croatians are Roman Catholic, and that this is a hot topic of dispute and ancient enmity. I decide to make a start with this language. First, I learn how to read and write the capital letters, and then, slowly, I graduate to lower case and joined letters. Some of the basic vocabulary reminds me of Polish.

Dushko is my guide to Belgrade. He takes me to visit the fortress of Kalemegdan, the great structure which commanded this corner of Europe during the time of the Austrian and Turkish empires and which the Russians and Partisans took over in 1944. We look down from its walls to the Sava river. Great lumps of ice are rushing along in the brown water. The Sava meets the Danube here, and the waters race eastwards along the boundary between

Romania and Bulgaria before reaching the Black Sea. I am close to the outermost edge of Europe.

On St Sava's day, the 27th of January, there are celebrations in the Orthodox church. I must see this. I go with Dushko, and there is a lot of standing and singing, with children reciting verses or prayers. Some holy bread is to be shared around at the end, but we don't stay for this. We go back again in the evening, but the musical part has finished. Dushko teases me. "I am trying to convert you to Communism, Bridget, but all we seem to do is to go to church!"

As for the Muslim influence, I see none of it in my daily routines, despite Nazan, Hurema and Ibrahim being from areas of Ottoman heritage.

One day, I go with Ildico to the ethnographical museum where there is an exhibition of attractive folk costumes from Slovenia, the north-eastern republic of Yugoslavia. Folk traditions are pushed hard in Yugoslavia, and I am very attracted by the Balkan music which is pumped out in every cafeteria and public building. The students I know feel it is thrust upon them and object. Most of them much prefer modern Western popular music which, although not forbidden, is less easily available. Another time, I am enraptured by a performance of *The Merry Widow* to which I go with Ibrahim. My diary:

> *What a glorious entertaining spectacle. I love that heavenly music, romantic or not. How I imagine myself whirling again to that da-da-dee la da-da-dee la da dee as I did in Hungary. What an array of costumes, what ecstasies of music, the Hungarian folk song tradition being very prominent.*
>
> *On the way home, I was in a mood to reach for the stars high in the black night sky. We danced in the streets and skated on the ice and sung. We found a little restaurant where we heard the true music of this land from a small gypsy band with a woman singer. Ibrahim drank beer, and*

I ate oranges. We wore each other's coats coming home. He looked crazy in mine which hardly reached his waist, and his was down to my ankles.

I realise how wildly lucky I am to be here in Yugoslavia, in Europe, to be experiencing all these wonderful people and friendships, sounds and sights and songs.

What a life of joys, mental challenge and satisfaction, of utter freedom like the wind, no responsibilities. Jenny said to me in one of her letters: 'Bridget, you don't realise what a struggle it's been to become responsible'. I don't envy her. I feel more like seventeen than twenty-two. My desires to settle have sunk gloriously into the background. I'm probably staying away from England now for more than a year.

However much I write like this in a good day, there are other times when I feel differently. My friends Ildico and Gordana and I spend hours talking about the men we know and what we expect from them, or will give to them. Like my friends in England, we are torn between wanting to be educated professionals and mothers and homemakers.

EARNING SOME MONEY

I knock on the door of a flat belonging to an old lady whose name I'd been given by the British Council librarian who knew that I needed to earn some money.

"Come in, my dear," calls Mrs Popovitch. The door is opened by Branka, her friend. Mrs Popovitch is Irish. She has married a Serbian man, is now in her eighties and bedridden but lively as a bird. We drink English tea prepared by Branka who is planning a visit to Maidenhead in England. My diary:

Mrs Popovitch planned that I was to give English lessons to Branka Zivcovic, who indeed had no opportunity to refuse.

163

She was coaxed into employing me. I am to give two lessons
a week at one thousand dinars per hour, which is about six
shillings.

Branka and I meet regularly after that. My diary notes that on
the 30th of January, 'I gave my first English lesson. It wasn't very
terrifying. The lady only wanted to talk. I felt a robber, pocketing a
thousand dinars afterwards'.

Her sister joins us sometimes. On the 7th of February:

They are so pleasant, these two sisters. I enjoy my hours with
them very much and we often go long over our time. Zaga is
going to Sweden, so we are going to talk about geography there.
Branka is going to England, so we're going to do maps, geology,
land use, art, architecture, history. I'm full of enthusiasm. It is
something I can get my teeth into.

Branka has strong Serbian nationalist feelings. She tells me about the
Battle of Kosovo Polje in 1389 where the Serbs were outnumbered
and defeated by the Ottoman army and how, to this day, they feel
threatened by the Kosovan Albanians, the Muslims in the south
of the country. This surprises me as my roommates, Nazan and
Hurema, seem to mix well enough with the other students. Branka
is also a piano teacher, and as part of my English lesson, she gives me
some tuition. I am very keen, and we do scales and simple pieces.
Her strong conviction is that I must learn to relax my fingers when
I play, which I find very difficult. Later, I chat and discuss a play by
Tennessee Williams with Zaga, and we do some work on verbs.

I advertise in the local paper and gain two more people who
want English conversation. Marianne is studying English literature
and Dragan Dragic is a geologist. The library of the British Council
has plenty of material from which to plan my lessons. Four sessions
a week at one thousand dinars is more than enough to pay for my

room in the student hostel. Having English as a first language is a great help in supporting myself.

The significant post – Belgrade

Back in England, my college friends are struggling with the challenges of teaching and the conflicts of love affairs. They are bound to earn their living, as indeed I am, but the pull of the open road has not left them. I receive letters which reflect my own dilemmas. From Jenny:

> *Teaching is quite fun now I've got used to it, but at first it was a terrific responsibility. Every time I saw a lorry roaring down the road towards Cardiff, Hereford, Ludlow, Lancaster etc, my blood would start roaring and pulsating with the engines, and I wanted to stick up my thumb and be away enjoying myself, watching other people carry on the jobs of life, and the brief glimpses of so many different kinds of lives, and be part of theirs for that fleeting moment as houses, faces, hills, mountains flick past. But instead, I had to go to work. Bridget, you can't imagine the struggle it has been to become responsible.*

A further letter from Jenny describes that her parents are threatening to throw her out. She had been to Ireland over the Christmas period where she'd met her boyfriend:

> *I went home exhausted from the first trip and in an emotional chasm of nothingness. I slept all the days and went around feeling as if I'd reached old age before my time. My parents, who really do care about my welfare, were really worried and think the boys are dragging me down.*

She writes how she had been so much in love, but he 'won't face his feelings and tries to be the big man'. There are several more pages of this. It is the dilemma of young women in the 1960s. We are encouraged by society to get out, become educated and work in the professions. At the same time, it is still considered immoral to have mature adult relationships outside of marriage. We all seem to be pulled in conflicting directions.

Jean is a friend who has a teaching job in a seemingly idyllic rural English village. But there is no peace here either. Her letter:

> *I was talking with my ardent, religiously keen landlady. The latest is: "Miss Batterbury, is it true that you are an atheist?" Two people interviewed me at my cottage last night and told me I was lucky that I hadn't been asked to go and see the two vicars in the village. "The church is here to help you, you know." I'm fed up with being discussed. And I don't need any help, let alone from the church.*

My friend Mary goes back and forth to Ireland to see her Damien. The open road, the hitchhiking, this is what we all do, and it can lead to superb friendships or singing sessions in pubs but, occasionally, something less pleasant. While on her way to Holyhead for the ferry to Dublin, Mary finds her way out of such a predicament:

> *Last lift from Bangor was with a policeman. "Won't you spend half an hour with me?" over and over again. He drove straight past the entrance to the dock and along the sea road. Well, I thought to myself, this just will not do. So I said: "Well I wouldn't mind so much if there was fish and chips in it!" Eager to please, he turned, thankfully, back to the town and, eventually, with me yanking the steering wheel, back to the boat, where I was able to get out.*

Mary plans to give in her notice at Easter so that she can finish at the end of the school year. Tonie has left her job in Birmingham and moved to a hotel in north Wales. She expects to marry her Welsh lorry driver boyfriend soon. We are an unsettled group of should-be teachers.

Another college friend, Sarah, wrote to me as she had passed through Belgrade on her way to Greece. She had left college with great dramatics owing to her unplanned pregnancy, and terminations were still illegal in Britain:

I was back home when I got your letter, but perhaps it was as well that I didn't get it in time to meet you in Belgrade for I couldn't have been very cheerful company. The actual operation was pretty straightforward, but the mental results were shattering. I was plunged into desperate depression for two or three days. Have since been told that this is the general thing, something to do with balance of hormones. But at the time it took me completely unawares, and I was a helluva wreck and could hardly stop crying.

I am to this day filled with horror and sorrow for what this young woman went through, travelling to Greece and returning afterwards, all alone.

Other correspondents are fluent on political matters. These young men are all writing in English, a second or even a third language.

Sergi from Sabadell in Spain has been a regular penfriend now for almost a year. This is the time of Franco's dictatorship and its travel restrictions. Sergi, however, is attracted by socialism and would like to visit Yugoslavia. He writes long pages describing the fascist dictatorship, and then:

It seems the most probable that after Franco, some prince grandson of the last Spanish king will come to rule our Spain, but if it's so, he won't last longer than a year. Of course, I don't recommend you to be in Spain by then.

Although he wants to visit, he understands the difficulties.

Of course I can't go to Poland, Hungary or Yugoslavia because in the Spanish passport this is written, in big letters, ALL THE COUNTRIES OF THE WORLD EXCEPT RUSSIA AND SATELLITE COUNTRIES.

Yugoslavia seems to be a socialist and yet a little democratic country. For the present I'm getting more and more committed with the cause of the revolution. The anti-Franco opposition is getting very strong, and the arrests are very common. Just the last week about twenty men were arrested in Sabadell.

Is it very difficult to get a job in Yugoslavia? And for a short time? What do you speak there? German? Do many people speak English or French? I would like very much going to Yugoslavia over the summer. How much are the lowest wages in Yugoslavia? The £3 a month you pay in the hostel – are they for food, for bed, or both?

Theo, who had spent a few days with me in Poland, also writes regularly. He explains how difficult it is, with different languages, to be clear what each other means.

When I was speaking with a few East German boys, they told me that they had in their country real democratie (Demokratische Deutsche Republik), though we two do associate the word democratie with something else. So, I can tell you that I am a socialistic-minded person, but what do you understand with that, the socialism of the USSR, of the USA, of China, of India, of Yugoslavia, of the DDR, of the Labour Party etc.

Though there are people in Polen and Yugoslavia who do not agree with their life, I think there are less there than in Holland, for most of these people have an ideal to live for (i.e. being as rich and comfortable as in W European countries).

Theo is writing about what I am finding, which is that many of my young student friends are committed to building socialism in their country.

Tom from Poland also writes faithfully. He sends me some Kashubian songs and music. I have asked him about his feelings for Germans:

You think I'm dislike all people in Germany. No, it is not a truth. I like not this men only, in West Germany, who will not peace in all world. This are nazist, militarist and fascist, who go in Hitler's way. Therefore, impregnate anxiety in fact, that in West Germany Kurt Kiesinger, a chancellor of government, that West Germany National Socialist Party has seats with the elections in government, too. This signify not peace; this signify confusion in world politics.

My family keep in close touch with me. My sister Helen is preparing for the birth of her baby, as big an adventure for her as anything I am doing:

I have my time full here, cleaning, baking cakes, knitting bootees, taking pills and reading. I'm calm and peaceful and content with my lot. I think of you rushing all over the continent in your duffle coat and wellies and just accept that we're differently constructed.

My brother Richard relates 'I had cards from three girls from three different European countries: Yvonne Koski from Poland, Nicole Grenier from Paris and Yvonne Somebody from Stockholm. Quite a Casanova'.

My mother is thinking about going to Israel this summer. I still plan ultimately to go there myself, and she informs me that our hosts, the Keller family in the kibbutz, would like to know if I am coming. She is in her third year of teacher training:

> *Teaching practice is looming ahead. It is from the middle of February till middle of March. Secondary school this time. Don't know how I shall get on – perhaps better. I've applied to be in a girls-only school.*

And later:

> *Have started teaching practice. No serious troubles with discipline. But am taking huge boys of fifteen to sixteen tomorrow. We are working on a theme of youth hostels.*

My darling grandmother, who had been born and grown up in Chile, writes in her neat handwriting:

> *It will be wonderful to see you again. Time passes so quickly so it won't be long before you return. I like the photo printed on your articles. I hope you manage to get a varied and sufficient vegetarian diet. I expect fruit and vegetables vary in the different countries, and the languages must be a problem, though I feel you are gifted with a facility to cope with it.*

And to keep me on my toes, she finishes her letter in Spanish:

*Le envió cariñosos saludos mi querida nieta, y, hasta la vista,
se despide, su abuela.*

*I am sending you loving greetings, my dear granddaughter,
and see you soon, goodbye, your grandmother.*

My father has sent me my article about Hungary, which was
published in *The Journal*, and deposited the £6.6.0 in my post
office account. My sister Rosie too sends a series of affectionate
letters, about her anticipated Easter job in the Lake District and the
complexities of her love life.

All these letters have had long and complex journeys. First
the sender had to find an envelope and paper and sit down to
concentrate and write, often in a language which is not their
own. Then the stamp had to be purchased, the correct amount of
payment for a different country, which often means lining up in a
post office. Once dispatched, the letter is sorted and put in a bag
which heads for the train station. Letters from Britain then must
be transferred onto a boat, so the words are now travelling over
the sea. They must then be sorted and put on more trains. Once
at the requisite city, they are then organised again for the regional
town or village and from there put into the correct postman or
postwoman's bag for delivery. He or she then walks the streets,
putting those meaningful words into the correct letter box. It is an
amazing international cooperative effort. My letters from England
complete this process in four days. If the sender wants it to take
less time, then airmail is the newest and most expensive method.
However, in 1967, most trans-European letters are transported by
land and sea.

Thanks to the postal services, I am still included in my network.
This world at home could be mine, right now, but I am engrossed
in something different.

Let's go to the Danube gorge

"Come on, Dushko, let's go to the Danube gorge," I say merrily
to him, early one Sunday morning. "It's only a hundred kilometres.
We can go there and back in a day."

He's always ready to oblige and good humouredly agrees. We
head for the road towards Smederovo out of Belgrade. My diary:

*We passed through one remote place after another, crossed
mountains, walked along muddy roads. We saw village
markets and a peasant wedding. We walked twenty-five
kilometres or so and were very tired, a little lost and laughing.*

In one of the wide-open earthen landscapes, country people pass
us walking to market. Some are in carts, but peasant women with
swinging skirts and long competent strides are making their way,
carrying baskets containing hens or eggs. How I admire them.

Finally, we realise we'll never get to the Danube gorge, so we
reluctantly decide we'd better head back to Belgrade. My diary:

*Eventually, we found a railway station, by itself without a
village, and a train came along. We took it as far as a real
road. From there we got a lift to a village in a horse-drawn
cart. Here, everyone came and gazed at us. They were dancing
in the street. We never thought we'd get back to Belgrade, but
at last a lorry came and took us there. It was a relief to get
home. We both shouted with joy when we got out in Slavija.*

What appeals to me so much about this land is its openness,
bareness, spaciousness. During the course of this visit, we have
seen little villages far from roads, on hilly bumps, isolated with
just a track towards them. I am compelled to think about who
lives there, what do they do, how do they live, how do the women
marry and bring up their children? They seem so far away from my
normal European life.

Not having given up hope of getting to the Danube gorge, another time I persuade Nazan, my roommate, to come with me. This time, we will take a whole weekend over it. Once again, we follow the remote routes, sometimes walking, sometimes getting a lift in a lorry or a cart. By now it is the 20th of March, and the weather is kinder.

At one of the open landscapes, we see some long, low thatched buildings with walls made of tied bunches of maize stalks. A great horned brown ox with a white face is nibbling straw beside a cart which is loaded with red bricks. Two villagers are loading an ox-cart with bricks. With Nazan translating for me, I learn that this is a family brickmaking business, a private enterprise which is allowed in Tito's Yugoslavia. The two men and two women are surprised by my interest.

We get as far as the village of Golubac beside the Danube. Here the river is as wide as a lake, and we can see Romania on the other side, with Russian barges chugging upriver. There is a rock in the middle of the expanse of water, and I learn that it is known as *Babagaia*, a Turkish word meaning 'old woman'. The story goes that in the times of Turks, a man put one of his querulous wives on the rock to starve.

Startlingly, at the edge of the village rise the walls of a gigantic castle with square and round towers, built into the rocks at the water's edge. The villagers' houses lean right up against the base of this structure, in its shadow. There are no tourist signs. The castle is just there, not interesting to anyone. We climb up a bank to take a photograph. From there, we can see across to Romania and down on the rooftops.

GOLUBAC CASTLE

During the Middle Ages, the castle at Golubac became the object of many battles, especially between the Ottoman Empire and the Kingdom of Hungary. It changed hands

repeatedly, passing between Turks, Bulgarians, Hungarians, Serbs and Austrians. Since the time of Nazan's and my visit, it has been renovated and become a tourist attraction.
See *Wikipedia* for a full detailed history.

Nazan and I know that a great dam is being planned for the Danube, between Yugoslavia and Romania. We are not sure what we'll see. The rooftops below us, however, are probably going to disappear under water. As we make our way further east, along the barely surfaced road beyond Golubac, we arrive at a place called Donji Milanovac. We pass a school playground where little girls wearing red sweaters are playing with a ball. The sweaters are the same red tone of those of the market women in Bajmok. *This must be a standard Yugoslavian red dye*, I think. Deciding we have come far enough, we will see if we can stay here for the night. Nazan and some village women sort out accommodation at a simple, hostel-like inn where we can spend the night.

The women explain to Nazan that the village is doomed. The construction of the dam means that it will soon be drowned just like Golubac.

As the daylight fades, people begin to gather in the village centre. A man with an accordion begins to play, and people start tapping their feet. Soon a circle forms, and the dancing begins. Nazan and I are invited into the circle, first one dance, and then another. The sun lowers behind the village. The last minutes of daylight create a golden glow on the long, low houses with their red-tiled roofs and on the crumbling concrete of the village centre buildings. The simple church too is suffused with gold. As we dance, the people sing the familiar eloquent Balkan melodies. For me, it is a lament for what is there and what soon will exist no longer.

Next morning, which is a Saturday, there is a market in the village centre. The villagers are curious about us, especially about me, a person who doesn't understand their language. Dark-haired men, scarved women and curious children make a space in the group so that I can take a photograph. The geese in their baskets are for sale. The people are lively, attentive, concentrating, teasing each other, wondering at this unusual interest in their everyday activities. I am thinking about them, in this remote edge of Europe, in a village which will soon be under water. Where will they be rehoused? Who knows about them? Who cares about them? The labouring families – who built the houses from locally produced bricks and tiles, who live here, bringing up their children and sending them to school – all must be moved from Donji Milanovac.

Nowadays if we look on a modern map, we can see the town rebuilt higher up on the hill. Their original village has gone. Some of the children in my photograph may still be old people living in a replacement dwelling. Perhaps an odd girl or boy will remember the young, fair-haired English woman and her Albanian friend who danced with them. Fifty years later, this is my tribute to them.

Are we funny?

I write my third article for *The Journal*.

What's so funny about the English?

I was walking home through the streets on the outskirts of Belgrade. The winter sun was gleaming weakly through the leafless trees, and I was in the world of my own thoughts.

Suddenly, a sprightly young man of about thirteen years of age appeared beside me. He began to speak excitedly in Serbo-Croat, and I had no idea what he wanted.

On seeing my lack of understanding, he gave a low chuckle and said in a clear voice: "Do you speak English?"

I was rather surprised and said: "Yes I do. Do you?" He

chuckled again, murmured something unintelligible and scampered away.

I laughed to myself. Even such a youngster was able to tell somehow that this stranger had a particular strangeness that was English.

What exactly is so funny about the English? We figure in several Yugoslavian phrases. For example, when somebody makes a remark in all innocence which is immediately reinterpreted by a companion, this companion is told: "Don't be like an Englishman."

The normal reaction of a Yugoslav when someone says something he doesn't like is to answer back colourfully. If, however, he pretends he doesn't hear, or somehow tries to avoid the situation, he will again be accused of 'behaving like an Englishman'.

When someone in trouble goes into moods of silence and awkwardness, this is also referred to as 'English behaviour'.

The Yugoslavs regard us as an eccentric race, difficult to get to know, involved in a complicated phantasmagoria of social *mann*ers, very conservative, shy and polite, alternatively amusing and irritable, unpredictable, nevertheless largely likeable.

One lady from Belgrade visited England last summer and stayed with a family in Berkshire. "I was amazed," she told me. "They actually did say: 'Do you like your tea strong or weak, Mrs Vulicevic, and please help yourself to sugar.' It was just as I'd always read in books. And they really did talk about the weather. In fact, once we'd talked about the weather and the garden, it seemed difficult to find anything to say."

One experiences a revelation of one's own countrymen, meeting them in foreign parts. Here in Belgrade, when the snow was a foot deep and icy winds and frosts generally inhospitable, I helped two boys from London to find the British Consulate. One was sneezing, shivering and miserable with flu. All he wanted were the comforts of home, hot baths and some good, strong tea.

This is natural enough when one is ill and alone in a foreign land. He blamed the weather, not himself, for his misery. Yet he was clad in only a thin nylon shirt, a lightweight suit, thin socks and shoes.

Who but the English would think to traverse the severe Continental winters without at least a decent overcoat, warm underwear and a pair of boots?

The payment I expect for the article will really help my stringent budget. At £6.6.0 each time, that is equivalent to twenty-one hours of teaching English in Belgrade, at one thousand dinars, or six shillings, per hour.

Yugoslavian 'policeman' jokes

The Yugoslavian police are a target of jokes. I report a few in a letter to my friends in England:

> *Q. Why do policemen go round in pairs?*
> *A. Because one can read and the other can write.*

And:

> *Some policemen had been attending a course on criminology.*
> *Then, soon afterwards, two of them found a dead man lying*
> *in front of a post office. "Don't touch him," said one. "You*
> *mustn't touch dead bodies. Get out your notebook and write*
> *the details to report it to the police station."*

"I can't spell 'post office'," said the other as he began to write.

"Oh dear," said the first. "Let's move him in front of the bank and write the report from there."

And another

A man was travelling by train. He went to the WC to wash his hands. He saw a toothbrush there, so began to clean his teeth. A man arrived. "Excuse me, but you're using my toothbrush."

"Oh, I'm so sorry! I thought it was the latest idea of Yugoslav socialism!"

Springtime

The spring weather gives me the urge to move, and I feel the need to smarten up my appearance. I buy a pair of shoes for £2. At the market I buy two metres of tartan fabric and draw a pattern for a sleeveless tunic. I cut out the cloth and hand-stitch it together. It works out quite satisfactorily. On the 17th of March, I write to my mother:

I've decided to spend a little time and money on my appearance which is greatly neglected due to lack of resources. I'm making a red tartan dress, have bought some green-grey suede shoes and am buying a red blouse today. Just think, it is nine months almost since I left England. I seem quite apart from the old life now and don't miss it at all, except for conversation and familiar food. But I expect I'll be back in a year or so.

I tell my mother that I'm leaving Belgrade soon, travelling first back through Mezőberény on my proposed route to Czechoslovakia. She should reply to me at the home of the Gulyás family. My plan is to make a circuitous route north through Hungary and Czechoslovakia and then return to Belgrade on my way to Israel in the summer.

I obtain visas for my passport for Hungary and Czechoslovakia at the local consulates in Belgrade and organise my bags.

Gordana tells me: "Bridget, you can make some money in Czechoslovakia by selling cocoa, chocolate powder. They don't have nice chocolate over there. People want to buy the Yugoslavian kind."

They do? I decide to risk it, following up on my experience of cross-border smuggling with Isobel into Bratislava. I buy a kilo and wrap it up in small portions.

Financially, my twelve weeks in Belgrade has been neutral as I have been able to pay for my expenses out of my English conversation classes. I have accumulated two ring files of diaries from Hungary and now Yugoslavia. I pack the files neatly into a box and arrange to leave them at the student hostel for the time being. It is impossible to carry them with me. Then I buy a lightweight exercise book to continue my travel stories. The first entry is the 25th of March 1967:

Today I left Belgrade. I'd been there almost three months, through the bitter cold winter weather until the gradual arriving of spring. I'd had a fine time there, living with the students, keeping alive by the money I earned giving English lessons. But it was spring, and there's so much of the world to see, the sunshine, the warm spring winds, the breaking buds and new birdsong makes one long to move and explore. And in my fortunate life I can go when I want to, not having any responsibilities. So, all I had to do was pack up my few things, pay for my stay in the hostel and go...

I was piled with stuff. I had a heavy rucksack and two bags. I'd planned a route, to take about five weeks, and today I am visiting Silvy and his family in Subotica.

What a fine contrasting mixture of lands I'd be visiting,

plains and mountains, cold weather and warm sunshine, three different language families: Hungarian, German and Slavic. This flat, flat land which is now divided by three nations – Romania, Hungary and Yugoslavia – but which is in every essence Hungarian. The wide, endless plain, dotted by houses, lined by a few roads and bare acacia trees, full of sky, air and wind.

First I head for Novi Sad, the main city of Vojvodina, eighty kilometres away to the north. It is a quaint city of domed churches and has a bridge across the Danube. From here, I can take a photo of the spectacular Petrovaradin Fortress started in the eighteenth century with the purpose of holding back the Turks. Barges make their way along the river, leading from Vienna to the Black Sea, through and across the Iron Curtain. In the town centre, I meet some smiling women wearing country dress, blue, patterned full skirts and aprons over their ample hips, bright shawls and headscarves. One of them is wearing little heeled boots, another some short, rubber, waterproof bootees and the third some felt slippers. Footwear is always a big expense. They have come into town to do some shopping and smile happily when I ask if I may take their photograph.

Beyond Novi Sad, the road becomes more rural. I pass through Vrbas, Feketić and Bačka Topola. This part of the journey is one hundred kilometres long. I walk a little, sing a little. My diary:

How I love the concept of plain, huge open spaces and enormous expanses of glorious sky, wind ever fresh and invigorating, skyscape most lovely and changeable hour by hour, low villages clinging to the soil as toadstools grow, tree-lined roads stretching from village to village. There's so much air, so much freedom and so much privacy.

I got to Silvy's house at 5pm. The tiny house, in its garden surrounded by a high wall. The lettuce has grown large and

green. Mary the cat had two kittens. I was given a huge meal
of three eggs, paprika and special sweet bread for Easter.

It is now Easter time:

How fine it was this Easter Sunday morning, with the sun
streaming through the windows, cockerels crowing out in
the garden. There seemed to be light flowing down from
the sky to us in this house, and it seemed that everything in
our world was turned upwards and meeting the light from
the sky. The sheer power and communication between the
things of the world and the pouring sunlight, the straining
cockerel who proudly boasts his strength, the slender cat
in her private world with her little kittens, this feeling
of rebirth of spring, the miracle of life straining to go on
forever.

Easter Sunday dinner at Subotica in March 1967 is important. The
family has saved the best piece of ham from the Christmas pig. It is
served proudly on a white bedecked table with new-laid eggs and
home-made bread and butter. The hens have begun to lay again in
the spring light. Eggs, after the dark, non-laying days of winter, are
a delight. The meal is simple but strong, the true food of the season.

After dinner, Silvy, Petro his brother and I go out with some
friends, one of whom has an open-topped sports car. My diary:

We went racing over the plain, wind zipping past, singing
and ecstatic. We visited a friend in Bajmok and then went to
another along a muddy track where there was an old farmer
with a hat and a big moustache who opened the gate as if we
were royalty, and we rolled elegantly into his farmyard. This
farm has a white house, two cows and pigs and is heated by
an enormous clay stove which burns maize straw.

181

By evening, as the stars begin to twinkle, our group drives to Lake Palić:

It was beautiful indeed, no deeper than three or four metres over the whole area, the remains of an old lake which once had covered the Pannonian Plain, now used as a tourist resort, and reflecting the moon and stars and houselights by night in the water.

I learn, just as I am about to leave Yugoslavia, more about another ethnic group here in Subotica:

These people are descended from Herzegovinian settlers of the sixteenth century, one of the many immigrants to the Danube Plain in the conflicting and troublesome periods of Magyar, Turkish and Austro-Hungarian power. They still speak a Western Serbo-Croat dialect. The name of these people is Bunjevac, and the blood ties are still very strong. They are not so much mixed with the Hungarians, Montenegrins, Macedonians and Serbians who all live together in this part of Yugoslavia and who all uphold their own tradition. For example, we went to a name-day party of one of the relations; all the music and dancing was Bunjevac, in other words probably several hundred years old and stemming from a completely different part of Yugoslavia.

Skills of the economical housewife

In her kitchen, Silvy's mother is mixing something in a big bowl. I watch carefully. She drops several eggs into a pile of white flour and, using her hands, she kneads the ingredients together until she has a big, yellowish ball of dough. This she cuts into three sections. Two of the portions will be meat-free, partly for my benefit.

Using a long, wooden rolling pin, she rolls out one portion until it is paper thin. Then she cuts the dough into long, thin strips and then into shorter pieces. She drops the strips into a pan of boiling water, and when they are cooked, she drains them and adds freshly beaten eggs. It becomes a delicious panful of noodles with scrambled eggs. I never knew until this moment that country women make pasta in this way. For me, noodles, in the same way as macaroni and spaghetti, are something we buy hard and dry in a packet, then boil until soft.

Next, she rolls out another of the portions. This is to be cooked with a mixture made from crushed black poppy seeds mixed into a paste with sugar.

The third portion is mixed with chopped ham from their own home-produced meat.

This food is so simple and delicious. I have never tasted anything better.

I am impressed by her in other ways. When she breaks the eggs into a bowl, she uses her finger to squeeze out every speck of the white. At home, when we break eggs in the normal fashion, we let the inside drop into a bowl, and then dispose of the shell. There is always a little egg-white left in the shell, but we pay no attention to that. Silvy's mother, however, has known hunger. She wouldn't let one drop of egg white be wasted. She rotates her finger inside the shell, scraping out every speck.

Then, after washing the dishes in warm water, she throws the water out onto the earthen yard outside. The hens know the routine, and when they see the bowl coming, they rush over and get every single scrap of edible food from the washing-up water. Not a soggy crumb, not a fatty scrap, is wasted. And because washing-up liquid is not yet in use, the water is unpolluted. My diary records my ponderings. How would I like to be a Serbian woman with a little house in a village-town, animals I could take to market, living close to the land? My diary:

I like the life of the country people in Vojvodina. Their work is the business of living, preparing food, seeing to the garden, building and incessantly repairing and improvising round the house. They are largely their own masters with regard to time. Pleasure is in rest, enjoyment in each other's company, or nowadays an hour in the evening by the television. I wonder if a self-sufficient life could satisfy me, doing nothing but working for the basic needs of life. Maybe I'd get to like it. I have much admiration for these people, but I'm a spoilt, independent Western girl and not much like them.

On Thursday the 30th of March, I am on my way:

Silvy came with me to Horgoš, a little town near the Hungarian border. I turned and waved for a last time as I walked to the barriers with my load of stuff. The sun was shining, and I was impatient to get inside the real Hungarian frontier. I spoke my last few words of Serbo-Croat to the frontier guard.

Perhaps I'll never need to speak Serbo-Croat again. I am leaving Subotica, Belgrade, Serbia, Yugoslavia and all the friends I've made. There are pangs, a real kind of pain. I walk on into Hungary, along the road to new adventures. And there are heavy packs of chocolate powder in my bag.

YUGOSLAVIA CHRONOLOGY

1389	Battle of Kosovo. Spread of Ottoman empire
1918	Creation of united Yugoslavia
1939	Josip Broz Tito elected to lead the Communist Party
1941	Hitler's army bombs Belgrade and invades Yugoslavia
1944	Partisan troops and Red Army units enter Belgrade.
1945	Tito's Communist Party controls Yugoslavia
1948	Yugoslavia breaks with Stalin
1953	Death of Stalin
1956	Khrushchev's speech denounces crimes of Stalin
1963	Earthquake in Skopje
1960s	Yugoslavia the most liberal of the Communist states
1967	**Author's visit to Yugoslavia**
1970s	Tito leads the non-aligned states
1980	Death of Tito
1988–1989	Rise of Slobodan Milošević
1989–1990	Collapse of Eastern European Communist regimes after Berlin Wall comes down
1991–2001	Yugoslav wars
2004	Slovenia joins European Union
2006	Slobodan Milošević dies in prison at The Hague
2013	Croatia joins European Union
2021	Serbia, North Macedonia and Montenegro have EU candidate status. Bosnia-Herzegovina has applied
2014–2022	Cold War confrontations erupting between Russia, Ukraine and NATO

7

Between One Land and Another

ALFÖLD, MARCH 1967

OFFICIALDOM

"You must come with me," says the assertive Hungarian police officer in Békéscsaba. "You are not allowed to hitchhike in Hungary!"

At least, that is what I assume he means, from his gestures and arrogance.

Marika and I are leaving her office together. I'd gone there straight away after crossing the border into Hungary, which I'd got through without having my bags inspected. Hence my precious packets of chocolate powder are undiscovered. My first lift had taken me to Szeged, the regional capital, where I found the post office and sent a telegram to Mutti and Imre Bácsi to warn them of my arrival. Next, a Russian Land Rover-type vehicle stopped and took me as far as Békéscsaba. The driver told me his name, Bubla Pal, which made me think of horsemen galloping over the steppes. My diary:

He was really like some wild, grinning tribesman. He thought me hitchhiking with my flag was so amazing that he proudly showed me off to his friend in Békéscsaba. Pity his friend was a policeman and chose to make trouble.

This is the policeman who insists that Marika and I go with him to the police station. Clearly, I am a suspicious character who must be investigated. My diary:

Poor Marika went through a rigmarole for almost an hour, in which she was asked every imaginable question about her family, my family and Henry. Then they demanded my Union Jack. I argued. So then he threatened to keep my passport and said that he could get me sent out of Hungary in twenty-four hours. I had no choice but to hand over my flag that has helped me on many a journey through Europe, and now it has ended up in this humiliating situation.

When we arrive back at Marika's house in Mezőberény, Mutti welcomes me with her warm embrace. After hearing our tale, she says, "Oh, that's the smallest thing that's happened to us!"

A few days later, she and I are sitting by a pile of scraps of cloth in red, white and blue colours which she has managed to find. She cuts them out carefully, laying them all onto a plain cloth to make a patchwork Union Jack. I tack the pieces into the correct places under her direction, and then she gets out her sewing machine and stitches the whole thing together. I am really impressed with my new flag. I treasure it highly but resolve not to use it until I leave Hungary.

The family and I feel the tensions that this episode with the police has caused. We all are unsure about what we can safely do. This is also because of an unfortunate happening.

A TACTLESS MISTAKE

A few days before I'd arrived in Mezőberény, the post had delivered a letter to Mutti from my mother in England. She'd sent them a copy of the article I'd had published in *The Journal*, which the editor had headlined: 'The cold can't freeze warm hearts'. My mother had thought they would be pleased, but in fact, it had caused them a lot of worry. In this Communist country, every word is liable to censorship. People who have been reported making negative comments could be tracked down, penalised, fined, imprisoned, or harassed in many other ways.

I'd quoted the medical student, receiving free state education, who said: "I'd give ten years of my life in Hungary for one month in Las Vegas." I'd written about Mutti's German origin and her uncles who'd been sent to Russian camps after the war. And the old lady, Gittanéni, who had lost everything but her education and was living now in a few tiny rooms in Mezőberény. If any of the powers-that-be felt like it, all of these people could easily have been traced.

I have made the family who are so kind to me feel uneasy, and I reflect in my diary:

> *I was made to realise the trouble my carelessness can cause in this country. I don't always succeed in behaving differently from the way I would at home.*

As nothing further seems to happen, after a day or two, we begin to relax. My diary:

> *Friday the 31st of March. Mutti and I went to the market. I love it there, so many colourful peasants in their furs and sheepskins, the interesting variety of vegetables and spices for sale. Mutti bought me a red headscarf I'd been wanting for ages. It was nylon and so expensive I didn't want her to buy*

*it, but she insisted. This family's idea of hospitality is to pay
for everything for the guests. They pay my train fares, my
post, my paper, everything.*

The significant post – Mezőberény again

A letter from my sister Helen arrives on the 1st of April:

*We have a sweet little son; his name's Henry Michael, born
on the 15th of March at 4.40am. He is a great big baby, well
above average – 8lbs 12oz at birth. He is a very good-looking
little chap, tho' I say so myself, browny hair, huge blue eyes
and gorgeous, smooth, soft skin. Please don't say he'll be a
year old before you see him. He's out in his pram for the first
time today; the sun's shining; the sky's blue, lots of daffodils
around – everything's lovely.*

I am standing with Marika on the pavement outside their house in
Mezőberény when I open the letter. I let out a shriek, to Marika's
great surprise, because I am reading that the baby is to be named
Henry! Everyone in our family called her brother Imre by his
anglicised name of Henry. And now, my new nephew has the same
name. I am absolutely thrilled.

My father, brother and sister have all managed to post their
letters to reach me as I pass through Mezőberény. My sixteen-year-
old brother Richard has his version of the new baby's arrival:

*About half-eleven last Tuesday night, Mike came round and
said Helen had gone into hospital. After sitting biting our
toenails for about an hour, we went to bed again, and Mike
went home. Next morning, we phoned and found a boy 8lbs
12oz had arrived. Was to be Henry, then changed to Edward,
then back to Henry – better I think!*

Now I am an aunty! My home-making sister is thrilled and happy. My diary:

> *I never imagined I'd be so pleased to actually hear Helen is a mother. Why, I'm just longing to see the little lad. I'm thinking about arranging a quick trip home from Prague, if only my finances could stand the strain.*

My father writes too and tells me he has bought a caravan. More significantly:

> *I have also bought a minivan and am trying to sell the Cortina, tho' the second-hand market is in a glut state at the moment. I have had it resprayed and it looks like new.*

My brother is disgusted:

> *I suppose Papa has told you he has bought a stupid minivan. I HATE THE THING. Come, Richard, we mustn't be snobs. All the same, a minivan!*

I sit down immediately to reply and when my letters are ready, I decide to post them at the station. I get lost while I'm looking for it amid the grid-planned streets which all look so alike. As Marika says, Mezőberény's such a big town.

THE GYPSY CHILDREN

I'd been spellbound by the gypsy musicians I'd heard when I'd been in Hungary over the Christmas period, and I knew that as masters of the beautiful and famous Hungarian gypsy music, some of them are quite rich. But this is not always the case. My diary:

I met some gypsy children in Mezőberény today. They fascinate me, grubby, curly haired children, lovely young girls with babies, good-looking but bawdy young men. The women laugh and scream and live in grubby houses where the earth is the floor and goodness knows how many children sleep in one bed. Even being poor, it must be fun to be born and bred a gypsy, easily roused to anger or laughter. They live in cottages on the edge of towns and villages everywhere in Hungary. They don't move any more. Imre Bácsi said they used to move more when he was younger.

About ten of the girls came with me to the station where I was to meet Marika and Sanyi on their return from work. The girls were very friendly to me because of course I encouraged them. But I was surprised by their reaction when a man shouted at them. They silenced immediately, ready to run, as a dog who is often beaten crouches ready to flee before a blow from his master. And just as the dog is sprightly the instant the danger is over, so were these little girls. They sang and chattered again.

When Marika and Sanyi came off the train, the children sensed a different intolerant attitude to them and melted away without a second thought or word to me. I thought at first their feelings must be hurt, and I wanted to say goodbye to them, until I realised that I was thinking of them as though they were English people. They never thought any more of the whole situation, I'm sure, and certainly didn't criticise me for my manners.

One day, as it is beginning to clear up after the rain, I go out into the countryside to take some photos.

Some boys are fishing beside a pond with white, single-storey houses ranged behind in rows and the balance beam well completing the Hungarian landscape scene. My diary:

> *I was befriended by a fur-hatted young man of eleven years who tried to talk to me in Magyar. But even though he escorted me all the way back home, and never stopped talking, my knowledge of this language isn't much increased.*

When I get home I make a list, and the total I can manage is thirty-three words of Hungarian.

The 4th of April celebrations and taking leave

"Today is the day we are celebrating twenty-two years of 'Wonderful Freedom'," says Marika to me. I look enquiring. "It is the celebration of the day the Russians came to 'liberate' Hungary in 1945," she says.

The one good thing about this day is that it is a public holiday.

When I go out into the town, I note: 'Apart from the flags hanging outside the public buildings, nobody seems to be doing much celebrating'. There certainly is none in the Gulyás family house. I have been here now for nearly a week. Although the family's hospitality is as unfailing as ever, I know that I am a little bit of a worry for them. Also, they must fit me in with their daily working lives, Marika and Sanyi in their offices in Békéscsaba and Mutti at Mezőberény's telephone exchange. I know that I must leave.

On the family's firm instructions, I am to go by bus. I plan to have one more night along the way and then cross into Slovakia the next day. My route will take me over the Hungarian plain, the *Alföld*, to Debrecen. I will cross the area around Hortobágy known as the *puszta*, famed for its horsemen and pastoral culture. My diary:

I wanted to see the Hungarian puszta herdsmen en route. Well, I was thrilled to see them, but from the bus window only, on the way to Debrecen. They were herding long-haired, curly horned sheep. I hoped to see more later, but I never did. From Debrecen I took a bus to a small town on the route as the express bus wasn't for several hours. I began to walk, hoping to meet herders on the flat lands. At last, a farmer gave me a ride in his cart for eleven kilometres or so, and that was lovely. I was riding, jolting, along in the open air behind two shiny horses, being able to see right over the plain. Eventually it began to rain. After I left the farmer, it got even worse. I was soon drenched. But I was in real Hungarian puszta, seeing it at its wildest and most romantic.

At last, a car stops and takes me to Miskolc, the last large town before Slovakia where I buy my train ticket to Košice. It is obvious that if I really want to see herders and horsemen on the *puszta*, I'll need to come back another time.

8

Chocolate, Tea and Electrifying the Iron Curtain

Czechoslovakia, April 1967

Bridget tries her hand at smuggling

"*Čokoladu?*" I try my Serbian knowledge of this international word with two women attendants in a little shop in Košice. They look at me with interest, so I show them a small packet of cocoa powder which I had purchased in Belgrade and have smuggled into Slovakia, the eastern part of Czechoslovakia. They take it off to the back of the shop and look at it behind a curtain. Coming out smiling, they ask how much, and I tell them. "150 *krone* per pack." That is quite a lot of money for them, but they want it and happily pay up. Chocolate is a prized rarity in 1967 Slovakia.

I don't look like a seasoned smuggler, or feel like one. I am nervous, but I persevere. I find a few small shops in the main shopping street of Košice and, dashing from one to another in the pouring rain, I manage to sell six packs. I decide that is enough and keep a few for spares.

When I had been on the train, crossing the Hungarian/ Czechoslovakian border, the frontier guards asked me lots of questions. Where are you going? Why are you going? They tried in Czechoslovakian and Hungarian, and whatever I mumbled in reply caused them in the end to stamp my passport with a grumble. They didn't trouble themselves to look in my bags. My visa was in order, so they let me be. My little gamble with fortune has succeeded to this point.

My problem is with the weather. The rain pours down relentlessly. With my new earnings, and despite it being an expense I rarely allow myself, I find a hotel in the wide main street. This is going to cost me all of three hundred krone, two packets of cocoa, or about two British shillings, for the night. I will have a warm, comfortable room, and there is no reasonable alternative if the rain won't stop pouring.

I go shopping, which is something I seldom do. I buy an umbrella, an essential road map of Czechoslovakia and a novel in English. In a local pharmacy, I invest in some DDT, considered a great boon in 1967, to deal with anticipated insect friends. My smuggling adventure has paid for all these purchases.

Churches made of little pieces of wood

Never in my life have I seen such a little miracle as now appears before my eyes in the pouring rain of Košice. Next door to the museum, right in the centre of the town, is a small church made of tiny pieces of wood. It is the size of perhaps an English chapel but otherwise completely different. It is in three sections joined together, with layers of sloping roofs and arrangements of domes on the top. Every part of it is made from small pieces of wood, joined and overlapping. The three-dimensional geometrical structures are perfectly lovely. I am entranced, and although the great Gothic cathedral in the centre of town is much grander, I have seen plenty of those on my travels. A wooden church like this is a complete surprise.

In the museum, they tell me this church has been moved here from a village called Kožuchovce and that there are others like it in this remote corner of Slovakia. I know then what I'll do. My diary:

Suddenly I decided – bother this rain. I can't waste time. It's better to go out and get wet than to hang around a place, and my visa isn't going to last forever. I packed up from the hotel. Leaning against the cold wind and belting rain, I made my way north. I had to walk a lot. It amused me to think of myself, a lone English girl in this wild country, charging along in the rain with rucksack and umbrella. It got funnier as the countryside grew more mountainous, very beautiful rolling hills but no sign of the rain abating. Eventually, I began to walk along a muddy track to a village called Hervartov, literally in the middle of nowhere. I got a ride on a tractor and arrived in the centre of this mountain village.

> *There in the dripping trees was a dark wooden church, on a little hillock by the stream. All around me were sloping-roofed houses, many of wood with thatched roofs or wooden tiled roofs. There were many little barns, like miniature houses, and huge, raftered barns with mossy thatched roofs. Many of the barns were painted bright blue, which I'd seen before in Poland.*

The tractor driver calls over a man he knows, who beckons me and wants to show me the church. Dripping wet as I am, tired and cold, and unsure where I'll be spending the night, I follow him. I must prioritise looking at this church. Who knows if I'll get another opportunity. My diary:

> *The inside of the church was incredibly lovely. However could such a gem be found in such a wild place! It was, is, a Catholic church, and my guide and a couple of other people there genuflected respectfully as I'd been taught in my youth. The walls were covered in medieval paintings, excellently preserved, and worth so many million krone per picture as my guide constantly assured me. There was a wealth of intricate wood carvings and a little figure of 'sorrowing Jesus' as I'd seen in Bavaria. It was tiny, with only room for about fifty people.*

Children begin to peep inside the door of the church, and some of the older ones come in and smile at me. I tell them I am English. That does the trick. A few minutes later, a bandy-legged old man wearing breeches and an ancient cowboy hat appears in the church.

"You from the States?" he asks, with a distinct American twang. When I say I am English, he says: "I was in the States for twenny years before the war. But I come home to my kids. Where you stayin' tonight? You stay in my house. C'mon."

He leads me to his self-constructed cottage and shows me his bull and his pigs. I am taken into the house to meet his family. My diary:

There were ducklings in the kitchen. The house was so clean, and his daughter-in-law was busy working. She wore a simple peasant costume, a white lace cap, a pleated skirt with a hoop arrangement underneath that swished around as she worked.

My host's name is Jan Marsalek. He proudly acts as interpreter to his family and friends that evening who all come round to visit. I get stares of amazement when I light up a cigarette. "We know girls smoke in the towns," he says. "I seen 'em smoking in the States. Girls don't smoke here."

As we make conversation, I tell them my name is Bridget. The pronouncing of my name normally results in someone saying Brigitte Bardot. In Hervartov, no one, young or old, has heard of the French film star. Western radio, films or TV barely exist. My diary:

There was home-made bread and fresh eggs for my supper. They ate potatoes with jam, and I had some too. The house was warm, well lit, and the food was good. My bed had a feather down cover, and we all slept in the one room, grandfather, daughter-in-law, son and me.

I've stayed in farmhouses in Poland and in Mezőberény in a traditional Hungarian family home. I've spent weeks in student hostels and the last two nights in, what for me are, luxury hotels. But I've never stayed anywhere like this. There is no bother about bathrooms or washing. The outhouse is in the yard, as with all these country houses. There's no need to dig out clean sheets, to scrub the corners of the guest room and all the palaver that accompanies having visitors in a modern home. My bed is prepared on a long wooden seat, with rugs underneath me and a feather duvet on top. My steaming damp clothes are drying with the heat of the wood-burning stove. I'll smell deliciously of wood-smoke tomorrow. There I lie in the heart of the family home, snores and smells together. I am cosier and happier than I could ever be in the most splendid hotel.

HERVARTOV'S COLLECTIVE FARM

Bread is baking in the huge oven in our combined living room/bedroom as I emerge from slumbers. Jan's daughter-in-law and I greet each other in Serbian/Slovakian pidgin, and she presents me with delicious apple bread.

Wearing a borrowed pair of her boots, I head out into the rain and try to take a photo of the church with a long, slow exposure. Then Jan Marsalek takes me to the collective farm. In a large shed, a group of men are sawing the wooden tiles from which they make the roofs of their houses. And in this long shed is a row of cows, all being milked by hand. In another shed, young male cattle are tied up. They look flighty and troublesome.

My companion is able to explain. "They are bulls. We keep them whole, not like your bullocks. It saves the expense of castration, and then we can see which are the best ones for reproduction."

I am surprised. A bull farm!

He takes me outside, and across a small narrow valley, dividing Hervartov from the next commune, we can see the ploughed strips of private small farmers. "*Feudalizmus!*" he explains. I'm not sure if he approves or disapproves. The rain just keeps on and on, but I decide to move along and hand him one of my saved packets of cocoa. He arranges for me to ride on a tractor to the town of Bardejov. I bid goodbye to Hervartov, that unforgettable village.

Bardejov in the rain

It is very unlikely that British people would see pigs or chickens running around inside the walls of our carefully tended historic towns like York. But here, in this extraordinary little Slovakian town, this is just what I find. The sun is peeping out from the clouds. The walls around the medieval town of Bardejov are overgrown, with tumbling plants hanging and little houses built into the shelter of ruined towers. Why waste a good wall if it can be used as part of your house? And if there are scraps of food for pigs and chickens to pick up, it is an added advantage.

I am dropped off in a large, cobbled square with a tiny town hall in the middle, a lovely church with four pinnacles on its tower at one end and rows of little houses on every side. This is a fairytale village just sitting there waiting to be appreciated. The town museum provides me with a brochure for visitors printed in black and white on cheap paper, in Slovakian, Hungarian and German. Later, I cut out the pictures and stick them in my diary. The leaflet is about post-war economy and politics, as well as history. Bardejov is pictured with winter snows on its rooftops, the church tower and walled remains dominating the sloping roofs of the houses. There are no cars in the square outside the church and not a sign or advertisement to be seen anywhere. This is frugal Communism, but modern too. Large factories nearby with big, square buildings and neat chimneys appear proudly in the leaflet. I'd seen some of them along my route.

Bardejov was taken by Soviet troops of the 1st Guards Army on the 20th of January 1945, and the leaflet shows two great tanks mounted in a war memorial near where they passed over the frontier into Poland. But that is not my route. I follow tiny roads further into the wilds. In little towns like Zborov, Vyšný Mirošov and Krajná Poľana, I spot mysterious shop names in what I realise is the Cyrillic alphabet, and I buy a newspaper written in that language.

I walk past a huge Hungarian castle on a hill. In Zborov, there is a large, fortified church, in ruins, presently used as storage for electrical equipment, causing me to think that there is no sympathy for religion in what is now a Communist state. At last, I spot another church of wood, peeping between the trees, in a little village with no signpost to tell me its name.

NEARLY IN RUTHENIA

This little corner of Czechoslovakia is in the extreme east of the country, bordering the former region of Ruthenia.

Who has heard of Ruthenia? Harriet Wanklyn's book, The Eastern Marchlands of Europe, which I had read in Belgrade, shows pre-Second World War maps of Czechoslovakia. In that map, the Slovakian end extends like the tail of a lizard much further east than now. The end of the tail is Ruthenia. Ruthenia and Slovakia had been part of Hungary prior to the First World War, but after the Treaty of Trianon in 1920, when Hungary's boundaries were severely cut back, Ruthenia became absorbed into the new state of Czechoslovakia. In 1939, after Hitler had invaded Czechoslovakia, Hungary took hold of Ruthenia once again. At the end of the Second World War, the Soviet Union grasped Ruthenia as war booty, and it became incorporated into Ukraine. This eastern corner of Slovakia, which I'm now visiting, still has Ruthenian inhabitants who speak Ukrainian. This explains the shop signs and the newspapers in Ukrainian Cyrillic lettering.

When this area was part of Hungary, the Slovakians lived mainly in the mountainous fringes of the empire, while the Hungarians dominated the fertile valleys and lowlands. In summer, the Slovakians would seek work on Hungarian farms. The socialist government was seeking to reduce this underemployment by policies such as rural collectivisation and the building of factories in these outlying areas.

BODRUŽAL NUMBER TWENTY-THREE

"*Bonjour, madam. Où allez-vous?*" a man calls out to me from number twenty-three as I walk along the village street.

Am I imagining things? Is someone talking French, here in this remote corner of Eastern Slovakia? He is a cheerful oldish man wearing trousers which are more patch than cloth.

"*Vous parlez français?*" I respond, putting down my heavy bags. He is quick to realise that I am not French.

"Sure do, missis. I lived in Canada. Long time ago. Where you from? Why you here?"

I tell him I like the wooden churches. His name, he tells me, is Peter Ilke. "You come stay in my house."

His chubby, head-scarved wife is called Maria, and she invites me into her kitchen. "You want some tea?" asks Peter. I am damp and so tired I am almost unable to converse in any language other than my own. All I want to do is sink down in a comfy bed. A cup of tea? Hot, strong, brown – now that would really revitalise me.

Maria pulls out a pot of red jam from her cupboard and puts a spoonful in a cup. "Raspberries," explains Peter, as I look bemused. She pours some hot water from a saucepan into the cup. So, this is tea! It is hot and sweet, and it does revive me.

I use this little story in the article I write for *The Journal* about my visit to these remote areas, and the editor headlines it: 'A nice cup of tea was just raspberry juice'.

Peter and Maria tell me that they are very poor, both suffering from bronchitis and living from a small pension. They have two cows and two hectares of land. As well as Slovakian, English and French, Peter speaks German. Our conversation ranges across all these languages. A quadrilingual pensioner – I am impressed.

A bit later on, we have a visitor. The word has got round that there is a foreigner in number twenty-three.

After the usual courtesies and a few squirmy smiles, this man, wearing a gingery cap and dowdy old clothes, asks, via Peter, "Why are you in Bodružal?" I tell him I like wooden churches. "Who knows you are here? Did you go to the police station in Krajná Poľana?"

I gradually realise that I am being interrogated by the local Communist Party official. Of course I didn't go to the police station. Even though I vaguely know that I am supposed to do this in Czechoslovakia, as in Poland or Hungary too, I never did. I am successfully tiptoeing my way around, and the only time anyone made a fuss was once in Békéscsaba. However, Mr Ginger Cap mutters about this and that, and as I can't understand him, I act dumbly and submissively, leaving the conversation to take place between him and Peter. At last, he goes home, and Peter and Maria present me with a cosy bed.

The rain continues to make life difficult. Next morning, after a breakfast of eggs and home-made bread, with raspberry jam tea, the cloud cover lifts. I head for the church, St Nicholas of Bodružal, which I love as much as the other two I have seen. Like the one at Hervartov, it is made entirely from small pieces of wood. The roofs and sloping sides are created with small overlapping shingles, the horizontal sides being made from longer narrow planks. The small round domes are topped with even smaller umbrella-like shapes. The eight layers of satisfyingly shaped structures of the main church and the six of its belltower make an attractive wedding-cake-like wooden building. The tiny cross on the peak seems to overshadow an Islamic moon. I think it may signify the defeat of the Turks by Christendom. The whole church is surrounded by a wooden wall protected with a little roof of shingles. I manage to take a photograph despite the rainy, gloomy weather. Unfortunately, Mr Ginger Cap follows me around which is very irritating. Obviously, he needs to check in case I am a capitalist spy reporting on Slovakian secrets.

I return to the house for my bags. Peter and Maria won't take any money when I leave, but I am very happy that I still have a pack of cocoa to give them. Neither I nor they know at this moment that the farewell photo I take of them will appear in a British newspaper. My diary:

> *I left the village in the sunshine and was full of rejoicing as I walked on along into the Beskidy hills bordering Ukraine.*

When I passed through a village, everyone stared at me. Children followed me. Old women appeared in every window. "Have you anything to sell?" one of them asked. I felt like a travelling pedlar.

I decide that I'll take a photo of myself. Dushko has lent me a camera, one of those that folds out like a concertina, and it has a delayed-action shutter. I set it up on a stone, run a few yards away, turn back and walk into my picture. It is a long time until I have the film developed and see it. But when I do, I smile at myself walking up the slope, dressed in a denim skirt and light jumper, with my shoulder-length hair tied back. My blanket is attached to my rucksack; I am carrying a little grey bag with my daily food inside and have a sturdy stick in my right hand. In the landscape behind me, poles are carrying wires, presumably for telephone connections. The trees are yet without their spring leaves, and the road stretches off into the distance without a vehicle in sight. I really do look rather like a travelling pedlar.

At midday, I decide to write to my family:

Hello, everyone. At this moment, I'm sitting by a stream in one of the loneliest valleys in Europe, in the Beskidy hills, part of the Carpathian Mountains, close to Ukraine and the Soviet Union. The Polish frontier is about ten miles north, and the Soviet one a little further east. It's been raining for five days solid, except for about two hours yesterday and a bit of beautiful sunshine this morning. Birds are singing and not a house is in sight. The people, when you see them, live in tiny villages quite far apart. There were big battles here in the Second World War, and it's easy to imagine the feelings of soldiers as they marched and drove in lorries and tanks along this end-of-the-world place.

I tell them about the little wooden churches with their domes and spires, exquisite medieval paintings and wood carvings. I write that my rucksack is very heavy, filled mostly with winter clothing, but I don't mind. 'I'm as strong as a horse', I write. My letter:

The wind is blowing up and rain is on the horizon. It's great because I have very little money, so I never know where I'm going to stay at nights. I vary from luxury hotels to four-in-a-room peasant homes. Just where I am or where I'm staying tonight is a mystery at the moment.

Although Ukraine, a republic of the Soviet Union, is nearby, this is not a place which I am able to visit. For someone like me, wanting to travel independently and unrestrictedly, obtaining a visa is completely out of the question. The Eastern European countries where I'm wandering make visiting difficult although not impossible, and somehow, I have been dodging the regulations. As I am thinking in this way, what should come along, in this frontier zone, but a jeep carrying a group of smartly uniformed soldiers.

"Hey, young lady," calls out the driver. They are all smiling at me, good-looking young men, and acting unlike any border guards of my previous experience. We chat for a few minutes, some of them knowing a little English. They are relaxed, so I expect they don't really care if I am a capitalist spy, and they obligingly arrange themselves in a group in a scrubby field so that I can take a photograph. Somehow, I don't think the local Communist Party bosses would approve.

Their presence, though, reminds me of the political sensitivity of this region. I am in the Slovakian part of Czechoslovakia, remote from the west of Europe, close to the great Soviet Union. Moscow is always on the lookout for enemies, for spies and refugees. I need to be careful. The great tanks and armies of the USSR are not so far away.

Apart from this jeep, I walk for four hours, and not a vehicle passes. I arrive at a junction. Two young girls are there, and one of them gives me the address of her aunt in the town of Stropkov, which is where I am heading. A scooter stops for me, and I balance on the back with my bags, the kind young driver dropping me off at the aunt's house. I include the story of what happens next in my article for *The Journal*:

A tiny, perky woman opened the door. "May I stay the night here?" I asked. Knowing only that I was a foreigner, she drew me in and smothered me with kisses.

"Of course, of course," she said gaily and pointed to a bed by the stove where I could sleep. She gave me pancakes and chatted to me non-stop, though I couldn't understand what she was saying.

A few minutes later I was taken out by her husband and herself in their car, and we drove into the forested hills. I had no idea what was happening to me.

We stopped in the middle of the forest. The woman signalled to me to help her collect sticks for the fire. I'd heard a lot of strange stories about these people and hoped I wasn't going to be sacrificed or anything drastic.

The man brought a huge gun from the car and disappeared silently into the trees. A few moments later, two more cars and a motorbike arrived. And before long, I realised I was in the midst of a highly organised gang of poachers.

We women built up a roaring blaze while the men went hunting for pheasants. When they returned, we prepared the supper of roasted fat and onions on sticks which we ate around the fire.

The still of the evening was broken only by the crackle of the fire, the sound of our voices and the hooting of the owls in the forest around.

Back home in Stropkov, my bed by the stove in the kitchen is warm and cosy, and in the morning, when I try to pay, my hostess says: "Pooh! It's nothing." I'm glad I still have a packet of cocoa to give her.

INTO THE LAND OF THE ORE MOUNTAINS

I am now heading westwards into the Slovakian Ore Mountains. My diary:

I had a lift in an ancient rattling lorry in which my bones got thoroughly loosened. The mountains were high and sometimes forested. We had to climb and descend into narrow valleys with little towns, Bzenov, Klenov, Margecany, quite busy but very isolated except for a railway line. What a lot of factories, quarries and dust there was. My driver plunged through streams, up and down banks and through mud baths with amazing confidence. He's been born and bred in this place. At Gelnica, I was so surprised by the charming little town that I decided to stay the night. Could only get a room in the expensive hotel but managed it for seventeen krone, half the price of the one in Košice.

I am seeing for myself people from these different cultures: German, Slovakian and Hungarian. My diary:

The Slovakian Ore Mountains, Erzgebirge in German, were colonised by German miners in the Middle Ages and later. Many of the Germans remained until the Second World War, and many were forced to leave later. So, they left the land which their forefathers had settled years ago and returned to Germany, where nobody really wanted them and the main thing in common was their language.

In the evening, my diary includes my ponderings:

The contribution of post-war Slovak Communism is mainly in a mass of badly designed factories and extremely ghastly blocks of flats, strictly utilitarian and not always well looked-after. The Germans who still remain here stand out from the Slovaks, but they are becoming Slavised. Most of their children don't know German. Post-war civilisation didn't encourage it.

Many of the towns here owe much to German foundation, despite Slovakian claims otherwise. In fact, even now, Hungarian, Slovak and German are spoken by most people over twenty-five.

Next day, the sun returns. I have jam-filled bread buns and water for breakfast, followed by a cigarette. I continue upstream along the river Hnilec, through Mníšek village, and walk along an even tinier winding road until I arrive at *Stará Voda* in the early afternoon. *Stará Voda*? It means Old Water, I can guess, the words being similar in Polish, Serbian and Slovak. My diary:

Stará Voda is a little mining village at the foot of high mountains, forested and still snow covered. Here I discovered German families, with tidy and well-cared-for houses and gardens. The first house I went into, they were scrubbing and cleaning non-stop. I was made welcome by an old couple, he a Slovak and she a Swabian, which is how they refer to Germans. They have a heifer, a calf, two mother goats with three lovely kids, fruit trees and potatoes. My bedroom has a view over the mountains, and I am given a luxurious old-fashioned feather bed.

German Settlers

This area was colonised by German settlers as long ago as the Middle Ages. They came as miners and town builders. Another later immigration at the end of the seventeenth century was of 'Swabian' Germans, who came after the defeat of the Ottoman Turks. In the Nazi era from 1938, after Hitler had taken over the Sudetenland in Western Czechoslovakia, Slovakia was briefly a German protectorate. After the war, most German speakers fled to Germany or were captured and sent to Siberia. Thus, although I do find people who still say they are German, and certainly most people the age of my parents speak the language to some extent, it is certain that the people I meet have experienced huge troubles and changes in their lifetimes. The latest is life under the domination of the Soviet Union. I sense, however, that now, in 1967, there is relative stability under the Communist regime and some appreciation of a better standard of living for the people in these remote villages. What lies ahead in the future, who knows?

Conversations during three days in Stará Voda

"You're not married?" says Mrs Podalinsky, who is looking after me at *Stará Voda* number twenty-four. Although she is German, she has her husband's Slovakian surname. "Why not? You should have children by now, a big strong girl like you."

We are sitting with a mixed group of neighbours, younger and older. A young girl is fiddling around with her hairdo, and the older women are curious about this odd person who has arrived in their village.

I've told them how happy I am about my new nephew, and that has elicited these remarks. I muddle along in my German saying things like, "I want to see the world," and "Good husbands don't turn up every five minutes." But they are not convinced.

"Pooh! We have lots of handsome young men in the village." They hustle together, chattering and giggling, and name one. Heads nod encouragingly. "He'd make a good husband for you!"

Someone brings out a photo of a wedding procession, a *hochzeitszug*. A man, probably the bride's father, is leading the parade. The bride is next, wearing a white, knee-length dress, white shoes and veil, followed by six or so young girls also in white and carrying bouquets. The families of the bride and groom follow, women first, then men in smart black suits and black hats. They are parading along the village street towards the church, past the house where I'm staying. A group of villagers, mainly scarved women, is watching the parade go along. I am told that gypsy musicians will lead the procession on its return from church. I am deeply impressed by the simplicity of this wedding train, so much so that I am pressed to keep the photograph and later paste it into my diary. However much the simplicity of the wedding photograph attracts me, I am not tempted to meet this handsome young man with a prospect of marriage.

In the evening, I walk along the village street with Mrs Podalinsky. We are gazing at the sky. "Do you have a moon in your country too?" she asks.

This question makes an impact on me. I include it in the article I write for *The Journal*:

She was entirely serious. This old lady was born and bred in her village and has never travelled further than her own two legs could carry her. She is typical of the older peasant people in Slovakia with her entire lack of schooling.

But don't think she is unintelligent. She can speak three languages fluently – German, Slovakian and Hungarian – and a lot of mental agility is needed to change from one to another of these vastly different languages. She cleans the village school at nights and acted as interpreter for me.

INTO THE MOUNTAINS

"*Schnell, Brigitte. Komm.* The bus will leave soon." Mrs Podalinsky wakes me up.

It is 5.15am, and I clamber into the vehicle which is half bus, half lorry. I don't know where I'm going or what I'm doing, but off I go with the workers. My diary:

We wound high up, following the steep mountain stream. Gangs left the bus here and there to work in the forest, until there were only two women and me left. We marched up a snowy track through the forest, armed with pickaxes, rucksacks and buckets. I had no idea where we were going. We got snow in our boots but marched upwards for an hour or so. Eventually, we came to a mountain hut where the trees were cleared. The women had come to clean the hut in readiness for a group who were to arrive in the afternoon.

Mice had made short work of the blankets which were full of holes, but the little two-roomed mountain hut was charming. The women set to work, scrubbing, fire-lighting, brushing and washing, and I helped where I could. How they worked! When they'd finished, you could have eaten a meal from the floor.

Later, back in *Stará Voda*, I learn more about the lives of the women who live in this remote village. My diary:

A family woman is up at 4am. She gets breakfast, children ready for school, milks the cows and is ready for work at 6am. She has a hard day working in the forest. At 3.30pm she is back, has a quick meal, washes and changes, goes to the shops, makes the evening meal, milks the cows, puts the children to bed and does all the other endless chores. She drops into bed about 10.30pm. Next day, it's the same, and that's her life. Eat, work and sleep.

One old granny told me how she had been struck deaf when she was eighteen years of age and has had no cure all her life. She suffers from many aches and pains and can't sleep. She said: "Dear God, how much longer do you expect me to live and suffer this life?"

One young woman has been deserted by her husband who has left her alone with three children. Another lost her five-week-old baby. Their life is hard, here in the mountains.

From Mr and Mrs Podalinsky, I learn that although *Stará Voda* is so isolated, it was much more so before the Second World War. My diary:

People until then were entirely self-sufficient. They built their own houses, grew their own food, reared their own meat, spun and wove their own clothes, made their own furniture, had their own horses for transport. They worked like slaves.

When there was no work for the men, the family went hungry, and that was that. There was no railway, only a little radio, certainly no running water or electricity, and five or six months a year of winter.

The older generation now appreciate easier living. "Jetzt ist viel besser!" Now times are much better. There is always food in the shop, and a little work, thus money, is available. Life is better for the peasants in Slovakia now; there's no doubt about it.

Mrs Podalinsky invites me to go to the school with her where she works as a cleaner. My diary:

Children start at three years old. They have a long day at school, roughly the mother's working day, 7am to 5pm. They sleep and eat four times a day at school. But how naughty those children were. The young teacher had practically no control over them. Her life must have been a misery, thirty shouting, screaming roly-poly kids.

Back home, Mrs Podalinsky cooks wonderful food for me – everything I like, including my favourite poppy seed cakes. "Brigitte, would you like an apple?" she asks me. As most of the food I've been eating is very stodgy, the thought of a round, juicy apple is appetising. She pulls down a ladder and climbs up into the attic. When she descends, she is holding two or three apples, tiny, dried-up wrinkled things, nothing like I had imagined. She hands them to me proudly. Fruit – at the end of a long winter – this is a luxury. I realise that she has stored them since the harvest of the last autumn and quickly, I express my thanks and enjoy chewing the dried apple. These I now realise are the apples in the strudels and pies she has often made for me.

Shopping in Poprad

My bags are really heavy. As I leave *Stará Voda* the next day, I realise I need to improve my equipment. On my back, what I call my rucksack is actually a simple, tough army-store haversack, and it holds all my belongings. My woollen blanket, with my name cross-stitched on it by my grandmother, is strapped onto the top. It has kept me warm during my months of travels. The haversack contains my winter clothes and my stationery, consisting of my diary, pen, ink, scissors and glue. I have two cameras, one for black-and-white photos and one with colour transparency film. Together with basic toiletries and DDT, the whole adds up to a considerable weight. I carry a cloth bag in one hand, which holds my daily food, water and little red petrol-cooking stove, and my sturdy stick in the other.

I have often been told that Czechoslovakia is the place to buy outdoor gear, and that the prices are reasonable. I decide to do some shopping. I eventually get a lift which takes me all the way to Poprad, a relatively large town. Here, I invest in a well-designed rucksack with a bamboo frame and small tent, both of which will save me from spending money on hotels.

And so, newly equipped, I walk away from Poprad. My diary:

I suddenly saw the beautiful outline of the Tatry Mountains against the sky, snow-covered, fantastic shapes. It was thrilling to walk in the wind heading for the mountains, but it was very cold. I got to Starý Smokovec, a town of hotels for visitors to the mountains, the sort of place I hate. I decided to camp somewhere, trying out my new equipment.

It was very late, almost dark, with no time to mess around. So, I plunged into the snowy pine forest and put down my tent in a snow-free clearing. It was very cold. I put on every item of clothing I possessed and, inside my one-person tent, I tied my blanket around me. The wind began to howl. I was afraid it would snow or rain, and as I lay there, horizontally, not able to sleep, I began to feel afraid of the bears and wolves which are in these forests. I decided it was no fun camping alone. My body temperature was lowering as I shivered constantly. I realised that there are some things I am afraid of, and one of them is being alone in wild forests at night.

"I will pack up and go to a hotel," I said to myself. I wasn't that far from Starý Smokovec, and I'd surely find somewhere.

When I stuck my head out of the tent, I saw the moonlit sky and the pines blowing. It seemed peaceful. Why had I been afraid? I thought of smart hotels, how they treat raggedy-looking people like me with condescension, and I thought, on the whole, I prefer the forest.

So, I shivered back into my tent and, overall, was quite happy, despite the cold.

I wake with the first light and birdsong. I crawl out of the tent, so stiff from the cold that every movement is difficult. To warm myself up, I try to light my stove to make some coffee, but the matches are too damp. I have sticky sore eyes and am cold throughout my body, especially in my back. I have a feeling of hunger and yet not hunger. I pack up my tent and scramble onto the road. Walking is difficult as my body is frozen stiff and inflexible. My diary:

The worst thing about such a feeling is that you aren't in the mood to appreciate things. Anyway, I saw a lot of fabulous mountain scenery. I passed peasant plots and huge collectivised open fields side by side. I jogged along, walking quite a few kilometres, and then the sun began to disappear behind the clouds. I was dreading another freezing cold night when a car stopped to offer me a lift.

Then, a strange thing happens. Usually, when a car stops, I ask the driver if they are going to my place of destination. And so, I start to say that I am heading towards Ostrava, but only a croak comes out of my throat. My whole face and head are still frozen with cold, and I can't speak. I hadn't realised it until this moment.

The driver and his wife look at me kindly. They decide to help this strange foreigner who can't speak properly and make space for me in their car. I sit in the back next to their daughter while the car drives westwards. The warmth inside the car helps me to thaw out a little. They take me all the way to the city of Karviná where they live, over an hour's drive away. When they invite me to stay in their flat, my relief is unbounded. The first thing they do is run a bath for me.

This is the first bath I have had since the previous autumn, and I thaw out comfortingly in the hot water. Once heated through, I am able to speak to my kind hosts and tell them my story. They give me eggs, bread and butter, and hot fruit-juice tea, and then get out a book of pictures of their country which we look at while smoking good cigarettes and drinking wine.

Ilona and Josef Struppova – you helped this foolhardy young woman to come back to life!

PLUM TREE PARADISE

The Struppova family bring me to the city of Ostrava next day. This is the Silesian area of Czechoslovakia, the Moravia-Ostrava industrial belt. My diary:

> *Coal mines absolutely everywhere, and of course were formerly in Germany. The industrial area went on and on. The smuts and dirtiness, bright-clothed people, green patches in-between, all reminded me of Newcastle and the colliery villages. Sweet sadness!*

While in Ostrava, it is strange to think that I am less than a hundred kilometres from Zawoja, the village of fleas and wooden houses in Poland where I was last August. Wrocław, home of the four *zbereźniki*, Tom, Julo, Dionysus and Marian, is just on the other side of the mountains which I can see from here. It feels like I have made a big circle since I left them.

I am travelling through the Moravia-Ostrava water gap. Rivers from Ostrava flow north into the *Odra*/Oder, which I had sat beside in Słubice and which runs into the Baltic Sea in Poland. South from Ostrava, the rivers flow into the Moravia, which then flows into the Danube. I've seen the Danube in Austria, Hungary and Serbia, in Donji Milanovac, where it would soon be flooding that village on its way to the Black Sea. I feel myself in the heart of Europe, truly in Central Europe.

Prague, the capital of Czechoslovakia, is my next destination. I shall visit historical places and importantly collect my post. All my correspondents have been asked to send letters to me Poste Restante, Prague, to arrive by the 15th of April.

A motorbike stops for me, but as we leave, my bags and my own weight overbalance it. Almost immediately, it crashes to the ground, throwing the driver and me across the hard road and landing on top of us. Luckily, there was no more harm done than a few bruises and scratches. Apologetically, the young driver decides to leave me behind. The next car to stop for me is driven by two Romanian holidaymakers. They speak to me in French, which should be a relief, but I find difficulty in getting my tongue round the language after so much German.

They are going to Brno, but I need to stop somewhere for the night and ask them to drop me off at a village called Nemojany. Here I find a pretty orchard, and I ask the owners if I may put up my tent there. Bemusedly, they agree. I sit with my notebook and pen:

The plum blossom is in heavy bud, and the sky is blue-gold above. The sun is setting behind the forested hill. Birds are singing all around me. The village is small, of red-rooved houses. High on the hill behind is the domed village church. Insects are buzzing in and around my little tent. I'm grubby and tired from a long, hard day and must get this finished before the sun sets. This is one of my little paradises. I'll probably freeze in the night, but that is part of this life.

However, I don't freeze. The householders approach me. The tall, strapping, healthy man, although a pensioner, looks about forty. "Why do you want to sleep in your tent? Here we have a nice bed for you." That is the gist of what they say to me in Czech. They feed me with poppy seed rolls for supper, and the same for breakfast, before seeing me off on my way to Brno and then to Prague.

THE YEAR BEFORE THE PRAGUE SPRING

I meet three boys – Milan, Josef and Pavel – who, like me, are hitchhiking out from Brno in the direction of Prague. An open-backed lorry comes along, going all the way to Prague. *Dobrý, dobrý.* Good, good. We clamber up into the back. For the next few hours, we sit, wind-blown, in the open air, with views over hills, mountains and valleys. It is too chilly and noisy to chat. Our driver drops us off, at the boys' request, on the outskirts of the city. It is too late to find accommodation, and we have our tents in which we can sleep without paying. The boys are competent campers, and we build a fire in the woods where we make coffee and chat in the moonlight.

"Bridget, are you sad? Why you cry?" asks Milan in the morning when we crawl out of our tents. I have acquired a splinter of some sort in my eye, probably during the windy lorry journey. It is painful, and my eye is watering constantly. The boys look but can't see anything. I'm going to need some medical attention.

Nevertheless, my priority is my post. Milan knows the city, and at the main post office, in the Poste Restante, there are letters waiting for me. My correspondents have timed it nicely, as today is the 18th. I am pretty well on target. I can't wait to open all my letters, but first I must sort out where I am staying. Milan, Pavel and Josef are hitchhiking to the spa town of Karlovy Vary, close to the border of East Germany. I find directions to Ulica Řehořova to meet Milada Santruckova, a student friend of Dushko's. He had written to her, telling her I would be coming around this time, and had asked her to find somewhere for me to stay.

"Bridget, welcome," she says when I knock on her door. Slim, short and dark-haired, she smiles at me. When she sees my weeping eye, she says I must go to the *Červený Kříž*, the Red Cross. We go first to the student hostel.

Milada is friendly, but also cool. I think I am making her nervous. I sense an atmosphere of awkwardness, uncertainty, in Prague. The three hitchhiking boys were keen to get out of the city. The day is grey, and the streets are drab, people passing by with lowered eyes. Once she sees me settled in the student hostel, Milada leaves me without arranging to meet again. This is odd. Usually, I find young people keen to chat with me and practise their English. But my eye is hurting, and I am cold and tired. So I let things be.

Červený kříž – the Czechoslovakian Red Cross

At last, my turn comes. I've been sitting in the waiting room of the Red Cross clinic. The patient nurse examines my sore eye. She finds the source of the problem and manages to extract the splinter. She asks me if I want to see it, and I look. It is so tiny that I have to make a special effort to focus my eyes on the cause of all the discomfort. Relieved from pain, I feel a huge sense of gratitude to Czechoslovakia's Red Cross. There is nothing to pay. This is free socialist medical care.

THE SUBSTANTIAL POST – PRAGUE

Once again, the international postal service is keeping me in contact with the world beyond. My father is travelling in the Netherlands, visiting art galleries, and invites me to join. His travels, however, don't fit in with my itinerary. My sister Rosie is struggling through the third term of her college year studying institute management, after working in a café in the Lake District during the Easter holidays. She tells me about our new nephew, baby Henry:

> *He is funny. You don't think about babies seriously until there is one in the family. He mostly sleeps and eats, and when he's awake he looks about him in a most serious way.*

My father also writes:

> *Henry was very busy at his sleeping work when I last saw him.*

My mother is planning to visit Israel in the summer. After returning to Yugoslavia later this year, this is still the plan I have in mind myself. She writes:

> *It would be lovely indeed if you were also in Israel then. Hurry up and let Gerd at the kibbutz know. It helps to know who is coming as they have many summer visitors.*

Jenny sends me a card with news about my college friends who are still working in Birmingham as teachers. They seem so far away and remote from me here in gloomy Prague. Jenny writes:

> *You didn't surprise me on being a real aunty, Bridget. My cousin, the bishop of Newcastle's daughter, is marrying a*

Catholic from Belfast, causing great outrage according to my mother. Mary is going to Ireland for Whit. She is also planning to go to Romania with Damien. She's a lucky girl to have such a great chap and company on such a trip.

Sergi, my Spanish correspondent, still hopes to go to Yugoslavia. Living as he does in the restrictions of Franco's fascist Spain, he longs to experience socialism:

I think it will be difficult to get a job in a hotel reception because I don't speak a word of Serb. Never mind, maybe I can find something else. But please send me that book of Serbo-Croatian language. I'll manage to send you the money. If it's not too much trouble for you, when you go back to Yugoslavia, help me in any way to go there. I'll be very much obliged to you. A million thanks for all what you have done and will do.

I feel restless after reading my letters. I ask myself what I am doing so far from everyone who means so much to me and toy with the idea of making a quick journey to England home over the Whit weekend to see my new nephew.

Now my eye is better, I tell myself that I can enjoy being in Prague, which I know is a wonderful city, full of history and palaces. But it doesn't work. I feel at a loose end, without a clear sense of direction. The palaces and grandeur of Prague just don't fit my fancy right now. Little wooden churches attract me more than great city cathedrals, and town life is expensive. My diary:

I say to myself, "Bother touring around Czechoslovakia, looking at historical things and lugging my rucksack." I'm not really interested in doing this alone. I've seen so many places now. In other words, I don't feel like a tourist.

So, I've decided to buzz off to Cheb, on the frontier, the town I'd seen from Hohenberg on the German side of the river Eger, and try to do another article in The Journal. I have about five shillings in Czech money, and after buying my tent and rucksack, I am very short of funds. But anyway, I hitched out of Prague. A German gave me a lift as far as Karlovy Vary. I was surprised how much German I now know and understand. He was fat, kind, middle aged and lonely, and intelligent. But these ingredients add up to one total.

He tells me: "*Ich habe ein kleines Haus.*" I have a little house. He says I can stay there, but of course I am not interested. He buys me lunch anyway, and we shake hands on parting. I'm heading for the frontier lands again.

CHEB

I'm in Cheb and have obtained a bed in a sports hostel with the help of Petar, a young man whose mother is the hostel supervisor. This is the town I had observed on my visit to Hohenberg last autumn, when I was looking from the West into the East. Now I plan to do it the other way round. I'll settle for a few days and learn more about the German/Czech interaction. On my first day, I explore the countryside. My diary:

I wandered off into the fields where I discovered the old German farms falling into disrepair. What a symbol of fallen pride! I wandered as far as Františkovy Lázně, its German name Franzensbad. It was another German spa town, full of pompous, unlikeable buildings and holidaymakers.

I write an essay which I call 'The People who Have Suffered for Centuries', which is the first stab at a possible later article.

All around the town, in the small plain of the river Ohře, are the huge old German farms. At one time, they belonged to prosperous farmers, but now these well-cared-for buildings and lands have changed character. The land is collectivised and farmed by Czech workers. The buildings, used for housing machinery and animals, are entirely neglected otherwise and have not been repaired in any way since the war. It is a sad and desolate sight. These lovely old buildings will be used until they fall to pieces, and then what will happen?

I asked a peasant why the buildings were so dilapidated. "They were German farms," he said. "No one wants to live there or work on them."

West Germans who used to live in this area come back to visit their former homes. They take photographs of the decrepit buildings, go home and show their countrymen the state of Czechoslovakia since the Germans left. They don't always report on the improved conditions of the Czechs and Slovaks. They don't always see the prospering collective farms in the rest of the country. They see the grubby, smoky factories, compare them with their own immaculate establishments and don't see that these factories mean food and clothing for the people.

225

In Cheb

The main street is on a hill, with old, unmaintained houses and a cobbled road surface. A few women disconsolately shop in the state-managed store. The area of newly constructed blocks of flats feels more vibrant. The blocks are not more beautiful in any sense, but they emphasise modernity. These are the places where most people live, in preference to the old Germanic town houses.

As I wander around, children are playing in the muddy, unkept surroundings of the blocks of flats. I take a photo of two white-coated women leading twenty toddlers from a kindergarten, each child holding onto a long, white string as a way of keeping them all together.

Most impressive are the allotments. Under collectivisation, former smallholders and farmers had been given allotments of land, and here, near the blocks of flats, are neat rows of spring vegetables and fruit trees. This is where the fresh produce for the families of Cheb is being produced.

I WALK TO FRONTIER ROADS

There is an international crossing point between East and West, traversing the Iron Curtain, a few kilometres north from Cheb, but that is not what interests me right now. It is the little roads, the back roads between the villages. Here, in a tiny woodland glade, is one of those barriers that cut country folk off between one village and another, with an invisible but impermeable line.

I follow one lane until I reach two harmless-looking red-and-white swing barriers stretching across the road, like those for a rural railway crossing. A round white-and-red sign indicates 'Stop'. A bicycle and a motorbike are parked near the barriers. Three smartly dressed men are reading details on a sign which warns them about the forbidden crossing. I am standing near their Volkswagen Beetle car, left with its doors open wide, and I take my photograph. Their car registers KEH S 817, a West German nameplate. On the other side of the barrier, which is in the no man's land between the Communist and capitalist blocs, are some rows of cut-down logs. Forestry workers must be employed to keep the boundary clear.

Further along, I manage to get close to the river Ohře, which is the Czech name for the Eger. The water moves slowly here, the wintry trees reflected in its stillness. The view looks innocent, but it is not. On the other side of the river is a white boundary stone, brightly painted, meant to be seen. The flat, mown-down field, bare of vegetation, is cut like this so that the guards can spot anyone trying to escape. There is a wooden hut which must be where the guards are on duty. Behind the hut, on the other side of the river,

is a steep bank, at the top of which are the towers of Hohenberg Castle and, behind them, the spire of the village church.

This innocent view is a political statement about the Europe of 1967. People's lives are separated by this strip through the countryside.

ELECTRIFYING THE IRON CURTAIN

Petar's mother is of German origin and his father Czech. This is a rumbustious mixture. She is the manager of the sports hostel and friendly to me. She talks to me in German. "This country is crazy. I wish we could move to Germany. Here, everything is expensive, and nothing works properly." But she has married a Czech, and her children are Czech too. She is stuck here and feels imprisoned.

Her husband is hospitable to me but keeps out of the way. Petar is sixteen, a tall, slim young man. Having a girl staying in their hostel, from behind the Iron Curtain, across which he cannot pass, is a novelty. We decide to do a little exploring together. The frontier here runs along a high, forested ridge and, sticking out above the trees, is a television tower. Petar and I agree that I'd get good views from there. Another curiosity – the dome of a little chapel peeping above the trees on the ridge – had been visible from the sports hostel when I arrived yesterday. In the morning, it seems to have disappeared. Have I been imagining things? But no. Petar assures me it had been there. We think we'll go to see what is what. My diary records rather nonchalantly one of the most astonishing events in my travels:

Although we knew the television tower was on military territory and forbidden, we thought maybe we'd be allowed to go. We went to the place where the little chapel had been and saw the bombed-down ruins. Fancy that had happened when I was in Cheb. It may be that it attracted too many curious visitors on the sensitive military frontier. But now it was no more.

Everything was quiet, so despite warning notices, Petar and I wandered along until we came to the tower. We saw the actual Grenze and the guarding soldiers in their towers and the electric wires.

At the tower was one old civilian man. We asked him if we could go up the tower. He told us to get away, we shouldn't be here at all. So, we retreated by a different path that headed back towards Cheb. We were in a clearing, on a hillside. From there, we could see Hohenberg, in West Germany. Busily gazing westwards, suddenly we were surprised by two soldiers charging down the hill towards us, one holding on a leash a huge Alsatian dog straining for our blood and their machine guns at the ready.

What is this? We were told to stand still, and one of the soldiers looked as if he'd be glad to shoot us. The other was more polite.

We had to sit in the forest, waiting for an armoured car to take us to the HQ, which the soldier with the Alsatian went off to get, while the other, who was friendly and kind, kept us on guard.

At last, the armoured car arrived. I was blindfolded, and I didn't know if Petar was there or not because he told me later that the horrible soldier had his hand over his mouth. We sat in this vehicle, bumping over the forested tracks, not knowing what would happen to us. I didn't dare move. I could feel the dog's breath next to me, and I was scared it might bite me.

We arrive at our destination, and there waiting for us is a double line of armoured soldiers with batons, through which we have to walk the gauntlet. It feels melodramatic as we are such an unlikely threat. Then we are taken into a room with a uniformed officer. My diary:

The superintendent didn't speak good German. He questioned first Petar, and then me, alone, in German. It wasn't particularly frightening because we hadn't done anything. I supposed they must have believed whatever story I managed to come up with because they didn't take my cameras from me.

But then we had to wait, without speaking to each other, with a guard sitting on a stool in the corner of the room.

Our guard is nice, though, and we manage to exchange a few words. Probably the situation is making a little variety in his day, an odd-looking English girl and her youthful Czech friend nosing about along the border. We ask him how long we would be sitting there, and he answers, "Four or five hours." My diary:

We worried about Petar's mother, who would certainly wonder what was happening to us. When Petar had been questioned, he had given his family's details. Now, he told this friendly guard that his mother's health was not good, and please not to contact her. Petar then told the guard that I was hungry, and please could I have some food. What's more, he said that I was vegetarian, and please could he bring me cheese or eggs. The guard left.

When he returned, he said we could have food after we'd been there for two days! We didn't know if he was joking or not. So, there we sat.

Then the superintendent came in. He'd been convinced of our harmlessness. We were to pay a fine for expenses, benzine and general alarm, including electrification of the wires! He said that, as I was so hungry, we'd better go home for some food! We were quite surprised, and I was relieved that he hadn't taken my films from me.

We were blindfolded again and taken back to the edge

of the military zone. The driver saluted, bade me a good holiday, said, "Don't go near the Grenze again," and let us go.

So, we have been responsible for electrifying the Iron Curtain! Thus, I learn that it isn't always switched on. And I have learned something else. When I'd been with the ox team near Neualbenreuth, and looked over into Czechoslovakia, I'd seen the clearing in the forest. I'd been told that this is where the soldiers had their headquarters. Now I know this from personal experience.

This foolhardy episode is the closest I have come to the Cold War paranoia of the line separating East and West. We are young people with no particular reason to attempt crossing it and are merely curious. It is a matter of good fortune that the soldiers on duty have taken our escapade lightly. The officer in charge perhaps showed his sense of humour when he recommended that I should go and find something to eat. What if he hadn't let us go? We'd been blindfolded, driven to a secretive camp with a ferocious dog breathing in our faces and made to walk the gauntlet. Then, when shut in the room with the soldier guarding us, my fears about Communist gaols were rather too close for comfort. Who would know how to rescue me? Not a soul from the outer world has any idea where I am. Petar, however, is something of a hero. He has a story to tell, not least how he asked the guard for food for his vegetarian friend. When we get back to Cheb, we go to the house of his friend Liba. My diary:

Petar told them all about our adventure, exaggerating all the details. We ate good food, eggs, bread and butter, and tea, followed by delicious custard pies, fruit pies and blackcurrant wine. And I sat through a long film of Robin Hood, in Czech! When we got back to Petar's home, very late, we had to go through the whole story again. This time, his parents assured us they were not amused. I was glad when it was bedtime.

The next evening, Petar, Liba and some friends and I go dancing. I am not impressed. The music is ten years out of date, as is the style of dancing. I write about the young people:

> *The teenagers are crazy about modern clothes and beat music; everyone is crazy about cars. The women want to have as easy a life as Western women who they think have very little work and lots of pleasure. It is undoubtedly the women who are the hardest workers here. The young people want to travel. The trends from Poland in the north to Yugoslavia in the south are the same. The people want to be as we are in the West. Whether they are East German or Hungarian, Pole or Czech, despite idealism about Communism, individually and in their private lives, all these people want comfort and freedom.*

WHAT NOW?

It is three weeks now since I left Yugoslavia, and I am having one of my unsettled phases. I am free and independent. My sister, in contrast, is married and happily enjoying her new lovely baby boy. I hatch plans about visiting my friends and family in England.

I shall go to Munich and collect the diaries from Poland and the Munich months, which I have left in storage at the *Wohnheim* of the Agfa factory. From there, I'll make a quick trip to England to see my new nephew and pick up the money I've earned from *The Journal* articles.

My plan is then to return from England to Munich and to head through Belgrade again on my way to Israel, where my mother will be spending some time in the summer. Only one objection to this plan is forming itself in my mind. I've visited four of the Eastern European Communist countries – Poland, Hungary, Yugoslavia and Czechoslovakia – but not Romania or Bulgaria. I need to think about this. Can I somehow fit this in?

MY BRITISH PASSPORT

I cross the border at the road junction between Cheb and Schirnding in West Germany. My British passport, that blue cardboard-covered document which I hold in my hands, means that I can go west, but Petar, who lives in Cheb, cannot. Nor can his family, nor Milena in Prague, nor the peasant families I'd stayed with in Slovakia. The electric fence and mined zones are not so conspicuous at the border crossing to Schirnding, but I know they are there, the Iron Curtain which is holding the people in.

The last entry in my Czechoslovakia diary is about going to the dance with Petar, Liba and their friends. Then, on the bottom line of the last page, where there is no more room, it ends:

We walked home in the rain. Screams, shrieks etc. Quite a pleasant night on the whole.

There the record stops. The next day, I cross the border into the freer air of the West, but the diary which follows this one is lost. It hasn't survived the decades. I must continue the story without it.

CZECHOSLOVAKIA CHRONOLOGY

1867	Dual Austro-Hungarian monarchy. Czechs dominated by Austria, Slovaks by Hungary
1918	Republic of Czechoslovakia founded, including many German speakers in Sudetenland
1920	Treaty of Trianon. 750,000 Hungarians find themselves in Czechoslovakia; same number of Slovaks in Hungary
1938–1939	Sept, Munich Agreement, after which German troops occupy Sudetenland and set up Protectorate of Bohemia and Moravia. Slovakia nominally independent
1944	At end of Second World War 'liberation' by Red Army. Stalin grabs Ruthenia as war booty
1947	Forced expulsion of 2.5 million German-speaking population
1948	Communist government established in Czechoslovakia
1953	Death of Stalin
1956	Khrushchev's speech denounces crimes of Stalin, followed by 'Thaw'
1950s	Antonin Novotny's neo-Stalinist regime
1967	**Author's visit to Czechoslovakia in spring 1967**
1968	Alexander Dubček becomes president. Beginning of Prague Spring. Soviets invade Czechoslovakia. Dubček removed
1976	Charter 77 statement on human rights.
1980s	Gorbachev in USSR encourages hopes of relaxation
1989	9 November, Berlin Wall comes down. Velvet Revolution. Havel elected president
1990	Free elections in Czechoslovakia
1993	1 January, Czech and Slovak republics separate
2004	Czech Republic and Slovakia join the European Union
2014–2022	Cold War confrontations erupting between Russia, Ukraine and NATO

9

Gypsy Summer

ROTKREUTZPLATZ YOUTH HOSTEL

We are sitting on the steps outside the youth hostel in Munich, five of us, waiting for the hostel to open. There are a young man and woman from Southern Rhodesia, Brian from Canada, Bill from the US and me.

The usual conversations have taken place. Where are you from? Where have you been? What are your plans? And, of course, we have exchanged names. We agree to meet at the little tavern over the road after we have checked in.

Soon we are sitting at a table, telling each other more about ourselves and our adventures over glasses of German beer.

He is on the other side of the table from me, so our eyes meet. He has an appealing smile. Amongst all our chit-chat, I learn that he is from an Irish-American family, which explains his dark hair and blue eyes. He has done his two years' service in the US army, one year of which was in Korea. He has found the return to civilian life unsatisfying and taken a cargo boat to Europe. Like the rest of us, he's been hitchhiking around, in his case through France, Spain and into Morocco, and now he's come to Germany because here it is possible to find a job. And he is very low on funds.

We smile across the table. He hears my story and tells me later that he has never met a girl like me, hitchhiking all alone.

The rules are clear. Three nights in a youth hostel is the maximum stay allowable. After that, the five of us move to the Thalkirchen Campingplatz beside the river Isar and jointly rent a caravan.

To England to collect some money

I am thinking how I can organise visits to Romania and Bulgaria on my way to Israel via Belgrade. First, I plan to make a journey to England because I have some money to collect there from my articles, and I must see my new nephew. I only have a few Deutschmarks left. Bill has almost none.

"Would you like me to leave you my tent?" I ask him. He could stay on the campsite for a couple of Deutschmarks every night while he looks for work in the city, and he is glad to agree.

"I'll be here when you return," he promises. I've only known him for four days. How can I be sure? I'm gambling with my tent, which is the roof over my head. But it's that smile again. I'm going to chance it.

In these days of the open road, it is quite simple for me to set off from southern Germany to England. It will cost me almost nothing. Sometimes, if a lift deposits me in the centre of a city, I will need to pay for a tram or a bus to the outer edge of town, but the only certain expense is the ferry across the English Channel. That costs just over £2 each way if I buy a pedestrian-only fare at the ticket office.

Thus, on the morning of the 8th of May, I take the tram to the edge of Munich and head northwards along the Autobahn. I'm carrying in my bag the diaries from Poland and Germany, which

I collected from the Agfa factory, and the latest, the notebook from Czechoslovakia. My youth hostel card is my ticket to cheap and safe overnight accommodation on the way. I arrive easily in Cologne that evening, a journey of 460 kilometres, equivalent to nearly three hundred miles. There is no time for looking around. I'm focusing on getting home.

The next day, the 9th of May, I get as far as Dunkirk in France, having hitchhiked 320 kilometres, two hundred miles. There's a good ferry service from there to Dover, and I take it the following day. After crossing London, I hitchhike to Birmingham because I want to meet my college friends.

THE NEWS

"Bridget, he sounds gorgeous," says Jenny. I'm telling them about this American, and I've left my tent with him. Their eyes light up.

My friends are teaching small children in multicultural Birmingham. We are all young women absorbed by our longing for the perfect love but who also need to earn a living. They all have complex relationships and bring me up to date with their news. Tonie wants to marry her lorry-driver boyfriend and return to live in Wales. Jenny has abandoned her unstable relationship with her boyfriend from Dublin and is unsettled. Mary is the only one of them who is enjoying her teaching job with infants and is enamoured with Damien, also from Dublin.

"But what do you do when you love him?" sighs Jenny. We share our most intimate thoughts and feelings, sitting together in Mary's bedsitting room with its old furniture and ancient, green-enamelled gas cooker. I might have shared this life. I could, and perhaps should, have started teaching, going through my probationary year like them.

IN NEWCASTLE

My father hands me over my post office account book when I'm home in Newcastle. There are three payments each for £6.6.0 from *The Journal* articles I wrote from Germany, Hungary and Belgrade. That is nearly £20, a fortune for me, enough to keep me going with my camping and hitchhiking lifestyle for at least a month.

"Why don't you tell the television people about your story?" suggests my father. "A wandering young woman behind the Iron Curtain could be a matter of interest. And they'll pay you something." He had been interviewed himself recently about his beekeeping stories, so he knew that they pay.

"Yes, we would like to interview you," says the news-desk person at BBC North. "How about on Tuesday? Can you be here for 5pm?"

I agree. But this sets up consternation in our family. I look such a sight. My sister Helen takes me in hand.

Her new son, darling little baby Henry, takes up her whole life, but she'll see what she can do. The baby is two months old, and I'm ravished by his big eyes and chuckling face. Lucky Helen.

"We'll have to do something about your hair," she says, and we try combing my shoulder-length hair into a more flattering shape, a few snips here and there.

"Now you can't wear that dress," she says. I rather like my home-made tartan sleeveless dress, which I'd cut out myself from some fabric purchased in the market at Belgrade and hand stitched. But this won't do. Fortunately, we are similar in size, so I try on several of Helen's. We choose a maroon shift dress with coloured flowery sprigs.

She sits me down on a sofa, discussing my posture. "Be sure you don't press your legs against the seat so that your calves splay out," she says. I say that I will try to remember.

I appear on television, and it all passes by in a blur.

While I am at home, a letter arrives for me which had been forwarded from the Belgrade student hostel to my father's address in Newcastle. It is written in Serbian, and of course is typed in Cyrillic, on grey official paper. What on earth does it say? It looks and feels officious.

When I am at the BBC, I tell them about this letter. They are curious and ask to see it, so next day I take it down to the studio.

"We'll see if we can get it translated," they say. And after some investigation, they track down their Bulgarian interpreter in London. That language is sufficiently close to Serbian to enable him to translate it.

The message goes something like this:

From the Principal Post Office, Belgrade
   You have been sent some illegal substance through the post. It is absolutely forbidden to send organic matter into Yugoslavia without special permission.
   We have destroyed the contents and ask you to inform the sender of this regulation.

The sender's address is added:

Mrs Barrow
8 Rayfield Grove
Swindon
Wiltshire
United Kingdom

Now why on earth would the mother of my friend Mary, who lives in Swindon, send organic matter to me in Belgrade? I contact Mary, who phones her mother.

"I saw some lovely daffodils around the time of St David's Day," she tells Mary. She knows my attachment to Wales and the tradition of wearing a daffodil on the 1st of March. "I thought how much Bridget would love them, so I packed them up in a shoebox and sent them to her."

I tell the BBC people the reason for the grey, sombre reprimand from the Belgrade postal office. They really like this story. They ask if they may interview me for Radio Newcastle and put on a man with a strong voice to read the translation. I am pleased because I get another £5 for this. Then, even better, the item is chosen for the national radio's Home Service to go out across the country, and I get another £5. Along with my TV appearance, for which I received £10, I have now earned £20 from my media successes. I am becoming rich. This is as well as three six guinea payments from *The Journal*.

On the 26th of May, passing through London on my return trip, I dive bravely into the journalistic world. When I am in my grandmother's house that evening, I write an excited letter to my family in Newcastle which explains what happens:

Dear Family,

I went to the Geographical magazine office. The editor was very decent. They told me my photos weren't much good, but he said, "Go ahead, my lass, do us an article on Romania and Bulgaria if you're going there. We'll give you some films so that you can play about more with them. Get things from different angles etc. Get good photos and an interesting article and you're in." (Or something like that.)

They said if I can get back again to Hungary and do some better pictures, they'll take the article. I should get about £80 for each article. I was so surprised. I said: "Well, that's a good capitalist incentive for me to explore Communist countries."

They gave me six 35mm colour and 12mm black and white films. They keep copyright on these, but they said I can keep personal photos and have any copies I want for myself.

After leaving them, I again pluck up my courage and knock on a grimy door of a third-floor office in Aldwych. I've identified this address from the *Writers' & Artists' Yearbook*:

> *The agent was a genial capable Scotsman, and I showed him, and a journalist who worked there, my articles for The Journal. They said the articles were first class (I'd never have thought so), told me how I could have improved them and where they were good.*

I left with a kind of agreement to do five articles of two-thousand-word length, on 'Winter behind the Iron Curtain' or 'Girl alone behind the Iron Curtain', or similar. They encourage me to write a book too. I am ecstatically happy and tell my grandmother all about it:

> *Gran was thrilled with my adventures. I spent all evening making bloomers and am off early to Dover tomorrow. Hope to get beyond Paris! Never know your luck.*

My grandmother sets me off from her suburban house with a gift of £10. My father had also given me £10, so I am returning to Munich with the grand total of £68.18.0. This will keep me going for a few months.

I hitchhike to Dover, cross the channel and head straight for the German autobahns to Munich. There have been a series of unpleasant Autobahn murders around this time, but I manage without difficulty. I must see if Bill is still there with my precious tent.

HE IS STILL THERE

I track him down at his new job in the US army's transit hotel in Munich. He had been living in my tent but now has better accommodation.

I am rich and tell him about my fortune. While I was away, he was so short of money that he had been choosing between eating and smoking. Smoking usually won. He was down to his last Deutschmark. His shoes had holes in them which he padded up on the inside with his mother's letters.

He had been to look for work at the US army's hotel in Munich. The manager told him they had nothing at present, and he could come back again in two weeks as there could be something then. But he went back after a week, walking all the way from the campsite across the city because he couldn't spare the money for the tram. The shoelaces on his shoes had been broken so many times that he could no longer tie up his shoes properly. The manager noticed.

"OK, young man," he said. "We will find you work as a wine waiter. Come in on Monday."

The job included free use of a shared bedroom in the hotel's staff quarters, with meals provided. His fortunes are looking up. However, he was so completely penniless that he had written to his parents in the US, who sent him a loan of $130.

I like his ways. When we are out on a narrow path, he always wants me to be in front. This is partly so that he can see that I am safe, and he is keeping an eye on things. I am happy because I like to see what is ahead, the unrestricted view. He has never met anyone who always crosses the road to be on the sunny side, and I say he is the only American I have ever met who likes to walk.

The campsite becomes a meeting place for our gypsy summer. This will be the base for me to write my articles and to plan the next stages into Romania and Bulgaria. My sister Rosie and brother Richard join me, making their way there in July. Rosie, who is eighteen, four years younger than me, first travelled to Finland where she stayed with a penfriend. It was simple then for her to hitchhike to Germany. Richard, who is sixteen, made his way through France. He often waited hours for lifts as a lone male, but he gets there in the end. Mary has decided that one year's teaching is enough for the present, and she and Damien join us, along with Mary's younger sister Liz.

Bill works in his hotel, and I spend time stretched out horizontally in my tiny tent, writing about my travels.

Mary and Damien need short-term work too, and Germany is the place for this, they have heard. Mary finds work as a dishwasher at a restaurant called Kreutz Kampf. Damien gets a job on a building site, but after falling into a hole as he was pushing a wheelbarrow, he feels that is enough. He moves to Kreutz Kampf to work as a cleaner. He doesn't take kindly to the officious overseer who sends him to clean one floor after another constantly. "Jeez, what do you think I am? A bleedin' yoyo?" he complains. Sometimes I think we don't have the correct German attitude to work.

Rosie supplements her meagre funds by collecting empty bottles and taking them to the campsite shop in exchange for cash. Liz spends hours on the river Isar tumbling over rapids on a raft. Thus, our little group of Brits, one American and one Irishman live our gypsy life during the summer days.

HIPPY SUMMER OF LOVE

I cut out an article from Bill's July edition of the American journal, *Time Magazine:*

'*The hippies have emerged on the US scene in about eighteen months as a wholly new subculture, a bizarre permutation of the middle-class American ethos from which it evolved. Hippies preach altruism and mysticism, honesty, joy and non-violence. They find an almost childish fascination in beads, blossoms and bells, blinding strobe lights and ear-shattering music. Their professed aim is nothing less than the subversion of Western society by "flower power" and force of example.*

'*In their independence of material possessions and their emphasis on peacefulness and honesty, hippies lead considerably more virtuous lives than the great majority of their fellow citizens. This helps explain why so many people in authority, from cops to judges to ministers, tend to treat them gently. In the end, it may be that the hippies have not so much dropped out of society as given it something to think about'.*

BUT US?

In the age of The Beatles and Rolling Stone culture, are we, in our hitchhiking lifestyle, our love of the outdoors and our miniscule budgets in the same vein as the emerging hippy culture? We are not taking hallucinogenic drugs or decorating ourselves with flowers and beads like the hippies of the USA, but we, in our youthful inexperience, are certainly questioning Western materialistic values.

BACK TO HOHENBERG – THE WATERMILL ON THE IRON CURTAIN

I had always planned to revisit Hohenberg to investigate its little watermill which is right on the Iron Curtain boundary, and Bill comes with me. Once there, we follow the winding lane down from the castle towards the river and knock on the door of the house by the watermill. It is opened by a smiling woman with her eight-year-old daughter.

"Yes," she says, "this watermill is still working." Yes, they do live right on the *Grenze*, the frontier between West Germany and Czechoslovakia. She and the little girl take me to the rear of their house. Amid the wild flowers and the grass, on a post about eight feet high, is the sign saying *LANDES-GRENZE*, which means 'country border'. And near that is a small white boundary stone saying DB, for *Deutsche Bundesrepublik*, the German Federal Republic, or West Germany.

The girl, with her white kerchief tied around her hair, her speckly dress and black boots, looks just like Little Red Riding

Hood as she gazes up at the sign. At the top of the riverbank, the rounded edges of the flat fields on the Czechoslovakian side are mown short and stretch backwards to the forest, with its sharply cut side. The guard posts must be along that tight edge. Anyone who tries to cross the open mown fields would easily be spotted. This is the background to the mill family's life.

But far from being depressed, the family is cheerful and welcoming. Bill and I chat with them, and the father lets me take his photograph as he works shovelling manure.

Not only do they grind the corn at this mill, they also bake the flour into bread. While we are there, they load the bread into their horse-drawn cart. Two strong horses, one chestnut with a white blaze on its forehead and the other a bay, are harnessed. The miller, his son and the grandfather ride on the cart up the narrow lane towards the castle and the village. The boy is about eleven years old. He has a cheerful round face topped with a Bavarian hat, and he helps to deliver the freshly baked bread to the customers. Grandfather, smoking his cigarette and holding the horses as they pause, shows me his watch on a chain for the photograph. The father guides the horses through the streets, past the black and white half-timbered houses, until every loaf is delivered.

I stop to think. This is June 1967. The Iron Curtain is winding along the river's course behind this little family's mill, and here they are grinding and baking as in days long gone. It is a strange, ironic, fairy tale.

Yet these are the days of the Cold War between the Communist East and the Capitalist West, and we are still personally affected.

Bill has completed his two-year compulsory army service, but the war in Vietnam is ongoing. Young American men are still being conscripted, many against their will. Bill is obliged to be enlisted in the reserve force and could be called up at any time. He has been transferred to the US army reserve at Frankfurt, in Germany. We have no reason to worry, surely?

Hungarian interlude

Those yet-to-be-explored lands of Romania and Bulgaria are unknown and mysterious to me. Rosie stiches her big Union Jack onto her rucksack. She is coming too. We leave our little group in Munich, and together we head east.

Soon we are in Hungary, heading for the Hortobágy *puszta*, the region of the *Alföld* where it may be possible to find handsome farm animals long lost elsewhere: long-horned cattle and curly horned sheep. I imagine horsemen with flowing capes, the Wild West of Hungary.

As we walk along a quiet country road, we can see ahead of us the long, low thatched roofs of collective farm buildings. They would be just the same as many other such buildings these days except that, here in the *puszta*, the buildings are thatched. I have my colour transparency film and am looking for the right opportunity to take photographs.

Rosie stands back as I tiptoe cautiously forwards. No one is expecting us. There, behind the building, is a dark-haired young man, loosely dressed in shirt and grey trousers, forking hay onto a cart for his two white, long-horned oxen to eat. I am so excited – my first sighting of the long-horned cattle. I watch as he yokes them onto the cart and then leads them towards the great balance beam well where he draws water for them to drink. There are three horns between the two beasts, as one of them has lost a horn. These are raunchy, bony animals still doing useful work on the farm. A suntanned, fair-haired little boy watches me, the stranger, taking photographs. A sign above the open entrance to the barn reads *Tilos a Dohányzás*, No Smoking. This is a message for the workers. No private farmer would need to put this above his barn door. I am having a glimpse of old Hungary in the new collective system.

We move across some fields where workers are raking straw into a row of stacks. Grunting around among the dry grass and stubbles is a herd of black pigs.

"Free range bacon production," says Rosie. "These pigs don't know how lucky they are."

We approach a group of pig herders who are supervising their rummaging. An older man, a teenage boy and a younger one have whips with red bobbles on, and their black dogs have bells on their collars. We make friendly exchanges in two incomprehensible languages. A shepherd joins the conversation, and when he sees me taking photographs, he brings over his star performer. This is a ram with curly horns and impressive male genitalia. The ewes and lambs are distantly visibly across the open space.

On a hot summer day, this is a timeless almost-medieval scene, except for one thing – we are seeing collective farming under Communism. Because I can't speak Hungarian, I cannot ask what the workers feel about it. I can only see that they are proud of their animals and happy for me to take photographs.

LANDSCAPE ARTISTS

The great nineteenth- and early twentieth-century Hungarian artists Gyula Rudnay, János Tornyai, Béla Endre and Munkácsy Mihály painted these open landscapes of the *Alföld* and the *puszta*. The huge straw-roofed houses and villages, the watery meadows, rows of long, single-storey houses, with their sheltered balconies beside the ponds, and the people living and working in them belong to a lost world.

THE COLLECTIVE FARM GOOSE WOMAN

What is that we can see ahead of us? A cloud of white creatures is crossing the fields ahead of us, honking raucously.

Coming closer, we realise that an enormous flock of snow-white geese is waddling along beside the watery ditches, following someone. There she is, a sturdy woman with a straw broom, spotted navy scarf protecting her head from the sun and a short-sleeved blouse tucked into a knee-length skirt. We realise with wonder that we have met a lone goose woman. She is leading her enormous flock around on the unfenced fields while they graze and pluck at the sun-hardened stubbles in the hot summer weather. They must belong to the collective farm, the buildings of which we can see far away in the distance.

"How many geese?" we ask with hand gesticulations. She understands, but we can't pronounce the answer. We are left to guess. Hundreds, perhaps thousands. The flock of noisy, waddling white birds are all under her control. They know what she expects of them and follow her lead as she crosses the road and goes on her way. We are astonished at the skill of a person who can control such numbers of honking intractable creatures.

Then, a little further south along a road with almost no traffic, we see a group of women hoeing in a dry-looking field of pepper plants. Their bright clothes, lots of reds and blues, stand out in the burned corn-coloured landscape. When they see us looking at them, they beckon us over.

"Come, take our photograph," their words and gestures imply.

They are sturdy country women, the sort of women I admire, motherly, sociable, working as hard as they must, but not too hard, in the heat of the sun. And we, with our rucksacks, our foreign brightly coloured flag and our ignorance of their language, have appeared from nowhere and then disappear again.

Onwards now, we continue south to Yugoslavia.

Belgrade is our stepping stone to the East

As well as eating delicious cakes in a Turkish café in Belgrade, we spend the next week sorting out our finances and getting the necessary visas stamped in our passports for Romania and Bulgaria at their respective embassies. I buy a long, blue notebook. From the 25th of August, I use it to write my diary, and after the gap since leaving Czechoslovakia in May, this one has survived.

My post was waiting for me at the student hostel in which I had formerly stayed in Belgrade. A whole year has passed since I started my travels in Berlin and Poland, and during those times, from one set of forwarded addresses to another, I have kept in touch with family and other friends like Sergi in Spain and Theo in Amsterdam, Tony in Munich and Tom in Poland. But now, the flavour of the letters is changing. Looser links are slipping aside. Life is moving me along. I have letters from my mother and my father and, of crucial importance, letters and two cards from Bill. He tells me that he has been repaying the loan to his parents. He misses me, and I miss him.

In Belgrade, we stay on a dirty campsite with no water in which to wash. It is certainly time to leave for our exploration of those two curtained-off countries, Romania and Bulgaria. My diary:

We made the big effort to get out of the dusty outskirts of Belgrade, past a horrible smoky, stinking slaughterhouse where women in rubber aprons were cleaning guts out in huge black barrels. Bits of offal and burnt ribs of cattle were littered around, yellow fatty smoke belched disgustingly

*from the chimneys. The lowing moaning of cattle awaiting
slaughter must be the most pathetic sound on earth.*

This is a depressing start to our day. Through the open door of the
factory, we catch the eyes of some of the women as they work, but
we don't approach them. I cannot imagine living in a world where
I would be glad to have such a job in order to support the family.
We sheer away from conversations.

The dockside area of Belgrade is so filthy and dusty that we
are glad when we get a lift. There are few cars, but we estimate that
among those, there is high likelihood of one stopping for a couple
of harmless-looking girls like us. The great Union Jack Rosie has
stitched onto her rucksack is always a help. Two middle-aged
Yugoslavian men stop and offer to take us through the frontier into
Romania. My diary:

*This is a sandy area of Yugoslavia, on the plain, where
the wild winds blow up from Djerdap, piling dunes and
scattering sand over the crops. So, trees are being planted to
control the dunes, and the whole area has become a pleasure
garden. These men took us for a meal in a shady restaurant.
We drank šljivovice, wine, and ate meat and onions. I had
cheese and fried eggs, tomato and onion salad, with sheep's
cheese to end.*

*We photographed camels by the wayside from a circus.
The hot, dry climate must have suited them excellently.
We drove away from Vršac, a dusty and bedraggled town,
towards the Romanian frontier. The wide plain stretched all
around, flat and dislike. How huge, immense and arching
wide the sky seemed. Suddenly, a storm was looming,
thunderclouds hanging over the small, flat round world,
dissected by a tree-lined road through its diameter. A church
spire sticks up ahead. The drivers tell us it is a Romanian*

village, Hungarian in origin. It is now peopled by Romanians, Hungarians, Germans, Serbs and Bulgars. The plain seems endless. A single balance beam well is silhouetted black against the sky, an outline grim and dark, and looking lonely.

The Romanian frontier lies ahead. We feel fairly secure in the car with these two kindly men who will drive us across the border. There is no need to worry about crossing that no man's land on foot, it seems. Nevertheless, there is always uncertainty. What if the guards are unpleasant, unfriendly and make difficulties? The night is drawing in, and we have no food.

10

Piglets, Shepherds and Buffaloes

Romania, August 1967

Autostop? Ha ha ha

Our entry at the border post into Romania was so unexpected that I wrote it up later in an article for *The Journal*:

> *"English, eh?" said the Romanian frontier guard as we handed him our passports.*
>
> *"Where's your car?"*
>
> *"We have no car," I said. "We're travelling on foot, by Autostop."*
>
> *"Autostop?" he said, blinking. He called his friends. "Two English girls travelling by Autostop," he said, and they stared at us and roared with laughter.*
>
> *The car we were travelling in across the Yugoslav-Romanian frontier was examined by the customs officials. Our rucksacks were lying on the ground. Suddenly, the guards again burst into a roar of laughter as the Yugoslavian drivers scrambled into their car, turned it at breakneck speed and disappeared backwards across the plain towards Belgrade.*

"*They've left you, ha ha ha,*" *said the official.* "*Autostop good in Romania, eh?*"

Presumably they'd been caught smuggling goods across the border and were making great haste homewards.

We laughed too. "*It doesn't matter,*" *I said nonchalantly.* "*We'll walk.*"

"*Where will you stay?*" *he asked.*

"*In our tent,*" *I said. They laughed at that too.*

Evening was falling over the open frontier land between the two countries. A thin drizzle was dropping onto the brown, corn-stubbled earth. The road stretched onwards straight ahead, merging into the misty skyline.

We headed for the village that we could see ahead of us, where we planned to buy some food and then camp on the outskirts. We were no sooner in a shop than a crowd of some twenty people congregated around us. We spoke in German and asked for salt and bread. Women's heads nodded together knowingly.

"*Tourists from Germany,*" *we heard them say.*

The shop assistant showed us the most expensive and finest quality foods, automatically associating strangers with lots of money.

A German woman came up. "*Good evening,*" *she said.* "*Are you from East or West Germany?*"

"*We're from England,*" *I said and pointed to the huge Union Jack on Rosie's rucksack. She translated it into Romanian and twenty pairs of eyes opened wide in amazement.*

The magic words had been spoken. English girls. From England. On foot. Invitations began flying around us. "*Come to our house to stay.*" *And various hand gestures indicated bed, food and sleep.*

In the end, we were chaperoned by the kindly Frau Sabin, a German woman married to a Romanian. We were given the best room in a spotless cottage with grape-laden vines growing round the doorway. We drank milk and ate paprikás, tomatoes, grapes and ham. This was accompanied by white bread, the finest to be had.

Thus, we experience our encounter with Romanian hospitality in the village of Deta. Next day, using our basic German, we are able to chat with the family about their life. These are the early days of the regime of President Ceauşescu. Helga Sabin is our hostess. Stan, her husband, has a question for us.

"Do you like Roger Moore?" he asks. They are intrigued to meet people from the country where Roger Moore lives. We are quite surprised, as neither of us watches much television. We vaguely know that he plays the lead role in the British ITV series, The Saint, and mumble something or other.

"How about holidays?" I ask. "Would you like to travel to England?"

"Of course," Stan replies. "But we cannot do that. We only have twelve days of holiday in a year. We can't have Christmas or Easter, as they do in Serbia. It is forbidden."

"Do you go to church?" I ask, thinking this may be a delicate subject.

"We are not forbidden to go to church. But it is much discouraged. Children who go to church often progress badly in school. And if we have a Christmas tree in the house, we must keep it secret. The children don't tell their friends about it."

Helga, who has fed us and provided comfortable, clean-sheeted beds, says: "Every woman needs to work outside the home. It is essential. Grandmothers often look after the children, or else they may go to nursery school for a small fee."

We feel the restrictions. Yet there is no deep sense of oppression in this house. The family happily pose for a photograph. The state is not yet so paranoid, in 1967, that we are a risk to the Communist world of Romania.

Deta market

"Eeeeeeeeeeeeeeeeeeee," the piglet screeches as it escapes and runs amok among the crowd of people in the market. Sunday is market day in Deta. The piglet is soon caught and held up by one of its back legs for us to admire.

"For you." The men show us. "Cheap, lovely piglet. Good bacon for Christmas."

"Take it to England," says another. "Beautiful piglet from Romania."

Everywhere there are horses with gleaming coats harnessed to wooden carts. They must be precious animals. Cows are tied to the carts and offered for sale, beautiful cream- and brown-horned animals. Women with deep headscarves shading their eyes, wearing brightly coloured clothes and their best Sunday slippers, smile for us.

"*Din Anglia*," we are learning to say. We are from England.

We watch the transactions, money passing from one hand to another. We have never seen such a market before. There is a man selling white wooden ladders some as long as six metres, wheelbarrows with wooden wheels and brooms made of twigs. All the traders bring their goods on horse-drawn carts, beautifully crafted wooden vehicles, some with rubber tyres but many with metal bands around the narrow wheels. There is not a motor vehicle to be seen. This is a sight from times long ago, with cheerful, sociable people. Once they have done their buying and selling, they crowd round meat which is smoking on a portable metal grill and tuck into what last year's piglets have become: sausages and bacon. Bottles of some alcoholic liquor circulate. Merriment and laughter are all around.

Here too is a gypsy wagon, like a small-version one from a Wild West film. Its rounded frame is covered with cloths of various colours, and its narrow wheels have metal bands instead of tyres. The father of the family is driving, smoking a cigarette as he goes, his children peeping out from behind him. A woman in a long, red skirt turns away from us as I take a photo. It was rather impertinent as I hadn't asked their permission, but they are too timid, perhaps, to object.

The men in the market are mainly dressed in modern clothes, jackets and shirts, sometimes with ties. Their hats are either sheepskin or felt. The cooper is wearing white, broad, country-style, woollen trousers with a black waistcoat over his white shirt.

As we leave the market, we are offered a lift in a peasant cart, and we rattle along for ten or so kilometres to the next village.

A lift then takes us to Timișoara, and from there, a car driven by two West German boys stops. They are driving and drinking wine. My diary records that:

They were generally showing off and playing the rich Western European in primitive Romania. Then one wet his pants, a

*just punishment for his gluttony in our opinion. We insisted
on leaving them in Arad.*

We are heading east now, towards Transylvania, the Land Beyond
the Forests, and into the mountains. A land of mystery to us, tucked
away in the realm of Communism.

Truly, where are you from?

We are clambering up a mountain path when we see a small family
approaching us, father, mother and girl of about twelve years of
age. They are dressed for hiking. The girl's brown, shoulder-length
hair is in two plaits. She looks like a little German girl.

"*Guten morgen,*" they say. Aha. Germans. Here in this wild
place. And we reply in kind.

"*Woh kommen Sie her?*" they ask. Where have you come from?
They have never met westerners before, but to our surprise and
delight, they speak English.

"Keep following this path," says Herr Staffend. "You will find a
cabana, a mountain hut, and you can stay there."

"And when you return, come and visit us in *Hermannstadt*,"
says Frau Staffend. "This is our town. Romanians call it Sibiu."

They tell us that up in the mountains we may come across the
summer shepherds who live there with their flocks. The *ciobanii*.
This certainly appeals to me. Transhumance, people moving up
into the highlands for the summer. Perhaps we'll be lucky.

"*Auf Wiedersehen.*" We take their address and wave them
goodbye, certainly hoping to see them again. My diary:

*We had to walk up and up and up, along a narrow path,
between trees beside a rushing stream. The peaks above
sometimes peeped through the clouds. I was thrilled to see
ice-carved summits. Rosie was rather tired, but she kept*

going. I was as strong as a horse as I had eaten so much bread and jam lately. We arrived at the cabana.

Bine Ati Venit, said the sign over the entrance gate. We are realising that Romanian is not such a difficult language as Hungarian or Serbian. It reminds us of French, bien venu. Welcome.

There are several hikers here, and we have a little room with a lovely view. The blankets smell of DDT. We cooked rice, peppers and tomatoes for our supper.

THE MOUNTAIN SHEPHERDS

After eggs and the last of our cherry jam for breakfast, we are ready to make a day-long expedition into the mountain heights. Some boys are going the same way, well dressed in hiking gear and proper boots, whereas Rosie are I are flip-flop wearers. It won't stop us. We've climbed Snowdon in Wales in flip-flops before. The young Romanian hikers are happy for us to tag along.

"Bring your cigarettes," one of them says, because he knows I'd like to meet some shepherds. "They always ask for cigarettes."

We pass through the green upland meadows around the cabana. We see the Great Window, *Fereastra Mare*. The window is between two huge peaks surrounding a rounded scoop of land. One peak is 2,282 metres high and the other, Coltul Bolaceni, is 2,290 metres. These are serious mountains compared to Snowdon at 1,085 metres. My diary:

> *It was lovely up there, huge, rocky glaciated peaks. It got very steep, and we had a few terrific climbs. The air got quite thin, so we had to have frequent halts. We were around two thousand metres. I was quite exhausted a few times and thought I'd drop but wouldn't admit anything in front of the boys. At the top there were terrific views in all directions. Then the mist came down.*

We pause so as not to lose our path. Crunching footsteps sound, and marching with long, confident strides comes a man driving three donkeys. The mist is no deterrent. The donkeys know the way. They pick their way across the loose stones of the scree, their load of checked-cloth bags across their backs. The shepherd glances in our direction. He is wearing white trousers and a black, sleeveless jacket over a white smock. On his head is a round, black felt hat. He crosses our line of sight for a few seconds, and then he and the donkeys disappear into the mist.

He must have been down to the lowlands to collect supplies. Now I've seen one of these mysterious shepherds of the hills. I had my camera handy and had been able to take a couple of photographs.

As the mist clears, our little group continues on its way. We are following a recognised hiking trail, so despite being at heights of over two thousand metres, Rosie and I are in good hands with our friends.

And then, on the grassy slopes with the bare, rocky peak of Urlea in the background, we see a thousand sheep, heads down, nibbling at tasty mountain grasses. Two *ciobanii* have seen us. Knowing that hikers may have cigarettes, they approach us. Our companions engage them in conversation.

"English girls, from England," they say. We smile and stare at them as curiously as they stare at us.

"*Mulţumesc Doamna*," they say to Rosie, as she hands them a packet of our cigarettes. Thank you, My Lady. I am breathless with happiness at this encounter.

The boys translate all my questions to them, and later in my diary, I write what I have learned:

The shepherds spend four months in the mountains, in huts a little away from the high peaks. Our cabana was one before the First World War. Our hut is 1,401 metres. They graze the flocks, this one of a thousand sheep, right up to the summits of around 2,400 metres. Urlea, at 2,475 metres, is in the background of my photos. The flocks are from lowland collective farms and include a few privately owned sheep. The shepherds live in small groups, usually threes. They wear traditional costumes, shawls woven in tartans by the women, leggings of wool, embroidered shirts and shoes of leather made by a man in the village. Such supplies as they need are brought up to the high cottages on donkey back. They eat a food called mămăligă, a mixture of maize, water and milk. The sheep supply milk, wool and meat. They climb a thousand metres and return to their huts each day.

But now we must separate from the boys who have been our guides and return to our cabana. They are moving onwards, but we will get back safely with a couple who are going the same way as us. He is a German-Romanian, an artist, and she a Hungarian-Romanian. We communicate in French.

That evening, over our cooked evening meal of spaghetti, tomatoes and paprika, to which the man donated some welcome bread, we chat a little. He tells us a little about the Romanian part of the Great Hungarian Plain, here called the *Banat*.

The complete collectivisation after the war, he says, has rendered the land much more profitable. Mechanisation is efficient, and sufficient, and the peasants enjoy better standards of living than before. There is a tractor factory, with a Romanian patent, at Arad.

I am always keen to hear views on this theme. He is a moderniser, probably a Communist Party man. And it is interesting to note that, despite the completely traditional appearance of the shepherds we had met on the mountain pastures, the sheep belong to a collective farm. The ancient ways and Communism are integrated.

That evening, I write to Bill, and Rosie drops in a note:

Dear Bill,

As I'm writing this, I am in a bit of a bad mood, but why I don't know, because we just had a lovely dinner. I expect Bridget has told you all about it. Anyway, Romania is a very interesting country. Last night we camped in a potato field, the night before in an orchard, so we're alright for food. The other day, we climbed a huge mountain twice the height of Snowdon. At the top was a peak called the Great Window, but by the time we got there, a fog had descended, so it was a bit of a pity. But I was past caring. Bridget just charged off to photo some shepherds. Well, now I'm exhausted from writing this letter so will finish here.

Elizabeth Rose

I will post the correspondence later when we return to the lowlands, even though pushing the envelope through a letter box in a remote village will seem rather like sending it off in the wind.

In the morning, as we take our leave, we meet two teenage girls out of a picture book. Dressed in their pretty, hand-embroidered blouses, they've been washing all the sheets from the hostel. A rivulet running out of the forest is channelled into a hollowed-out log, creating a water trough in which they've been dowsing and rinsing the linen. The row of sheets flutters in a long line in the breeze. We had slept in those lovely clean sheets, but despite the smell of DDT in the room, we have learned that bedbugs are surviving the process.

SÂMBĂTA DE SUS MONASTERY

On the way down from the mountain, we decide to visit a monastery which we'd noticed on our ascent. I include the story in my article for *The Journal*:

> *The snowy-bearded, long-haired old father of the Orthodox monastery welcomed a Romanian family and ourselves to his office. He was talking to the mother of the family, who presented us to the old father as 'two young girls from England'.*
>
> *"From England?" He threw back his hands in astonishment. "Well, I never! We had some visitors from China only six months ago."*
>
> *To the old man living in his secluded mountain monastery, England must have seemed about as remote as China.*

The father is quite happy that we put our tent near the buildings, beside a little stream. Pilgrims are always welcome and may make financial donations.

I learn a little from other visitors who can translate for me. My diary:

The Orthodox monastery was constructed in 1656, by funds from a prince. In 1765 it was destroyed by the Hapsburgs. It remained in ruins for over 150 years, although visited by pilgrims. It escaped total destruction because of its isolated position. In 1936 it was reconstructed from old plans.

Formerly there were more monks, but now only eleven. They have eleven hectares of land. The state removed all monks who hadn't middle school education, and they were rehabilitated into normal life. Many went to night schools to complete their education and came back gradually. The state gives eight out of the eleven monks a wage, making them like 'workers'. Three are too old and are supported by the other monks.

Young people can join the monastery but must have middle school education at least. Men can only become priests, as distinct from monks, after having studied at theological college. The youngest monk at present is thirty-four years of age, and the aged father thought this to be very young.

I deduce that the state education means that suitably approved Communist values have been taught to the monks before they are entitled to financial support.

When it is time to leave the monastery next day, the white-haired old father permits us to take some photographs of himself and two of his monks. Standing in front of their wooden residence with its garden of bright flowers, he is leaning on his stick. The monk on his right has straggly, long, brown hair and beard in the Orthodox style. The one on his left is a modern man with a well-shaped goatee beard and short clipped hair. His expression is cynical. I can't help feeling cynical about him myself.

We drop a few lei into their collection box. As a farewell gift, the old father gives us some lovely honey. Then a white-coated monk approaches us from the garden where he was working.

"*Poftit, Doamna*," he says. Please accept this, madam. He is holding out some carrots which Rosie always loves to crunch, an onion and a parsnip. We are truly honoured.

WOMEN DOING THE WASHING

"Look at those two!" we imagine the cluster of young women saying to each other. They gaze at us, straightening up their backs as they wash their clothes next to the little stream that we have followed down from the mountain.

We are glad to rest for a while. Walking eight kilometres in the heat of the summer, downhill from the monastery to the next village, carrying a tent and all our gear, is hard work.

But so is the work of these women, splashing and rubbing the family's clothes as part of the weekly wash. We drop our bags, cooling our hands and faces in the stream while we observe operations.

Clearly there is both a modern and an old-fashioned approach to laundry. Two stout older women, wearing wide-brimmed straw hats and ankle-length black skirts, are bent over their bowls, scrubbing away with blocks of soap. But the two younger women, with short, brown, curled hair and knee-length skirts, give us knowing smiles. One of them is holding a cardboard box, a Romanian version of our Persil or Tide soap powder.

It is pleasant to wash clothes in the summer sunshine, by the stream, rather than struggling with carrying of water in the house. Such a thing as owning a washing machine is beyond imagination. A young lad, with long, suntanned legs, passes by, grinning at the funny foreigners. We exchange smiles and goodwill, and they don't mind at all if we take their photographs.

We are in Sâmbăta de Jos, and we are hungry. We would like to sit with the women and have a picnic by their stream. However, we need to buy essential food items. My diary:

> *I tried to buy bread in the village, but the shop was only open three mornings and one evening per week. We were out of luck and feeling faint with exhaustion and hunger. Eventually, I persuaded an old man in a back street to sell me half a loaf.*
>
> *I was standing there with my bread, and a small crowd of people had gathered. As usual, the first thing they ask is, "Have you come by car?" To own a car seems some kind of paradise. I was standing there with my bread, being stared at as a most extraordinary creature. Then a car came along, lost in the side streets, and all of their stares changed direction, so we escaped unnoticed.*

Our picnic lunch, with the half loaf of bread, and water from the well of a nearby house, was delicious.

A BUFFALO FARM

The same afternoon, one of the most surprising sights we will ever see on our wanderings meets our eyes. We are leaving Sâmbăta de Jos and heading towards Făgăraş. What are those animals, those black creatures with downwards-turning horns, hundreds of them, grazing on the flat grassland dotted with muddy puddly patches?

They seem to be placidly munching the grasses, unattended, but then we notice a young man among them, and another a little closer to us.

We manage to show our surprise and ask him in Romanian what these creatures are. "Bivoli," he replies. Buffaloes. Water buffaloes. We have some idea that they may be found in places like India, but here in Europe? In Romania?

"How many?" He tells us there are 350. They are part of the collective farm. The individual animals belong to particular people, and he himself owns two, his father three. Only three herders look after them as they graze the common lands of the village.

He tells us that there are three hundred cow buffaloes which give milk and that they are milked every day at 6am and 6pm. Of course we can come to the milking, if we want to, he says when I ask, so we plan to return in the evening.

A little further along, an ancient threshing machine is being operated from the engine of a tractor. Carts pulled by horses and buffaloes are bringing loads of wheat to be threshed. Women in headscarves and skirts and straw-hatted men are in constant movement amid the noise of the engine. They are forking the bunches of wheat onto the top of the thresher, which shakes off the grains and deposits the straw. This is a sight from history. And obviously this is the combined effort of the collective farm workers of the village.

More surprises await us. What are those flames, those great cuboid piles ahead? We arrive at some huge kilns made of clay bricks, where barefooted men are loading wood into the fires. Others are wheeling flat barrow-loads of clay from pits where water has been channelled. They dump the clay at tables where women are working. We watch them moulding the clay into brick shapes which they put in tidy rows and explain that they leave them to dry in the sun for about five days.

The bricks that are dry then are made into huge piles, the cuboid heaps we had seen. The bricks themselves are the kiln, with a space left inside the heap for the fires of wood which will bake them.

Two women, one wearing a yellow headscarf and one a blue, smile at our questions. What could be so interesting about their daily work? Everyone is barefoot and muddy, busy at their job. I think that this would be a child's dream, playing in the mud on a summer's day. The women tell me, in our mutual sign language, that the villagers organise their own work. They use their common land and sell the bricks once made or use them themselves.

Now we have encountered three summer activities of the local collective farm. I am overwhelmed, exhausted even, at all these new encounters. But we need to eat, and all I have is the remains of the half loaf purchased in the village earlier. The everyday needs of two travelling young women must be seen to before our appointment at the buffalo milking in the evening. We find a spot to pitch our tent, and Rosie stays there while I hitchhike to the town of Făgăraș. I need to buy food and some insecticide for those pesky bedbugs which we have brought with us from the cabana.

One good thing about being in Romania is that the language, being related to Spanish and French, is reasonably manageable. I know *pâine* for bread, *lapte* for milk and *ouă* for eggs.

By 6pm, I am back, and we go to the collective farm. The buffalo cows are in their stalls being milked. Each woman, we are told, milks twelve cows. We watch a young girl with a neatly parted black plait, a blue blouse and check skirt, with modern slip-on shoes. She is sitting on a wooden stool, one hand holding a small, enamelled cup and the other hand milking the two teats. The buffalo cow submits calmly to this process.

"Would *Doamna* Bridget like to milk the cow?" a yellow-scarved woman asks. There are clearly two colours of scarves. I have hand-milked dairy cows in England a few times, and I am glad to try milking a buffalo in Romania. Why not? It is harder than it looks, but I do produce a few squirts to rounds of applause.

We ask questions, and later I write all these notes in my diary. As well as the milking cows, they have eight bulls, 174 young stock and fifty-four calves. They have one hundred horses and ten tractors. All this is needed for their 3,300 hectares collective farm. And there are eight hundred workers from 618 families in the village of Sâmbăta de Jos. The collective embraces the whole village. They get paid for the hours that they work and also are paid in kind with maize, milk and grain.

They tell me they grow five hundred hectares of wheat, 150 of maize and 230 of potatoes.

We watch the milk from the buffalo cows being poured into churns. We are told that the total herd produces about 230 litres per day. In a shed, the people line up for their share of the daily milk. We take a picture of a stout woman in a red cardigan pouring a measured cupful into an enamel container held by a young boy.

Their village was collectivised relatively late, in 1962, only five years ago. But the big question is – what do they feel about it? My diary:

We were asked if there were collectives in England. When we said no, a woman said: "Don't get any either." And they all laughed in mutual agreement.

271

THOROUGHBRED HORSES FOR THE COBBLER PRESIDENT

Nicolae Ceauşescu is the son of a cobbler. He is now the president of Romania. He leapt to fame by climbing the career ladders of the Communist Party. And like all presidents, he is beginning to enjoy the trappings of power.

Rosie and I have spent a rough night in our tent on a dry, lumpy field. At least we had eaten enough, cheese, peppers and plenty of bread and jam which I'd bought in Făgăraş. We brew up hot water to drink. The villagers at the buffalo farm have told us about a horse farm nearby, with wonderful horses, so we decide to visit it.

We prowl around outside the gate, wondering how we might get in. The guard shakes his head sternly. "*Interzis.*" Forbidden. We gather we need permission from Bucharest to visit this very important stud farm.

A man approaches who turns out to be the German-Romanian artist we had met in the mountain cabana and who had told us about the benefits of collective farms. He seems to have authority and accompanies us through the gates. He doesn't seem to mind either if I take photographs. My diary:

We saw young horses learning to jump and to pull carts, and fields of mares and their foals. He tells us that there are six hundred horses there, on forty hectares of land. We see the grounds planned like parkland, with an attractive old country house reminding us of England. He also explains that the president of Romania's horse is stabled there, a gift from the president of Bulgaria.

When we started to leave, the director, an evil-looking man, and his chief staff were around, and they told us we couldn't take our bags out because it was forbidden to photograph. We had quite a fright, but it turned out to be a joke. But that awful-looking director made it seem not very like a joke.

It seems that our guide, whose name is Robert Moser, is held in awe by the officials. He gives us his name and address in Timişoara as we leave and says we are welcome to visit. He would like us to have a good impression of his country.

WEARY, TIRED AND DIRTY

Rosie and I wash our hair under a pump in the village street. She pumps for me, and then I pump for her. The weather is hot, and we are tired after a few rough nights in our tent. It is time for some civilised comfort, and we are lucky because we have had a kind invitation. My diary:

> We got a lift to Sibiu with a really excitable, cheerful Romanian who kept bashing me as he talked and gave us sour apples. He drove us right to the door of our friends.

Frau Staffend opens the garden gate. "Come in, come in, and welcome," she says. Ernst beams at us, while their daughter looks on shyly. Their garden is neatly cultivated with vines growing over a trellis and coloured, well-tended flowers. They understand well how tired we are and, being hikers themselves, are not surprised at our dustiness. My diary:

> Gertrude is a wonderful woman, busy, energetic, made us feel really at home. We had a lovely meal, served properly on plates with a tablecloth, knives and forks. We drank home-made redcurrant wine which made us sleepier than ever. Then we each had a good wash, and I wrote to Bill. We slipped between crisp, clean, white sheets. What a delight.

We stay with them for three days, and because we can communicate in English, we learn a great deal.

WHEN THE PRESIDENT COMES TO TOWN

Herr Staffend tells us this story, which I record in my diary:

> "*When the president comes to the town, we realise he is to be treated just like a king. He is not called a king, but it is the same thing. An enormous amount of money is spent on flags and flowers and decorations. From the houses is taken a large selection of the best hand-embroidered cloths, or lace, or tapestries. These are laid on the ground for the president to walk on, just like an emperor in old days.*
>
> "*The people are forced by the police to turn out on the streets and cheer him, because if they weren't forced, they would stay indoors. The cheering is pathetic from the size of the crowds that assemble. It is not from the heart.*
>
> "*No, the state and the people are not the same. The people, myself included, are waiting for the day when a change of government will come.*"

WHO ARE THESE 'SAXONS'?

The family we are staying with are known in Romania as 'Saxons'. Herr Staffend tells us more. My diary:

> "*Our ancestors originally colonised this area under the patronisation of the Hungarian kingdom in the twelfth century. These were wild frontier lands. They came to civilise it and control it from savages. They built up their own little colonies of culture, and now they are no longer loved. The Romanians have taken over their towns.*
>
> "*After the war, all German men from seventeen to forty years of age, women up to thirty-two years of age, were sent to Russia. They worked in camps, in fields, mines etc*

as slaves. Their homes, land, shops and factories were taken from them and given to landless labourers or to the state. Everything dropped in value as the new owners had not sufficient education to manage things.

"As all was nationalised later anyway, the new owners gained little.

"Later the German people were allowed to return to their homes, but it was often not possible to repair the extensive damages.

"One of my brothers managed to leave for West Germany. In three to four years, he and his family had a house and four cars, all of which would take a lifetime to earn here in Romania. The Germans here in Hermannstadt all want to return to Germany. But they are good workers. They are not allowed by the state to leave. Very few get passports. Even when they do, they must have very close relations there, as they can take no possessions or money with them.

"A young boy attempted to cross the frontier. He was caught, and the punishment was seven years in gaol.

"Children in this town can attend German schools, but they must learn an hour of Romanian every day. As only five per cent of children can attend high school, they must know Romanian perfectly to qualify for entrance. Children in German schools learn English; those in Romanian schools learn French. Teachers earn between 880 and 1,200 lei per month." Fifty lei is equal to £1 sterling.

"Many old people have to live on three hundred lei per month. Pensioners who worked for fifteen years for the state get five hundred lei monthly.

"Travel abroad is very difficult; even if permission is given, it is only to other Communist countries. It costs two thousand lei for a ten-day stay in East Germany, 1,100 lei *to Hungary, 1,200 lei to Bulgaria. This is almost impossible on the average man's wage of 250 lei [£5 sterling] per week."*

Like the people of German descent whom I've met and heard about in Hungary and Czechoslovakia, in Yugoslavia and Poland, the conflicts with Germans still seem to be everywhere. This year of 1967 is only two decades after the end of the Second World War. Memories are still fresh in the minds of all the people only a little older than Rosie and me, like the Staffends. We know that many of the German people from these lands welcomed the Nazi regime, as did plenty of Romanians. This is not a topic we bring up in our discussions with our kind hosts.

LOCAL LIFE

Shopping is done in state-run shops with state-employed staff who feel no incentive to be helpful or polite. My diary:

Service is very offhand. Only the older generation are sometimes helpful. For example, in a bread shop in Făgăraș, when I wanted to be served, the door was full of baskets preventing entry. A peasant woman was before me. "No servi," said the girls. The woman went away. I was annoyed. "Nu stiu," I said. I know nothing. They realised I was a foreigner so drew away the baskets. Ordinarily, I'd have been treated like the peasant woman. The girls, at their own convenience, had said the shop was closed.

When I tell this story to the Staffends, they are not surprised. They tell us: "Swindling too is common. Wages are low, so unless one works extraordinarily hard, as honest Germans do, the only supportable life is through exercise of a little swindle, for example giving wrong change or receipts for less money than taken. The shop workers put the difference in their pocket.

"Nothing works properly here," they explain. "We built this house ourselves, but it is hard to buy the necessary materials, and the quality is poor. Look at those door handles. As soon as we put them in, they start to break."

We learn that their ambition is to emigrate to East Germany. The *Deutsche Demokratische Republik*? That dour, unlovable place? But to them, life there would be better than here as Germans in Romania. The possibility of West Germany, now the borders are closed, is out of the question.

The family take us round their lovely old town with its charming little streets and houses on top of the hill. We climb up the town hall tower to admire the rooftops and can see the surrounding Carpathian Mountains bathed in a haze from the heat. Our hosts tell us how much dirtier and untidier it all is since the Romanian country people moved in. We visit the museum and see the fabulous folk costumes of the Romanian and Saxon people.

THE SIGNIFICANT POST – SIBIU

Every day, I write a letter to Bill and post it with my ready-purchased collection of stamps. He does the same to me, but I can only receive his replies at pre-agreed Poste Restante post offices. The next one will be Bucharest. While I am at the Staffends' house, I have a clean room with a table, and so I am able to write in comfort rather than sprawled out in a tent at the end of a long, hot day. I record in my diary that one day I'll have a lovely house for Bill rather like the Staffends', and I write telling him all about it.

DISCUSSING THE COLLECTIVE FARMS

Herr Staffend's English is excellent. Now I can ask all my questions about the issue that interests me so much: the life of the country people in this Communist state. I record the conversation in my diary:

> *Me: Do you have the same problem as we do in England, the young people all leaving the land, preferring city life?*
>
> *He: We do indeed. The young prefer life in the towns. But it's not the real reason. The peasants of Romania have their hearts in the land. But since it's been collectivised, they are no longer interested in farming. Besides which, their wages are much less. The young prefer to work in industries.*
>
> *Me: Are the people comparatively better off since collectivisation?*
>
> *He: No, definitely not. They receive wages in kind, wheat, maize, milk etc, plus a small hourly wage from the state. The state takes all the produce not given to the peasants. Even when they loan tractors and machinery to help with work, it must be paid for with a certain percentage of the produce.*
>
> *Me: But the state is giving more assistance to complete the mechanisation of agriculture, is it not?*
>
> *He: It is. But very slowly. We have five-year plans, on which development of industry, commerce and agriculture is based. Agriculture always suffers under these plans. Not enough help is given. Nevertheless, we are becoming much more mechanised. We have tractor-building factories in Braşov and Arad.*
>
> *Me: With mechanisation, is the land producing better crops than before?*
>
> *He: Certainly, it is not. Since collectivisation, the peasants have lost interest in the land. The Romanian peasants you see really love the land. When they had their own private little farms, they worked much harder than they would dream of doing now. In the summer, I saw them going to work at 3 or 4am. It was in their own interest to work hard. Now it is not. [He refers to a field we had looked at the day before.] Look at*

that field. There was a crop of potatoes which yielded twice or thrice as much before collectivisation than it does now. I've been here all the time. I've seen it.

Me: But the future of agriculture lies with the big farmer, not with the small, surely? In England, bigger farms are always more profitable, acre for acre, than small ones.

He: In England, yes. Here also before the war. There were boyars – lords – who had large farms and paid employees. I tell you, the boyars must have got not three or four times better crops but ten times. It was in the boyar's interest, as in English large farms, to farm his land well.

Me: Then why did the peasants allow their land to be taken from them?

He: They did it under force, of course. The peasants will never forget the way in which their land was taken from them. It was done gradually, by police and military persuasion. Those that persisted too long were very badly treated. They had to give it up.

Me: When was collectivisation completed?

He: The last village was reached four years ago, in 1963.

THE VILLAGE OF RĂŞINARI

A town of German origin like Sibiu, called *Hermannstadt* by our host family, is very different from a traditional Romanian village. The Staffends know that Rosie and I would be interested to visit Răşinari, about twelve kilometres south into the hills. We take the *Straßenbahn*, a rattling blue and yellow tram, all the way, unchanged since it was built in 1901. The local people use the service to and from Sibiu for their regular needs. We see village men dressed in their white woollen smocks and trousers, big, strong leather belts at the waist, and black felt hats.

As we wander the cobbled streets of the little town, we come across a group of women sitting outside their house on benches. Scarved, but otherwise dressed in ordinary fashions of the day, a couple are spinning their wool on hand-held wooden spindles. Another is embroidering a large tablecloth, a detailed, time-consuming effort, which she will probably try to sell to the tourists who reach the village. A bent old woman, dressed in black, sits among the group. A little girl is snuggled up beside one of the women, and I find myself thinking about this entirely different culture. Here are Rosie and I, visitors to a Romanian-German family whose lifestyle is not so very different from ours at home and whose daughter is being brought up with Western values much like our own. And yet, in Romania, this little girl on the bench is learning the traditional ways of the Romanian-speaking country people. We are all so much a product of chance, of the world into which we are born.

Saschiz

This theme, where one happens to find oneself when the dramas of history take their place, hits hard again the next day. Rosie and I leave our kind hosts and wander on through Transylvania. We pass Mediaş and Sighişoara, with their utterly charming historic Germanic town centres. At the end of the day, I write in my diary:

> *The sun was getting low as we left Sighişoara. We travelled on a little way; the scenery was green and glowing in the slanting light. Eventually, we came to a halt in this village called Saschiz. It has a lovely church tower, is surrounded by vines on little hills, German-type houses, double-storeyed with huge barns and steep sloping roofs. We found lots of plum and apple trees and put our tent down in an orchard.*

But it is not so much the beauty of this ancient town that affects us as the human story that we now encounter. My diary:

I was up at 6am, before the sun was over the hills, and sat by a lovely view of the village waiting for the sun to light up the buildings through the vines. A kindly Saxon woman invited us in for breakfast, and her story brought tears to my eyes. She described how she was taken at sixteen years of age to work in a slave camp in Russia after the war. She worked underground in the mines until she was ill, her back was injured and, eventually, she came back to this German village in Romania. She married, but she cannot have children. Her family have left for Canada and Germany, but she and her husband cannot leave. They have lost their fifteen hectares of land, and their life, she said, is hardly worth living. Her whole empty life is haunted by what might have been, and what cannot be.

Meeting someone with a story like this really rubs home the consequences of the terrible war on individual lives, the war that ended around the time Rosie and I were born. I can quite imagine that many of the older people among the German families we are meeting were pleased enough when the war was going their way. The regrets came much too late. I reflect that guilt and innocence are intermingled in us all, and none of us choose where we are born.

No significant post – Bucharest

We have been travelling for two weeks now in Romania, and Bulgaria beckons. We leave Transylvania, hitchhiking south from Saschiz through Braşov and the flat oilfields around Ploieşti to Bucharest. Here, I am expecting to collect some post. My diary:

A thunderstorm began. I had been longing to hear from Bill. We crossed the city, and a nice young student helped us find the post office. There were not any letters. I was terribly disappointed, but nothing could be done.

What can be the explanation? There were no letters from my parents or other friends. Perhaps the Romanian post is not as reliable as that of other countries. There is no way to know. This is the first time I've been let down.

We must head on. My diary:

> *Despite the rain, we hitched away south towards the Bulgarian frontier. We asked at a house if we could camp in their garden. I am not sure if they are gypsies or not. They gave us mămăligă for the first time, made from maize corn and tasty with cheese. A boy and a policeman turned up, and although I got a fright, they were only curious.*

THE HOSPITALITY OF THE ROMANIANS

Later, I write about the kindness of Romanians in my article about Romania for *The Journal*:

> *While we were in Romania, we never had need to worry about being cold, hungry or left to walk when we were tired. In a land where strangers are few, and where the people are largely confined within their own borders, any visitor is treated with great friendliness and interest.*
>
> *Because of the curiosity and generosity of the people, we had to buy hardly any food and never once paid for a night's sleep. Our £5 proved plenty for a two-week journey through the country.*
>
> *Teenage girls flooded us with addresses and wanted us to correspond with them. The boys asked about The Beatles. Cars and lorries often queued up to give us rides.*
>
> *So, if any English person should chance to feel she is not appreciated at home, and would like to go on a confidence-building holiday, let her take off to Romania with a rucksack. She will certainly begin to feel she really is quite an extraordinary character.*

We are saying goodbye to Romania now. It feels emotional. We have experienced nothing but hospitality; the language is manageable; and the weather has been glorious. Leaving our gypsy hosts, our bellies full of the cheesy *mămăligă*, we walk towards the frontier.

CRUEL REGIME

In 1974, the paranoid regime of Ceaușescu passed the State Security Act which obliged Romanian citizens to report all contacts with foreigners to the Securitate, the State Security Police. It also became illegal to have foreigners to stay. Page 253 of the 1988 version of The Rough Guide to Eastern Europe advises visitors not to write down addresses but to memorise them and to act discreetly in communal hallways when going visiting. For foreigners who fall foul of the Securitate, immediate deportation is normal, whereas Romanians are liable to be fined, beaten up, sacked, expelled from college or imprisoned. Rosie and I visited in the early days of Ceaușescu's regime and encountered the natural hospitality of the people before the cruel rules were enforced.

Romania Chronology

1143	Saxons invited to Transylvania by King Géza II of Hungary
1458–1490	King Matthias Corvinus, resisted Turks
1718	Turks finally driven from Hungary and *Banat*
1700s	Swabians moved into *Banat* area after defeat of Turks
1941	Romania joined Nazi invasion of Russia
1943–1944	Romania 'liberated' from Nazi Germany by Soviets
1945	Dr Petru Groza led government
1947	Peasant resistance to collectivisation
1949	Communist Party rule established
1952	Gheorghe Gheorghiu-Dej, a Stalinist, becomes general secretary
1953	Death of Stalin
1956	Khrushchev's speech denounces crimes of Stalin, followed by 'Thaw'
1965	Death of Gheorghiu-Dej. Nicolae Ceauşescu becomes general secretary
1965–89	Human rights abuses and economic mismanagement
1967	**Author's visit to Romania**
1989	Berlin Wall comes down. Nicolae and Elena Ceauşescu tried and executed
2007	Romania joins EU
2014–2022	Cold War confrontations erupting between Russia, Ukraine and NATO

11

No Means Yes

BULGARIA CELEBRATES ITS FREEDOM

Rosie and I can proceed on foot from one country to another here. A great iron bridge crosses the Danube river between the Romanian town of Giurgiu and Ruse in Bulgaria. This is the 'Friendship Bridge', built with the aid of the Soviet Union. The Danube is a splendid river. I'd encountered it at Vienna, Budapest and the soon-to-be-drowned village of Donji Milanovac in Serbia. On its way to the Black Sea, the river here acts as the boundary between the Latin-speaking world of Romania and the Slavic-speaking Cyrillic world of Bulgaria.

Rosie and I walk out of Giurgiu, optimistically putting out our thumbs, and soon a car stops. My diary:

A friendly French couple offered to take us right to Varna, almost as far as we'd planned to go. Yippee! In a luxury Citroen car too. We crossed the Danube on the long iron bridge. Once in Bulgaria, everything was different. The houses were mostly plain, dull and square-shaped with red, tiled roofs, all the same.

Lots of donkeys were doing the work, where we'd seen none in Romania. We crossed the Dobruja, a wild semi-desert-like area of huge, flat hills and valleys which reminded me of Spain. There were women in Turkish or Muslim costume working in the collective farm fields.

We have arrived unexpectedly quickly and tumble right into Bulgarian surprises. In Varna, we see red flags and posters of Lenin everywhere in the seaside town. Noisy music is blaring uplifting songs. Well-dressed, smiling people are thronging the streets. We learn that tomorrow is the day the people are going to celebrate the Liberation of Bulgaria, when the Soviet armies crossed the border on the 9th of September 1944. We cannot know if the people really want to celebrate this event, but the authorities must think they do because they are going to have a holiday, whatever the political motive.

Soon after leaving Varna, we are picked up by a pair of men who have totally the wrong idea about what we are doing. They drive us up into the hills into a wild oak forest. We are not afraid of them because, although they are greasy and smarmy looking, they aren't behaving threateningly. At the first opportunity, we get out of the car and head back along the rough roads in the hot sunshine. It isn't a pleasant feeling to be half lost on the forested hills, but we head downhill, back to the coastal roads, aiming for a campsite in the village of Obzor.

Once there, we feel really tired. We must settle down for a little while. The shops will be closed for the next few days, thanks to the Liberation celebrations, so unless we want to be hungry, we must buy food. With no Bulgarian language, we manage with smiles and nods. This is very confusing. It takes a little while to work out that, in Bulgaria, head-nodding means 'no', and head-shaking means 'yes'. We buy bread, tomatoes, cheese, jam and sausages, our staple diet. And after that, we actually do what other seaside visitors do. We swim and dive under the waves and sunbathe until we are red and sore.

Truly, the next day really is a holiday. My diary:

We heard bagpipe music and went to investigate. A big group of people were seated around tables, celebrating their festival. A man was piping, and they were dancing. They grabbed us and made us dance, elbows round each other in a big circle, men, women and children. It was exciting, though for us the rhythm was difficult. Then they called us over and gave us wine and food. Later, when I was a bit dozy from the wine, I managed to learn the dance.

We want to get away from being seaside holidaymakers, however. Next day, we head south through the tourist areas around Slanchev Bryag and Burgas. This is the Costa Brava of the Black Sea, where those who can afford it from Poland, East Germany, Czechoslovakia, Hungary, Romania, and Bulgaria itself, may go for package holidays. Only a few westerners like us seem to be penetrating the visa system. We wonder if we'll see any Russians. It is the unknown interior of Communist Bulgaria that interests us, and we head west away from the seaside.

Three young Bulgarian men pick us up in their Mercedes, and the driver speaks French. They tell us jokes which don't amuse us, but I later record in my diary:

The little fish asked his father: "What's that big shadow up there?"

"Oh, that's Queen Mary's bottom!" he replied: "God save the King!"

And the other:

> *One Englishman is an Englishman. Two make a journey.*
> *One Frenchman is a Frenchman. Two make a scandal.*
> *One German is a German. Two make a war!*

The stereotypes still apply here in Bulgaria.

They take us to the town of Jambol and tell us we must register at the police station, but we don't. I've never done this willingly in any of the Iron Curtain countries and see no reason to do so now.

THE SOUTHERN FRINGE OF THE IRON CURTAIN

The image in our mind of the Iron Curtain is of running from north to south, dividing Europe from east to west. But here in Bulgaria, it runs west to east, separating Bulgaria from Greece and Turkey. Rosie and I decide we'll head for Elhovo, not far from the Turkish border, to have a look around.

The river Tundzha trickles southwards through the arid landscape, and we pause to take a photo of the view near the Elhovo road sign. A scrawny horse is drinking from the river, and a few sheep are nibbling at the brown grasses. Ahead lie factory roofs and a landscape of low houses. Our lift drops us off in the town.

"Who are you? Where are you going?" calls out a uniformed policeman. At least that is what we assume he is saying as we don't understand the language. My diary:

We were trying to photograph someone in national costume when we were whipped off to the police station. They asked us question after question, with utmost confusion on both sides. They couldn't understand why we'd come to this place, nor could we in retrospect, except that we'd decided to follow the road to its end and see a bit of the south of Bulgaria. Anyway, they let us go in the end, seeming to be satisfied, but we had sneaking fears we were being watched all the rest of the day.

Our blue, cardboard-covered British passports save the day. The police seem to have realised that there is no reason for us to leave Bulgaria illegally when we could just walk trouble-free over the border into Turkey. Yet girls like us, rucksacks on our backs, are so unusual that we have drawn attention to ourselves.

We head south along the traffic-free road out of town and are attracted by the brilliantly coloured entrance gateway of Elhovo's collective farm. Amid the brown and beige colours of the landscape, this really stands out. I must take a photo of this before anyone tries to stop me. Rosie approaches the gate, and soon, half a dozen dark-haired workmen appear. We are not trying to gain entrance which would surely bring police attention to us. The men are friendly and curious. This must be the first time that two young, fair-haired girls from an unknown land have shown up, unexpectedly, at the entrance to their pig farm.

While Rosie and the men exchange courtesies, I take my photo. Todor Zhivkov, president and father of Communist Bulgaria, tops the display. A larger-than-life painting of him dressed in a smart beige suit with red tie and white shoes shows him standing proudly in front of an industrial landscape with lots of electric pylons behind. 'Zhivkov means Progress', is the implied message. A red star is hoisted above him. On the other side of the gate is the 1917/1967 message emblazoned in black and red which we can work out means 'Fifty years since the Communist Revolution'.

Below Zhivkov is an enormous Diagrama. This huge poster displays a happy pig beside a block graph of numbers. Despite not knowing Bulgarian, we understand that this is the five-year plan for Elhovo's collective pig farm.

Last year, the farm produced 950 pigs. This year, 1967, it is expected to produce 1,350, nearly half as many again. Each year the number increases until, by 1970, the farm is expected to produce 2,400 pigs, more than twice the original number. Who knows how likely this is to happen? But there the numbers stand, bright and clear, and the workers are in no doubt as to the expectations as they approach the gates every working day.

I hand Rosie the camera, and she manages to take a photo of the Diagrama, with me tucked sneakily in one of the corners. Although the number of pigs to be produced at the farm may be a great state secret, none of the men seem to be worrying, and after more friendly chat, we go on our way.

"Look, Bridget," Rosie says. "Those women in the field." We see a long row of women bending over plants in a huge, green expanse. As we draw closer, we can see the brilliant red of peppers that they are plucking into the folds of their aprons before putting into boxes. Soon Rosie and the women are chuckling together.

"Da," they say, shaking their heads when she mimes a request for taking their photograph.

"No," Rosie says, shaking her head. Then she demonstrates 'yes' in English, nodding vigorously. Soon we are all nodding and shaking and giggling together, our yesses and nos all muddled up.

Most of them are wearing large white scarves, folded so as to hide their hair and create a shade over their eyes, and we deduce that this is the Turkish or Islamic tradition. One or two women have scarves revealing a little hair at the front, so they will not be Islamic. Skirts and blue cotton blouses are the style here. The women may be poorly paid for their work, but it is sociable and out in the fresh air. They press red peppers and tomatoes on us. Those few will never be missed when the boxes are weighed at the collective farm.

We meander along the little roads, back to Jambol and towards Sliven. Three good-looking older women are sitting in the sun on a bench outside their village house. The green trees of their gardens are to their rear, behind the wooden fence. They are suntanned, colourfully dressed and indicate a welcome to us. Two of them are spinning fleece. They hold the distaff with wool in their left hand and work it into yarn on their spindle with their right. They are handsome and friendly and so pleasantly occupied in this gentle autumn warmth that I feel all is not wrong in the world.

In another place, we come across a family group sitting in the shade of their house. The dark-haired smiling father, with his wife and young daughter, plus black-head-scarved granny, are threading tobacco leaves onto strings. They explain that the leaves will be hung up to dry. Perhaps the tobacco will be smoked among the family and neighbours, or perhaps sold. Either way, the effort expended in stringing it is obviously worth it and will bring them a little capitalist income.

No Flowers in the Valley of the Roses

Very tired one evening, we ask if we may camp in the garden of an old, whitewashed farmhouse near Sliven. The family won't permit such a thing, and we are soon invited into the house. From our comfortable bed, we have views over rubbish dumps to the smoking chimneys of Sliven and the jagged line of hills behind. I am glad that we have arrived at a town because I am running short of film, and I know that in the morning we must do some shopping.

I am unlucky. It simply is impossible, in this large Bulgarian industrial town in 1967, to buy film. I have no choice but to be very economical with what I have left.

We encounter a colourful group of gypsy girls and women bent over a long trough filled by a waterspout. The girls can't be more than twelve years old, scrubbing, soaping and rinsing. Barefoot, laughing and chattering, Rosie involves them in sign language conversation while I take a couple of photos. Several of them are gathering water, carrying it away in buckets yoked over their shoulders, while others carry jugs.

"Stop. Stop. It is forbidden to take photos of gypsies." A policeman arrives and shouts at me. "Your films will be taken from you when you get to the frontier." I recognise the international words *granitsa* for frontier and *tsigani* for gypsies. Rosie and I smile, act as though we don't understand, and the gypsy girls and women melt away. We sidle off, feeling lucky that we haven't yet again been escorted to a police station.

We wander on, hitchhiking towards the Valley of the Roses. There are no flowers in sight, only the smoking factory chimneys of Kazanlak and dull, drab cottages, their poverty often hidden by clambering vines. Then we spy some golden domes through the trees. Our driver tells us it is *Shipka Katedrala*, Shipka Cathedral. The gold is from Russia, he says, three kilograms sent by Khrushchev as a gift to Bulgaria in 1962.

We decide to camp here. The woodlands are green and inviting, compared to the brown, arid lands we've passed through. My diary:

> *A boy called Stefan came. He asked us to his house, and we were glad because it was chilly and windy. Lovely clean house and friendly parents. We had a huge meal, and we were so hungry. Fried eggs, butter, cheese, tomatoes. We talked. Stefan speaks some English. They were critical of their country and its ways. He earns seventy leva per month, which is about £10. "It is almost nothing," he explained, "with the cost of living as it is."*

Next day, Stefan takes us to the golden-towered church of Shipka. He and an official girl guide show us round, and later, I put what they tell us in my diary:

> *It was built in 1902 by the Russians to commemorate the defeat of the Turks in the Russo-Turkish wars 1877–1879. This was the original Liberation of Bulgaria by Russia, the first time they did it. There had been a great battle at Kazanlak. The Russian soldiers had to cross the Shipka*

Pass first, under dreadful winter conditions. It really is a dreadful pass – Rosie and I had crossed it the day before. The mountains are huge, high and steep, and the pass is probably thirty kilometres long. We had seen the memorial to the soldiers who died at top of the pass.

What interested Rosie and me was how Stefan and the guide accepted implicitly the friendship of the Russians and the rottenness of the Turks. They told us that crowds of Russian people visit here, which is very suitable as their country had donated the church. Even the beautiful, gilded cloths in the interior were sewn by Russian girls.

From this tour, I begin to realise that I've encountered a more friendly attitude to the Soviet Union among the Bulgarians than I've come across in the other Communist countries. It had been the same at the dancing and parties in Obzor where they had been celebrating how the Red Army drove away the German occupiers to 'liberate' Bulgaria. Perhaps the Bulgarians have a more accepting attitude to the Russians.

Rich or poor in Bulgaria

It is autumn now, and the weather is changing. This makes sleeping in our tent more uncomfortable. But should this be a problem? Not in Bulgaria. I write about this in my next article for *The Journal*, with the headline 'English? But you must be rich!':

By our own standards, my sister and I are living on a shoestring. Yet to those villagers, in the extreme isolation of the Balkan Mountains, anyone who could come from so far away as England must be steeped in wealth.

In fact, the only things of any value we possessed were our telescopic umbrella, our tiny petrol cooker and our tent.

We had £10 to last out our ten-day trip through Bulgaria. We were great curiosities to the people who lived in the outlying districts. But when they realised that we too were poor, almost as poor as themselves, they were positively amazed.

"From England ...on foot... without a car..." Losing inhibitions about their tiny humble homes, they would invite us to inspect and then admire their children and animals.

Owning no car, television or private property, the Bulgarian's home is centred on four walls and a garden. To be without a house, however simple, is to be totally desolate.

Money barely enters their lives. They get paid a small wage from work on the collective farm, but it is largely paid in kind: wheat, maize or milk. They produce most of their food from their garden, meat from the pigs, milk from a cow, sheep or buffalo, eggs and flesh from the chickens.

To make a journey away from home is almost unheard of. One can't take one's garden along.

To the Bulgarian peasant, unfamiliar with such Western phenomena as hippies, Boy Scouts, mountain walking for pleasure, youth hostels or plain, simple travel on a low income, travellers like us are from a different world, not just from the other side of Europe.

"Please take a photograph of my baby," a young Bulgarian wife begged us as we stopped to rest in the hot autumn sunshine. The nine-month-old boy gazed at us with huge, brown eyes from his perch in his mother's arms.

The young woman was so proud of him we hadn't the heart to refuse. So, from our dwindling supply of film, we prepared to take a picture.

This was a great ceremonial process. Mother and baby disappeared into the cottage, reappearing some time later with sleekly brushed hair, shining faces and Sunday best clothes. The little boy was clad in a light blue satin suit and the mother in a black dress.

Oh dear, this will never do, I thought to myself. My sister went up to our models, ruffled their hair a little, to their considerable surprise, then stood beside me making faces at them to make them laugh.

Click. I took the picture.

"Look around you," said Rosie suddenly. "They all want their photographs taken."

Peering out of doorways and garden gates, curiously ambling along in our direction, were groups of women and children. Little faces, brown and healthy from a season of sunshine, smiled endearingly at us. Mothers pushed their children forward and signalled to us to take their pictures. We had to apologise and say the film was finished, but we felt incredibly mean and selfish.

I take the mother's address. Apart from that, we can do no more than hope that our smiles will leave them with a feeling of friendliness from strangers and that they will have something to talk about at the end of the day.

GABROVO – THE MANCHESTER OF BULGARIA

This is such a changeable country. After we left Stefan at Shipka, we had a lift which took us over the pass and down to the rainy other side of the hills. My diary:

Gabrovo, the Manchester of Bulgaria, and what a place! Like most of these towns, a lovely, respectable centre, flower gardens, fountains, statues, big shops and a huge town hall or Communist Party centre. Apart from that, shabby shops, scruffy places, cobblers, tiny cloth factories and miles of sprawling houses, some not too poor but many simply awful, mud and dirt right up to doorways, no pavements, unpainted, nothing but slums. Although, in our experience, such houses are usually much better kept inside than out. Still, even on main roads, conditions are awful. Huge factories, filthy, smoky muddy establishments, never painted, bearing enormous pictures of Lenin and the Communist Party leader Zhivkov, red flag and the Bulgarian red, green and white flag gaily flying as if to say: "Can't you see what a wonderful factory this is?"

After Gabrovo, we crossed over some lovely mountains, green pasture, lands sweeping up to rows and rows of wooded mountains receding blue into the distance, gleaming from the recent rain, cows grazing here and there, with women spinning as they guarded them. In one village, we passed Turkish women with brilliant scarlet in their costumes.

At last, we decided to camp. We chose a colourful village in the blue mountains. Had the usual crowd of interested observers as we pitched our tent in someone's garden. Were presented with tomatoes, a delicious crispy cucumber and a huge melon which we ate with our supper. On this side of the Balkans, nearing Sofia, everything is much greener and more attractive, and not so poor.

It is a perfect camping spot.

NASTY HAPPENINGS IN THE NIGHT

Rosie and I are settling down to sleep in our tiny tent when we are awakened by the sound of men singing drunkenly at the gate near the tent.

We keep still. A few moments later, the sounds become louder. We hear whispering around the tent and can see shadows. We arm ourselves with opened safety pins and the point of our umbrella. Hands begin to creep under the groundsheet. We are becoming angry. I get the camera and fit a flashbulb in. When they are getting really annoying, I open the tent and take a picture of the men as they flee from us, saying that in the morning I am taking it to the police.

They leave then, and we try to go back to sleep. A bit later, we hear more whispering around the tent. Two boys are crouching outside, trying to get friendly. I tell them in no uncertain terms to go. They don't. So I get out and head for the farmhouse to fetch the farmer, but I can't open the gate. He must have heard the noise because his light goes on, and this frightens the young men, so they leave. But they come back. I say if they don't go, I'll scream, and I do, and they leave again.

I go back into the tent, and all is quiet for a while. Rosie and I are really tired and hope that is all for the night. But no – we hear the noises again. Someone is trying to unzip the tent. I am beginning to recognise this fat young man. I am really angry. I get out of my blanket and threaten to hit him with the umbrella if he doesn't go. He begins to grab me. I chase him to the gate and hit him across the head with the umbrella. But he is stronger and pushes me to the ground. I am fighting him and screaming. Rosie comes up and we scream and scream. The dogs begin barking. The family come out from the house and the attackers disappear. We are taken into the house and given a nice warm bed. Our kind rescuers talk and talk, while we are both exhausted and longing to sleep.

In the morning, we wake to a beautiful day, and I write up the events of the past night in my diary. We have slept so soundly that it all feels like a dream pushed to the back of our minds, but I say to Rosie that if I see that man again, I'll go for him.

The family give us a delicious breakfast of home-made bread, fresh eggs, cheese from sheep's milk, tomatoes, cucumber and paprika from their garden. It is served with fresh buffalo milk and finished off with melon. A policeman turns up while we are eating, and he and the farmer speak together quietly.

It is time for us to leave, and one of the young married women of the family walks with us into the village.

When we get there, we see a crowd of people congregating around the policeman. Rosie wants to buy some cigarettes and lurking inside the shop is my assailant of the night before. We recognise the sleazy look in his eyes. He begins to walk quickly away down the street, and Rosie says: "It's him – go and get him!" Although people are crowding round, I don't hesitate. I chase him. I slap him over the face once or twice with my bag and pull his hair. He tries to get away, but I chase him again. Then he grabs me, and we begin to fight. The policeman comes rushing up and thumps him over the head with his bag and makes us both stop.

This is a serious situation and must be taken to an official level. This being 1960s Bulgaria, there are no handy police cars to be summoned. We are trundled onto a public bus to the town of Botevgrad seven kilometres away, our assailant, the policeman, Rosie and me. The unpleasant young man is fussing over his shirt which I have torn.

At the police station we are taken upstairs to report to the lieutenant. He calls a woman who has some sort of authority. I think she is probably a local Communist Party official. She speaks English and addresses us kindly. Both sides are questioned about what happened. We can't understand what our assailant tells the two officials, but they do not appear to be impressed.

"There are rules in this country, and he must be punished," the lieutenant tells us. But we are beginning to feel that the rogue has been humiliated enough and that we don't want any more trouble. In the end, they say they will not press charges if we really don't want it.

"Young men in Bulgaria are not used to girls like you," the woman tells us. "They wrongly interpreted what you were doing."

She is anxious that we do not leave the country with a bad impression, and we reassure her that we have been treated kindly through all our travels in Bulgaria. We know that such an incident could happen anywhere and tell her so. In the end, we leave the police station, after very reluctantly agreeing to shake hands with the loathsome young man and with me feeling abashed at my ungainly behaviour.

IN THE CAPITAL SOFIA

"There must still be Turkish people in Bulgaria who want to go to a mosque," Rosie comments. We are gazing through the crowds of a busy street in Sofia at a minaret adjoining the dome of a great mosque. We have little experience of Islam, and although we have chatted with Turkish women in the field at Elhovo, we have found few reminders of the five hundred years of Ottoman rule. The workmen in the mosque allow us to peep inside. We learn that it dates back to 1576.

Busy shoppers are crowding the streets. We pass the huge public baths and walk through the old market. Resting on a seat under a tree, we are wondering where we will spend our last night in Bulgaria. Soon we are chatting with a woman, and in a mixture of my Serbian, her Bulgarian and English, we realise we have been invited to her house. We try to negotiate a price, but typically she refuses any money. We take a rattling tram to her suburban house in a green residential area. It is quite unlike anything that we had expected, thinking she would live in one of the massive blocks of socialist-era flats.

"Three families live in this one house, sharing six rooms," Nedelya explains. She and her husband and two children have one room, and we are to sleep in a bed which folds out from under a sofa in the living space. Water is carried in from the tap in the garden.

"We are saving money for a flat in a block," Nedelya tells us.

In the evening, we are treated to a meal which has been cooked in the kitchen which is a shed in the yard. It seems that half of Sofia arrives, to meet us and to ask us questions while we eat. We know that our hosts will not accept payment, so we decide that the only way to repay this hospitality is to play a trick. In the morning, before we leave, we hide our remaining Bulgarian money under a pillow. Rosie writes a note in capital letters in English: FOR THE CHILDREN.

The autumn weather reminds us that our gypsy summer days must come to an end. We have managed to spend ten days in Bulgaria without needing to go over our £10. We are leaving what for me is the sixth Communist country of Eastern Europe I have visited. They are all so different. In Bulgaria we have felt a southern, almost Mediterranean, atmosphere. I am missing the man I left behind in Munich. Ten days is enough. We must return north.

OVER THE LINE

The Bulgarian border guards are indifferent to us. "*Dovizdane.*" Goodbye, we manage to say. Our blue passports make it easy, but it would not be the same for Nedelya and her family, or for Stefan and his friends. Rosie and I know that we are crossing an inflexible line.

We pass into Yugoslavia, the border guards stamping our passports relaxedly, and take a lift to a town called Aleksinac where we camp in a roadside field. It begins to pour with rain, and the tent falls down into the mud twice during the night. Next morning, we are on our way as far as the hostel in Belgrade, where we manage to recuperate. From there, we head for the Yugoslavian republic of Slovenia, bordering Austria, and arrive near the frontier in the same day, camping once again in a field.

Now we are crossing the Iron Curtain once again, heading out to the west. I have learned that it is not so difficult for Yugoslavian people living under their milder version of Communism to move in and out of their country. I remember Svetlana from Ljubljana who worked with me in the Agfa factory in Munich. And I know also that people from Eastern bloc countries may visit Yugoslavia under certain conditions. I have no knowledge about how difficult it can be for them, once in Yugoslavia, to leave the country as we are doing. There certainly must be restrictions or this would be a well-known way out.

"*Dovidenja*," we try as we leave the Yugoslavian frontier guards and are surprised when they reply "*Adijo*," which sounds like Italian or French Adieu.

We walk across the no man's land. Then, it is *Guten Tag* at the Austrian frontier. We accept a lift from two Turkish men who take us across the Austrian mountains to the outskirts of Munich. Things are beginning to feel familiar. How easy it all seems. By late evening, one more short lift takes us to the Thalkirchen Campingplatz.

"Bridget, Rosie," Mary cries. "Damien, look who's here!" They gather around, and amid hugs and explanations, they tell me that Bill is at the US army hotel. I will meet him tomorrow.

The visit to Bulgaria has been a landmark, and now the gypsy summer days are ending. Mary and Damien will soon be hitchhiking away to Israel. Rosie is returning to a new job in England. Mary's sister Liz and my brother have already headed back home. Bill has saved up some money. His own native land, the United States, is making a demand on him which he must escape. There is always politics, always impending war. I am no longer thinking about Israel. We must flee to the safety of the UK. To get there, we have a journey to make back through the Communist east, passing once again through Tito's Yugoslavia.

BULGARIA CHRONOLOGY

1396–1878	Ottoman Turkish rule of Bulgaria
1877–78	Russo-Turkish war reduces Ottoman rule in Bulgaria
1914–1918	Bulgaria allied to Germany in both World Wars
1939–1945	
1944	Soviet army crosses Danube into Bulgaria 8 and 9 September
1946	Communist state established, persecutions, collectivisation, industrialisation
1954	Todor Zhivkov becomes leader
1953	Death of Stalin
1956	Khrushchev's speech denounces crimes of Stalin, followed by 'Thaw'
1967	**Author's visit to Bulgaria**
1989	Berlin Wall comes down. Revolutions in all Eastern European Communist states
1990	First free elections in Bulgaria
2004	Bulgaria joins NATO
2007	Bulgaria joins EU
2014–2022	Cold War confrontations erupting between Russia, Ukraine and NATO

12

Tito's Land Is Holding Together

Yugoslavia, November 1967

Belgrade to Sarajevo

Bill and I are in Belgrade market. We have hurried here because he was called up, once again, by the US army. For five years after completing his compulsory draft, young American men like him remain on call as 'reserves'. When he came to Europe, he was obliged to register with a unit in Germany. Now the unit must be short of men, and they require him to do two more years' active military service 'for the duration of the conflict', the ongoing Vietnam war. He received his new call-up papers in Munich a few days ago. The sympathetic young man in the American Express office saw Bill's shock when he opened the letter and said he would return it as 'opened in error'. So now we are fleeing from the clutches of the American army, through a Communist land. We have come to Belgrade to collect the Hungary and Belgrade diaries I'd left in the hostel. The money he has saved from his earnings at the US army hotel is all carefully changed into $10 notes.

We change some money into Yugoslavian dinars. Bill buys himself a sheepskin hat in the market, and as I have a black fur one, we make a good pair. He buys some shoes for 6,800 dinars, while I am still contented with my usual flip-flops. A woman sitting on the ground selling wooden spoons calls me a *Deutsches Schwein*, a German pig, and certainly it was tactless of me to take a photograph of her without permission.

We leave Belgrade the next day, heading for the coast as the first step on our return journey to England. Our plan is to hitchhike 365 kilometres to Sarajevo in one day. My diary:

Our first lift took us to Šabac in a very roundabout way. We had a puncture in the middle of nowhere, in-between huge collective sugar beet fields. The land was flat and not very interesting, with the houses and villages truly isolated. Hardly any cars were passing through, and there was not even a television aerial to be seen. The people seemed to be living a sort of outback life. The settlement patterns and cottages were something like Vojvodina but more primitive, with less Hungarian influence. Occasional cottages were Turkish in style. We passed an enormous smoky sugar beet factory. Eventually, we arrived in Loznica, another backwards town with many enormous factories and new blocks of flats. It smelled like Communism, smoky, dowdy, trying to get somewhere amid the muck. We camped in an orchard, listening to noises of pigs, sheep and cows, very tired because we have a lot of weight to carry. We've spent all day travelling a hundred kilometres.

CROSSING INTO BOSNIA

This land feels unbelievably remote from civilisation. My diary:

The cars got fewer as the countryside got wilder and lovelier. By midday, we'd walked in the rain, lost gloves and gone back for them and progressed about twenty kilometres. Then we arrived at a Muslim town called Zvornik where there were mosques and people in Muslim costumes. We are now in Bosnia, in the valley of the river Drina. A fantastic old castle – is it Turkish? – on the hilltop. We bought a lot of sweet Turkish cakes and lemonade, and the man only charged us two hundred dinars. On we went, but no luck with lifts. About 3pm, a lorry picked us up. We drove along the Drina valley where a huge dam had been built and drowned the valley. Lovely mountains, golden trees, shining water. The road became a stony track. We got dropped off at an outback mountain village. Here is a sign, Sarajevo 146 kilometres! A long way yet to go.

On this day, we met a Muslim postman. He sat and talked with us awhile. Before he left, he astounded us by giving us ten thousand dinars. We couldn't refuse. He was only a poor man. How much percentage of his wage would that be? He was a saint. His kindness as an example of practising Islam will remain in my mind for years.

The road was following the Drinjača river. Our last lift took us to Milići, a real mountain village. There were many attractive peasant cottages, painted white, with wooden, steep shingle roofs, which looked like hats on little faces with two windows for eyes and the door the mouth. It is getting dark early now, so we had no choice but to set up camp for the night. We bought plenty of food in the village and camped beside the river, a twinkling, sparkly clean stream.

We were safely asleep when we heard footsteps outside our tent. They stopped, silently. We were frightened of bandits in this middle-of-nowhere place, but the footsteps faded away.

When we wake up in the morning, and clamber out of our tent, the people at the nearby house have been wondering who we are. We make friendly gestures and are invited to have breakfast in the garden area in front of their 'little hat' house. My diary:

> *The son is a policeman in Belgrade, here on holiday with his family. He encourages Bill to drink lots of little glasses of šljivovica, plum brandy, which will certainly set him up for the day. I have hot milk. They tell us they are part of a zadruga, which I understand to be a traditional patriarchal clan but which may now have evolved into a communal collective farm.*

After leaving them, we get a lift to Vlasenica, the last stage on an asphalt road. It is market day. My diary:

> *Vlasenica is a Muslim town on top of a hill, on the watershed between the Danube and the Mediterranean. We went to see the stock sale. People were mainly wearing baggy Muslim*

costumes, though some were obviously Serbians. The village was truly picturesque, with little hat houses clambering up hills on cobbled paths, and the marketplace in the centre had a lovely view over the mountains. It was a totally unspoilt village, like a scene from Baghdad. I bought a wooden pipe for two hundred dinars, and it is in tune.

As we amble on towards Sarajevo, our likelihood of getting lifts is minimal because only about six vehicles pass us in three hours, and all are full of animals. Eventually, however, we do get a lift with a kind woman. My diary:

Fantastic scenery, through gorges, along a high mountain plateau. It was dark when we arrived in Sarajevo, looking most picturesque, all set on little hills with lights. We looked forward to exploring it next day. We found a little eating place and had a long-awaited meal. Bill had beefsteak, and I had cheese omelette, chips and salad. At the campsite, we were turned away by the gatekeeper. "Fermée! Geschlossen!" Closed. So, we saved the money and camped on some waste ground.

This is not a good time to look at the sights of Sarajevo because it has been raining all night and we are soaked through. We finally drag ourselves out of the tent into the rain and bitter cold. My diary:

We had some coffee and a bite to eat in Sarajevo and then took a tram out of town. Some 'Ten-Ton Tessie' stood on my toes, which were freezing, and I only had my flip-flops on. We thought we'd never get a lift, but at last we did, going the whole 133 kilometres to Mostar. We passed through lovely scenery, now covered in snow! We were travelling down the

Neretva valley, a dam there empty because of lack of rain. Fantastic karst limestone gorges, at one place a waterfall spurting out of a rock. It took us until 4pm to get to Mostar, where it was sunny but bitter cold. We just didn't fancy getting out the soggy tent and sleeping bag, so we got a room for three thousand dinars. A room! With a big, cosy bed. We had a hot bath too. How long it seemed since we'd been clean and cosy at night instead of being huddled in our faithful but damp sleeping bag and tent!

Next morning, we look around the town, white limestone mosques and cobbled streets with tiny houses and a fantastic bridge over the Neretva river. We visit the inside of a mosque founded in 1677, carved and painted and from which there are lovely views.

From Mostar, we have a series of small lifts down to the Adriatic where the Neretva river enters the sea. From there, we have a hair-raising ride in a lorry along the winding, narrow coastal road, all the way to Split. After a quick glimpse of the Roman marketplace, we leave, not wanting to spend our small reserves of money in the coastal region where prices are higher. Bit by bit, short lifts of sometimes twenty-five kilometres at a time, we are getting closer to the Austrian frontier where we will leave Yugoslavia. We are elated when an American jeep stops. The driver is offering us a lift all the way to Zagreb, the capital city of Croatia. My diary:

We drove across the mountains by a lonely road across the wildest, highest limestone peaks in Yugoslavia, by ghostly moonlight which exposed the grey, cracking rocks. A moonscape. Few people lived there. An occasional house. The driver told us that the houses have enormous water storage tanks built under them, which have to last from snowmelt and odd rainfall. For there is no surface water at all for almost all of the year. The nearest village from some of those houses must be a day's walk on foot, along a rough track, or almost a day on a cart. None of the houses looked wealthy enough to have a car.

Once we crossed over the highest point – a mountain like Snowdon rising directly from the sea at 1,591 metres – the other side wasn't quite so desolate. There were a few trees and some more houses. We passed the Plitvice Lakes but couldn't see much in the moonlight.

YUGOSLAVIAN FAREWELL

This is a very long lift, and because our driver speaks good English, I memorise much of what he tells us and write it later in my diary. It summarises one man's opinion of life in Tito's Yugoslavia of 1967:

"I can tell you that life is much better now than in the Stalin era. Communist and capitalist countries are becoming more like

each other. Russia westernises, decentralises and introduces incentives and private initiatives. In the West, you have socialisation, trade unionism, welfare schemes for health, housing and pensions. As for religion, the party members attend church at Christmas. Although a true Communist is automatically atheist, many are still sentimentally religious.

"In the factories, workers' councils sometimes advertise their products to boost sales. Formerly there was no need (not a matter of principles) for advertising as there was only one product to be had anyway.

"As for travel abroad, passports are easily available. There is a $20 allowance of foreign currency per person which can be taken out. Although it is illegal, everyone obtains more, usually by exchange with visiting tourists.

"Working abroad is always allowed. Many non-skilled leave to work in England, the USA, Germany or France. Although many return, there is a large drain of professional people who stay away. This is a problem.

"We have many foreign visitors now. The Russians buy cigarettes, chocolates and nylon stockings. Czechs, who cannot get many Yugoslavian dinars, exchange crystal and porcelain for food and dinars once here. Of course, it is illegal, but which farmer would refuse a Czech who offered a lovely piece of crystal for some potatoes and tomatoes and bread?

"Education here from ages seven to fifteen is compulsory. We have three universities, in Ljubljana, Belgrade and Zagreb, and faculties at Skopje, Split and Sarajevo. Young people accept Yugoslavian Communism."

At the end of a long day, with the weather becoming foggy and bitter cold, this kind driver takes us to a youth hostel in Zagreb. He insists to the unwelcoming man at the desk that we be given a room, and we bid him a grateful goodbye. We are taken to a room like a prison cell with a cement floor on which we are supposed to sleep. Miserable, tired, hungry and cold, we prefer to camp outside. Over the night, the damp soaks through under the trees; the fog penetrates the cocoon in our tent, and a heavy crust of frost coats the outside.

As we drag ourselves out into the freezing morning, we see the people walking by on their way to work. They are clad in boots and furs while we'd been sleeping outside, on the ground, in ordinary clothes. We spend the last of our Yugoslavian money on a good breakfast of scrambled eggs and hitch away along the foggy Autobahn.

At the departure barrier between Yugoslavia and Austria, the border guard looks cursorily at our passports. "*Dovidenja,*" Goodbye, he says, and we reply likewise. We are crossing the Iron Curtain, not so rigid and frightening here as on other frontiers. We are leaving the land where, our driver had reassured us, young people accept Yugoslavian Communism.

Mine has been a long journey for over a year, exploring the world where half of Europe's population is trapped behind the Iron Curtain. I have learned that the people I met have the same aspirations as those on the western side, and many would like to leave, at the very least for a visit. But except for Yugoslavians, most cannot do this. They have to make the best of things within the Communist system. I am leaving them all behind.

In August 1966, the guard on my way into East Germany told me I couldn't walk in there. But I managed to get in, and continued on foot, hitchhiking and walking with my Union Jack. I have crossed the Iron Curtain back and forth several times, as well as many internal boundaries between Poland in the north and Yugoslavia in the south.

Now Bill and I are showing our passports at the Yugoslavian frontier. They are our tickets to freedom into the West. We have our reasons for escaping. The weather is wintry, cold and inhospitable to people on foot like us. We must flee to England where the US army may not be able to keep track of Bill. *Dovidenja.* Goodbye.

13

On the Aeroplane

JANUARY 1968

ESCAPING

I am looking out of the window of one of Icelandair's propeller-driven airliners in January 1968. We are crossing over the snow-covered mountains of Greenland, from which glaciers are slowly moving, blending in with the sea ice. We are now husband and wife, and heading west. This is the cheapest way from the UK to the United States and is my first experience of flying.

We have escaped from the grasp of the US army by arranging a quick marriage in England. Claiming that a postal strike had been responsible for loss of contact with the German base, Bill registered himself with the army unit in the UK. As a married man, he is unlikely to be called up. The ruse seems to have worked, and we are blissfully contented in our new roles.

Every minute we fly further and further westwards, leaving behind the continent of Europe, divided from north to south by the militarised barrier of the Iron Curtain.

It is almost two years since I was tempted across, travelling into the closed land of Poland. I was a young woman with little idea of what to find, adventurous, curious, often unsure of myself. Behind that electrified barrier, with its mined strips and armed guards, I have left a trail of friends.

In Poland are Marian, Julo, Dionysus and Tom, the last who, despite his privileged student life, would love nothing more than to be able to drive a car.

In Hungary are the Gulyás family, whose only son Henry had escaped in the 1956 revolution, leaving them devastated, yet who were endlessly hospitable to me.

In Yugoslavia, I have left behind Dushko, Ibrahim, Ildico and my Albanian roommates who will be continuing their studies in Belgrade, and Silvy with his family in Subotica. I have learned how well my acquaintances from the different regions of Yugoslavia mingled and got along. The wars of the past seem as though they could never happen again.

In the remote corner of Slovakia are the peasant families who fed me raspberry tea and a wrinkly apple at Easter. Along the Czech militarised frontier is Cheb, where Petar and I inadvertently electrified the Iron Curtain.

Then there are the people Rosie and I met in Romania, the Staffend family, who would like to emigrate to East Germany, and the shepherds in the mountains who will be taking the sheep up again when summer beckons. There are the dancing Bulgarians by the Black Sea and the women harvesting the peppers in the sunburnt fields of the collective farm.

All their lives are being played out amid the inculturation, the oppression and propaganda of Communism.

I have made my journeys behind the Iron Curtain, and now, perhaps, like my friends and my sister in England, I will begin to settle into married life, make a home and have a job as a geography teacher.

We are flying towards a contrasting world where we will be bombarded with the messages of capitalism, encouraging us to be consumers, to buy, buy, buy. There is always some kind of indoctrination at work. I turn away from the window and glance at the face of the man I love. We smile at each other, the same smiles as on that first evening in Munich across the table. Holding hands, we enjoy the moment as we fly through the air between one world and another.

14

Epilogue

MARCH 2023

It is over fifty years since I made those journeys. I travelled around during what looks, in retrospect, like an interlude of relative calm: after Stalin's death in 1953 but before Solidarity in the 1980s; after the 1956 Hungarian Revolution but before the 1968 Prague Spring; during the rule of Tito but before the Balkan Wars; after Ceauşescu's election but before his worst abuses from the mid-1960s.

Since 1989, the fall of the Berlin Wall and the collapse of Communism in Europe, the Iron Curtain no longer exists. Generations of Eastern Europeans are growing up in an entirely different world. Yet, as I write, in March 2023, Russia has moved into Ukraine and NATO countries are on alert. East and West face each other once again. The Cold War continues to affect all our lives.

Bibliography

The books below are ones I read or consulted while writing this book. I knew virtually nothing about these matters at the time of my travels.

GENERAL INTEREST

Anne Applebaum, *Iron Curtain*, Penguin Books, 2013. First-class summary of how Communist regimes took control of Eastern European countries 1944–1956. Particularly good chapter on ethnic cleansing, which applies to families like Cesary's in Wrocław and the farmers near Kunowice.

Anne Applebaum, *Between East and West*, Penguin, Penguin, 1994, 2015. She travelled from the Baltics to the Black Sea just after the collapse of the Soviet Union. A particularly useful section on little-known Ruthenia, whose famous modern sons are Robert Maxwell and the family of Andy Warhol.

Anthony Bailey, *Along the Edge of the Forest: An Iron Curtain Journey*, Faber & Faber, 1983. He followed the boundary from the Baltic to the Adriatic, mostly by car, at times on foot. He affirmed what the border guard had shouted at me. 'One is not allowed to ride into the DDR on a bike or enter it on foot', page 27.

Isabel Fonseca, *Bury Me Standing: The Gypsies and Their Journey*, Vintage, 1995. Frighteningly informative and particularly good on Roma/ Gypsies in the immediate collapse of Communism in the early 1990s.

Tony Judt, *Postwar: A History of Europe Since 1945*, Vintage, 2010. Reading this is like reliving my own or any post-war baby's personal history. Chapter 13, 'The End of the Affair', specialises in the Eastern European regimes at the time I was there. His book contains informative details about Auschwitz, the Berlin Wall and the Cheb area of Czechoslovakia.

Timothy Phillips, *The Curtain and The Wall*, Granta, 2022. An inspiring and up-to-date story of a journey from the Arctic, through Europe as far as Azerbaijan. The author meets those who lived along the Iron Curtain boundary, hears their stories past and present, and informs the reader of little-known background information.

Dan Richardson and Jill Denton, *The Rough Guide to Eastern Europe*, Harrap Columbus, 1988. This book is about Hungary, Romania and Bulgaria, dating before the revolutions of 1989. Thus, it contains advice to travellers when those countries were under Communism and makes clear the fearful consequences for Romanian citizens who talk to or play host to westerners.

Dean S Rugg, *Eastern Europe (World Landscapes)*, Longman, 1985. Includes descriptions of the landscapes and their historical development while Communism was still extant in Eastern Europe. Excellent chapter on how German speakers moved east, establishing municipal cultures between 950 and 1350 AD.

Timothy Snyder, *Bloodlands*, Vintage, 2010. This is for anyone who wants to understand the terrifying full story of Eastern Poland, Ukraine, Belarus and the Baltic states under Hitler and Stalin.

Harriet Wanklyn, *The Eastern Marchlands of Europe*, George Philip, 1941. Written when Hitler's Reich was at its peak, this geography book reflects the international boundaries and standards of 1939 and 1940. Good summaries of history and landscape.

THE COLLAPSE OF THE COMMUNIST REGIMES IMMEDIATELY AFTER 1989

Timothy Garton Ash, *We the People: Revolution of '89*, Granta, 1990. Reprinted with an updated chapter, as *The Magic Lantern: The Revolution of '89*, Atlantic Books, 2019. My favourite quote: 'Perhaps the most difficult thing of all for the historian to recapture is the sense of what, at a given historical moment, people did not know about the future', page 23.

David Selbourne, *Death of the Dark Hero, Eastern Europe*, 1987–1990, Jonathan Cape, 1990. Written after the fall of the Berlin Wall in 1989 but before the Soviet Union collapsed in 1921.

John Simpson, *Despatches from the Barricades*, Hutchison, 1990. Useful summary of background to Eastern European Communism and on-the-spot reports of the actual collapse in 1989.

ABOUT OŚWĘCIM AND CONCENTRATION CAMPS

Thomas Buergenthal, *A Lucky Child: A Memoir of Surviving Auschwitz as a Young Boy*, first published 2007. Profile Books, 2009.

Primo Levi, *If This Is a Man / The Truce*, first published in Italian, 1958. Abacus, 1987.

Primo Levi, *The Drowned and the Saved*, first published in Italian, 1986. Abacus, 1989. If I had been able to read this, and the above, before my 1966 travels, I would have mingled with Germans with less equanimity.

Margarete Buber-Neumann, *Under Two Dictators: Prisoner of Stalin and Hitler*, first published 1949, Pimlico, 2008. This is a poignant, classic example of the concentration camps from the point of view of a woman.

Nikolaus Wachsmann, *KL: A History of the Nazi Concentration Camps*, Little Brown, 2015. Thorough. Devastating.

Elie Wiesel, *Night*, originally written 1958. Penguin books, 1985. Another story of a boy telling how he and the Jews were taken from his home town in northern Hungary in 1944 as the war was ending. Has parallels with Imre Gulyás's story about Salomon.

POLAND

Marcel Krueger, *Babushka's Journey*, I B Tauris, 2018. A grandson follows the journey of his grandmother, a young German girl, from a farming family in East Prussia, which became the Masurian lake district of Poland after the war. During the Russian invasion in 1945, she was taken into camps deep in the Soviet Union, before later being rehabilitated in West Germany.

Jonathan Bousfield and Mark Salter, *The Rough Guide to Poland*. This contains very useful summaries of Poland's fluid and complex history. My copy is the seventh edition, 2009.

GERMANY

Anonymous, *A Woman in Berlin, my edition*, Virago, 2005. A woman's diary giving a harrowing account of the first few weeks after the arrival of the Soviet army in Berlin in April 1945.

Christabel Bielenberg, *The Past is Myself*, Corgi, 1970. The account of an English woman who married a German citizen and lived there between 1932–1945. An insider view of life in Nazi Germany.

R M Douglas: *Orderly and Humane: The Expulsion of the Germans After the Second World War*, Yale, 2012. Relevant to my visit to Hohenberg and to the many German, or part-German, people I encountered in various countries. A surprising account of the unnecessary suffering of German minority populations, who were mainly women, children and the elderly.

Astrid M Eckert, *West Germany and the Iron Curtain*, Oxford, 2019. Detailed and readable, focusing on the inter-German borderlands. Chapter on Iron Curtain 'tourism' applicable to my travels.

Anna Funder, *Stasiland*, Granta, 2003. This readable account relates the human stories of those who inflicted, or suffered, the pain of the *Deutsche Demokratische Republik*, the DDR.

Edith Sheffer, *Burned Bridge: How East and West Germans Made the Iron Curtain*, Oxford, 2011. A detailed account of the lives of people in Sonneberg, East Germany, and Neustadt, West Germany, separated by the Iron Curtain, which parallels that of the villagers of Posseck and Nentschau in my story.

CZECHOSLOVAKIA

Martha Gellhorn, *A Stricken Field*, University of Chicago Press, 1968. Describes the refugees fleeing towards Prague as Hitler began invading the Sudetenland in 1938. Sympathetic to Communism as she saw it at that time.

John Keane, *Vaclav Havel: A Political Tragedy in Six Acts*, Bloomsbury, 1999. Through the story of Havel, the reader can grasp the reality of everyday life in Czechoslovakia and the events of the Prague Spring.

Josef Škvorecký, *The Bass Saxophone*, Picador, 1980. Two short stories about jazz, love and revenge, written in 1963 and 1967 in Czechoslovakia. The author is a young musician, writing with strong imagery of the Nazi and then Communist era.

Rob Humphreys, *The Rough Guide to the Czech and Slovak Republics*, 2002. Contains a useful summary of the complex history of the two present-day nations and a useful description of the post-war city of Cheb on page 232.

HUNGARY

C A Macartney, *Hungary: A Short History*, Edinburgh University Press, 1962. If you want to cope with the endless ramifications and squabbles of the warlords during Hungary's history, I'd recommend it. I used it to learn about the Turkish invasions.

Anna Robertson, *No Going Back to Moldova*, Mainstream Publishing, 1987. Starting with a German/Hungarian childhood in the Austro-Hungarian empire, near the Danube, her story goes through the break-up of the empire, between wars when the village of Moldova finds itself in Romania, the Second World War, and then to post-war Communism. Her German-speaking family lived through all those changes.

Charles Hebbert, Norm Longley and Dan Richardson, *The Rough Guide to Hungary*, 2005. Contains a helpful summary of the country's complex history, as well as regional information.

YUGOSLAVIA

Peter Batty, *Hoodwinking Churchill*, Shepheard Walwyn, 2001. Detailed description of Tito's rise and fall. None of the players come out with honour: Tito and the Partisans, the Croats, Muslims and all other minorities, the Catholic and Orthodox churches, the Nazis, British, Soviets or Americans. All participated in atrocious cruelties.

Milovan Djilas, *Conversations with Stalin*, 1962. Pelican 1969. Originally a committed Communist, here he explains his gradual doubts and disillusion and his personal meetings with Stalin. Djilas fell out with Tito and was frequently imprisoned for his writings. When I was in Belgrade in January 1966, he had just been released from prison.

Slavenka Drakulic, *How We Survived Communism*, Vintage 1993. First published 1987. For anyone who wants to know how people, women in particular, coped with the dreary world of Communism, this is the book to read.

Tim Judah, *Kosovo: What Everyone Needs to Know*, Oxford University Press, 2008. A sturdy attempt at simplifying and updating to 2008 the complexities of Albanian/Serbian wars and their background history.

Ismail Kadare, *Broken April*, Vintage, 2003. Written in Communist Albania in 1978, it describes the horrific system of blood feuds in the mountains of Albania. At the same time, it seems to be an allegory of death and torture under Communism.

Ismail Kadare, *Chronicle in Stone*, my copy Canon, 2018. Written in 1971, in Communist Albania, it tells of a boy's life during the Second World War and is a fascinating glimpse into family life in Ottoman-influenced Albania.

Noel Malcolm, *Kosovo: A Short History*, Bloomsbury, 2002. For anyone who wants to fully understand this region and its background. I read both this and Tim Judah's book above to try to understand the background and later lives of my friends in Belgrade, Nazan, Hurema and Ibrahim.

Richard West, *Tito and the Rise and Fall of Yugoslavia*, Sinclair Stevenson, 1994. Although published in 1994, this has a readable account of how Yugoslavia went through the Second World War and how Tito took control. It also has a section on what was happening in Croatia while I was in Belgrade, all of which I was completely unaware.

Martin Dunford and Jack Holland, *The Rough Guide to Yugoslavia*. The copy I have was first published in 1985 so contains impressions of the united Yugoslavia before the wars of the 1990s. It is dedicated to 'the continuation of a free, non-aligned and socialist Yugoslavia'.

ROMANIA

Several books above include information about Romania. In particular, Tony Judt, *Postwar* from page 262 onwards and John Simpson, *Despatches from the Barricades*.

Acknowledgements

Max Adams, Fiona Hall and Timothy Phillips
Reading and commenting

Stephen Ashton
Editing, title and cover design concept

Biddy Carrdus
Proof reading

Imre Gulyás
Hungarian stories

Alison Hutchison
Reading and critical guidance

Diane Milburn
Reading and multi-lingual checks

Roddy Williams
Photo improvements

Janusz Zaręba
Checking the Poland chapter

About the Author

Bridget grew up in the Welsh border town of Hay on Wye, her family migrating to Northumberland in 1955. In 1966, she travelled alone, on foot, behind the Iron Curtain, writing extensive diaries and a series of articles for the Newcastle Journal.

Back home, she and her American husband raised four children and campaigned against nuclear power stations. *Cold War, Warm Hearts* is the second of her memoirs, following *Hay Before the Bookshops or The Beeman's Family*. She has also written a series of carefully researched local history books about the town of Morpeth in Northumberland. During her varied working life, she has been press officer for the regional anti-nuclear campaign, director of a renewable energy company, primary school teacher, and lastly college tutor to overseas students learning English. After 1989, when the eastern European countries opened up, she travelled and photographed extensively in the countries she had visited in 1966.

Cold War, Warm Hearts is the second of Bridget Ashton's memoirs.

It follows ***Hay Before the Bookshops or The Beeman's Family***

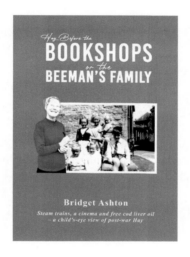

What they have said

"From steam trains to picnics in the castle, Bridget's new book, *Hay Before the Bookshops or The Beeman's Family*, has echoes of Kilvert's Diary as it lovingly recalls family life in post war Hay-on-Wye."

Joe Corrick, Journalist,
Brecon and Radnor Express

"This account of a post-war childhood was my holiday reading - and as compulsive as any page-turning thriller! Bridget captures beautifully the now-vanished world she grew up in, to create a book that is both a memoir and a fascinating piece of social history. The diaries of her poetic mother add another intriguing dimension to the tale."

Barbara Fox, author of
Bedpans & Bobby Socks and *When the War Is Over*

"A thoughtful memoir of one woman's childhood, with insights she has gained from her mother's life and personality, the family's rising and falling fortunes. With a father bent on an unlikely career as a beekeeper, things were not easy at home."

Alan Wilkinson, author of
The Red House on the Niobrara

"The times and the place both come to life vividly."

Mary Steele, editor of
Kilvert Society Journal

"If you want to know about life among ordinary British families at the end of King George VI's reign and start of Elizabeth II's, then read this book. Steam trains, ration books, strict schools, the new NHS. It's all there."

Ian Leech, journalist, editor of
Inside Morpeth

"The book presents a childhood memory of 1950s Hay-on-Wye before it became the bustling home of bookshops we so fondly know today. Its snapshot of Hay uses hand-written accounts from her mother's diaries."

Carrianne Lloyd-Ralph, journalist,
Wye Local

Letting the nine-year-old Bridget speak for herself guilelessly is the book's secret weapon! What a different world it was; and what an interesting family through which to encapsulate it.

Colin Pearson, academic and reviewer